C. S. Lewis
as Philosopher

Truth, Goodness and Beauty

EDITED BY

David Baggett, Gary R. Habermas
and Jerry L. Walls

Foreword by Tom Morris

IVP Academic

An imprint of InterVarsity Press
Downers Grove, Illinois

InterVarsity Press
P.O. Box 1400, Downers Grove, IL 60515-1426
World Wide Web: www.ivpress.com
E-mail: email@ivpress.com

InterVarsity Press® is the book-publishing division of InterVarsity Christian Fellowship/USA®, a student movement active on campus at hundreds of universities, colleges and schools of nursing in the United States of America, and a member movement of the International Fellowship of Evangelical Students. For information about local and regional activities, write Public Relations Dept., InterVarsity Christian Fellowship/USA, 6400 Schroeder Rd., P.O. Box 7895, Madison, WI 53707-7895, or visit the IVCF website at <www.intervarsity.org>.

Scripture quotations, unless otherwise noted, are from the New Revised Standard Version of the Bible, *copyright 1989 by the Division of Christian Education of the National Council of the Churches of Christ in the USA. Used by permission. All rights reserved.*

Index prepared by Wesley Grubb.

Design: Cindy Kiple
Images: Arthur Strong ©Ingrid Franzon

ISBN 978-0-8308-2808-1

Printed in the United States of America ∞

Library of Congress Cataloging-in-Publication Data

C.S. Lewis as philosopher: truth, goodness, and beauty / edited by
David Baggett, Gary R. Habermas, and Jerry L. Walls.
    p. cm.
 Includes bibliographical references and index.
 ISBN 978-0-8308-2808-1 (pbk.: alk. paper)
 1. Lewis, C. S. (Clive Staples), 1898-1963. 2. Theology. 3.
Christianity—Philosophy. 4. Truth—Religious aspects—Christianity.
5. Good and evil—Religious aspects—Christianity. 6.
Aesthetics—Religious aspects—Christianity.   I. Baggett, David.   II.
Habermas, Gary R. III. Walls, Jerry L.
 BX4827.L44C23 2008
 230.092—dc22

                                                            2007049464

P	21	20	19	18	17	16	15	14	13	12	11	10	9	8	7	6	5	4	3	2	1
Y	26	25	24	23	22	21	20	19	18	17	16	15	14	13	12	11	10	09	08		

To Antony Flew, in good friendship and admiration.

GARY R. HABERMAS

To the Gang who ventured across the pond with me
in the summer of '05 in pursuit of the
Three Great Ideals, including she who said,
"What women really want is Truth, Beauty and Goodness."

JERRY L. WALLS

To Evelyn and Leonard, in faith, hope and love.

DAVID BAGGETT

Contents

PART TWO: GOODNESS

PART THREE: BEAUTY

Foreword

Clarity is power. This is one of the reasons that, for more than half a century, the immensely popular books and essays of C. S. Lewis have launched into the world a nearly steady stream of new Christian philosophers and intellectuals. The stunning clarity of his thought and the scintillating crispness of what he wrote in expression of that thought have together stimulated generations of readers to aspire to some measure of that intellectual power and to at least a small fraction of the positive impact that Lewis has had in people's lives. I for one became a philosopher in part because of the influence of C. S. Lewis. He was a vivid role model and a potent stimulus that set me out on the very first steps of a great adventure, initially on the path of academic philosophy and then later on to a broader cultural calling as a philosopher.

I first read Lewis when I was in high school, and was completely mesmerized by his writing. His ability to cut through to the core of any issue, shine great light on the most central elements of Christian belief and display Christian theology's penetrating grasp of human nature were, in my admittedly limited experience, unparalleled. Moreover, in deftly managing the daunting balance between a keen and easy accessibility of language together with a real logical rigor of thought conveyed by that language, he presented to many of his readers an immensely attractive example of what a public philosopher could be and do. As a college student, I recall finding in his books sentences of such insight, and unexpected phrases of such perfection, that I would just sit and stare at the words, thinking to myself, *I wish I had been able to say it that way.* It was all so wise, and yet at the same time so simple. I was just astonished.

Simplicity is attractive. That's why political debate so quickly degenerates into sloganeering. People crave the sense of certainty and control that simplicity can provide. We all want "the simple truth" about anything but often find to our dismay that the full truth about most things of importance is hardly ever simple—except in the mind of a master. Simplicity that neither falsifies nor distorts is so rare that we seldom come across it outside works of real genius. And what makes the works of C. S. Lewis so noteworthy is that we come across such profound simplicity all the time in them. How could a young reader not want to think and write like that?

Lewis is most broadly known and remembered generally as a Christian writer. Technically he was throughout most of his adult life a professor of literature. But really, he was a philosopher. Philosophy is the love of wisdom, along with an unending desire to find it, understand it, put it into action and pass it on to others. Lewis brought a philosophical cast of mind to everything he did. And his philosophical instincts were astute. His way of being a philosopher was certainly distinctive, in engagement with great literature, through writing memorable fiction himself, and in grappling with topics of real life through his immensely popular books and essays on matters of faith. He didn't hold a regular position within a university department of philosophy, or publish in the technical academic journals run by philosophy professors, or even allow his own intellectual agenda to be dictated by the fads and styles of thought favored by those who paradigmatically think of themselves and each other under the honorific label of "philosopher," but he was a genuine philosopher nonetheless, and as such, has had a tremendous impact on the world. This book is a welcome exploration of what is behind some of that impact.

Tom Morris

Acknowledgments

Many thanks to our wonderful contributors, for their patience, diligence and expertise; to two research assistants whose help was invaluable: Brian Collins and Sean Turchin; to all the good folks at InterVarsity, especially Gary Deddo, who believed in this project and saw it through to completion; and special thanks to our dear friend and supportive colleague, Mark Foreman—and our hearty congratulations on the occasion of his recently minted doctorate.

Introduction

Jack of the Philosophical Trade

Jerry L. Walls

The first reaction some persons might have to the title of this book is to think "Interesting, but C. S. Lewis was not really a philosopher." And depending on what they mean, they could well be right. Professionally speaking, Lewis (1898-1963) was a teacher of English literature whose most distinguished academic position was the Chair of Medieval and Renaissance Literature at Cambridge University, a position he received in 1954. Before going to Cambridge, he taught for several years at Oxford, a university well known for its large philosophy faculty. Basil Mitchell, a friend of Lewis's, who studied and taught philosophy at Oxford, has remarked that if he had been asked to produce a list of philosophers at Oxford, "Lewis wouldn't have been mentioned among them."[1] In the world of Oxford's academic life, Lewis was a literary scholar; indeed, he was arguably the most accomplished member of the English faculty, though he never received a chair and was passed over several times when such positions were open.

But there is more to the story if we want an accurate answer to the question

---

[1]Cited by Scott R. Burson and Jerry L. Walls, *C. S. Lewis and Francis Schaeffer: Lessons for a New Century from the Most Influential Apologists of Our Time* (Downers Grove, Ill.: InterVarsity Press, 1998), p. 240.

of whether Lewis was really a philosopher. If we ask what he is best known for and which of his many books have been most influential, a number of titles that are distinctly philosophical will come quickly to mind. It is safe to guess that if asked to list books by C. S. Lewis, many persons who could not come up with a single title of his scholarly works in English literature could easily rattle off philosophical titles like *Miracles, The Problem of Pain* and *The Abolition of Man*. Moreover, his most famous work in popular theology, *Mere Christianity*, is very much a philosophical work as well. This is evident when he writes: "We are not taking anything from the Bible or the Churches, we are trying to see what we can find out about this Somebody on our own steam." This "Somebody," of course, turns out to be God, and the "steam" Lewis is using to drive his case is decidedly philosophical in nature: a variation of the classical moral argument.

Indeed, there is likely a connection between Lewis's philosophical fame and the fact that he did not receive the recognition and promotion he deserved at Oxford. His colleagues in the English faculty did not appreciate his popular works in philosophy and theology, particularly since those works had the aim of defending beliefs they did not share. In Lewis's day, Christianity had few vocal proponents in intellectual circles, and it was hardly to his political advantage to gain fame and notoriety as a spokesman for Christian orthodoxy, a position many of his colleagues viewed with disdain.

The full story of how a distinguished literary scholar achieved international fame as a popular philosopher is beyond the scope of this introduction, but it should be emphasized that his educational background was crucial in preparing him for this dual role. In 1922, after receiving a degree in Greek and Latin Literature, he received a degree in "Greats," which was a study of philosophy as well as ancient history. A year later, he took another degree in English, his eventual field of expertise. Not surprisingly, Lewis was awarded a "First" for each of his degrees, the highest possible grade.

Given this broad educational background, Lewis did not venture into the field of philosophy as a rank amateur, unlike several popular writers today. Rather, he had studied the subject with distinction with one of the world's great philosophy faculties. Indeed, at this stage of his career, he had decided that he wanted to be a philosopher. During his study of Greats, he was especially close to his philosophy tutor, E. F. Carritt, and learned a great deal from him. Apparently Carritt was impressed with Lewis's philosophical ability, for in 1924, when Carritt went to America for a year, Lewis was chosen to fill in for him. His first job at Oxford, then, was teaching philosophy. The topic of his lectures during that year, interestingly, was "Moral Good," an issue to which he would frequently return in his popular philosophical writings.

It was only when he received his position as Fellow at Magdalen College in 1925, his first permanent job, that his career direction as a literary scholar was set. But even then, part of the reason he may have gotten the job was because Magdalen was looking for someone who could teach both philosophy and English, and Lewis took an occasional philosophy student his first few years there. When it became clear that he would focus on English, Lewis was somewhat ambivalent and saw the move as something of a "descent" from the heights of philosophical reflection.[2]

Lewis's philosophical background was also crucial for another significant role he played during his years at Oxford. In 1941, Miss Stella Aldwinkle founded The Oxford Socratic Club as a forum where Christians and non-Christians could debate issues that divided them. In her search for a suitable president, she settled on Lewis, and he readily accepted the position, which he continued to hold until 1954, when he went to Cambridge. While this aspect of Lewis's career is not particularly well known, it was crucial to his overall apologetic mission. In a world-famous university setting, The Socratic Club demonstrated Lewis's conviction that Christian truth can stand up to thorough critical scrutiny. Indeed, Christopher Mitchell has suggested that apart from his published work, "no other activity that Lewis engaged in has proven more beneficial and far-reaching in its influence on Christianity than his participation in the Socratic Club."[3]

For our concerns, it is particularly significant that several speakers at the Socratic Club were prominent philosophers, including some notable atheists. As president, Lewis was typically expected to provide a rejoinder to the main speaker, and it was in this role that he gained his reputation as a formidable debater. It is another telling indicator of his native philosophical talent as well as his competence that he was able to stand toe to toe with leading philoso-

---

[2] Alan Jacobs, *The Narnian: The Life and Imagination of C. S. Lewis* (San Francisco: HarperSanFrancisco, 2005), p. 119.
[3] Christopher W. Mitchell, "University Battles: C. S. Lewis and the Oxford University Socratic Club," in *C. S. Lewis: Lightbearer in the Shadowlands*, ed. Angus J. L. Menuge (Wheaton, Ill.: Crossway, 1997), p. 329.

phers in public debate. Many came to the Socratic meetings to see Lewis perform, confident that he could always carry the day. Indeed, Austin Farrar, a distinguished philosophical theologian, makes this apparent in describing his own anxieties when he was expected to defend the Christian case at the meetings: "I went in fear and trembling, certain to be caught out in debate and to let down the side. But there Lewis would be, snuffing the imminent battle and saying 'Aha!' at the sound of the trumpet. My anxieties rolled away. Whatever ineptitude I might commit, he would maintain the cause; and nobody could put Lewis down."[4]

Ironically, the most famous debate of the Socratic Club was one in which many thought Lewis *was* put down. In 1948, shortly after the publication of *Miracles*, Miss Elizabeth Anscombe, a young Roman Catholic philosopher who was only twenty-nine at the time, read a paper criticizing one of Lewis's central arguments in that book. A vigorous debate followed, during which Anscombe obviously scored some points, for Lewis significantly revised the relevant chapter for a later version of the book. Friends and biographers offer different accounts of the debate and its aftermath, but some hold that Lewis was bested in the exchange and was demoralized by the experience. A. N. Wilson has even contended that Lewis was so humiliated that he gave up on formal apologetics and turned his attention to fantasy writing.[5] It was shortly after this event that he began his famous children's series the Chronicles of Narnia.

While Wilson's thesis is dubious, this famous debate is a rather good measure of Lewis the philosopher. On the one hand, it revealed his limitations, for it showed that Lewis had not kept up with the discipline and was not equipped to engage the sort of issues that had come to dominate Oxford and Cambridge philosophy. This is hardly surprising since he had turned his focus and energy to English literature over two decades before. But on the other hand, the argument he developed in *Miracles* is a provocative one that poses a profound challenge to naturalism, and in its revised version still has considerable force, as Anscombe herself recognized.[6] Indeed, it is worth noting that Lewis's ar-

---

[4]Cited by Jacobs, *The Narnian*, pp. 228-29.

[5]For a persuasive critique of this claim, see Victor Reppert, "The Green Witch and the Great Debate: Freeing Narnia from the Spell of the Lewis-Anscombe Legend," in *The Chronicles of Narnia and Philosophy: The Lion, the Witch, and the Worldview*, ed. Gregory Bassham and Jerry L. Walls (Chicago: Open Court, 2005), pp. 260-72.

[6]See G. E. M. Anscombe's introduction to *Metaphysics and the Philosophy of Mind*, vol. 2 of *The Collected Papers of G. E. M. Anscombe* (Minneapolis: University of Minnesota Press, 1981), pp. ix-x.

gument has striking affinities with powerful arguments recently put forth against naturalism by Alvin Plantinga, one of the world's leading Christian philosophers.

It is also worth pointing out that Lewis's philosophical work filled a void in an era when there were very few philosophers of stature writing in defense of Christian faith. While there has been a remarkable resurgence in Christian and theistic philosophy in the past few decades, Lewis wrote in a more hostile environment. It is a telling indicator of the dearth of Christian voices among the professional philosophers, as well as Lewis's role in filling this gap, that his popular works were engaged by academic philosophers looking for Christian dialogue partners. For instance, in the landmark volume *New Essays in Philosophical Theology*, published in 1955, it is Lewis whom Antony Flew takes as one of his targets.

The volume you hold in your hands provides impressive evidence that Lewis's philosophical legacy is a substantial one, with lasting significance. These essays show that Lewis had interesting things to say on a wide range of philosophical topics and that his writings provide distinctive and penetrating insights on fundamental issues of perennial concern.

Earlier versions of most of these essays were read at the C. S. Lewis Summer Institute, Oxbridge 2005. This was the sixth convening of the Lewis Summer Institute, a triennial event sponsored by the C. S. Lewis Foundation and held on the campuses of Oxford and Cambridge Universities. The theme of Oxbridge 2005 was "Making All Things New: The Good, the True, and the Beautiful in the Twenty-First Century." In Oxbridge 2005, the Summer Institute initiated a philosophy symposium as one of its offerings, and several of the papers here were read as part of that symposium. Others were read at other sessions, including two keynote addresses.

The great classic triumvirate of Truth, Beauty and Goodness is a particularly apt framework for engaging C. S. Lewis and philosophy. These magnificent ideals are not only at the heart of the classic philosophical enterprise, the tradition into which Lewis was initiated in his Oxford philosophical training, but they are also of crucial significance in the Christian vision of reality he came to embrace. Before his conversion, Lewis sought truth, was enchanted by beauty, and aspired to goodness, but he struggled to find a way to hold these goals together. In an oft-quoted passage describing his preconversion mindset, he wrote: "The two hemispheres of my mind were in the sharpest conflict. On the one side a many-islanded sea of poetry and myth; on the other a glib and shallow 'rationalism.' Nearly all that I loved I believed to be imaginary; nearly all that I believed to be real I thought grim and meaningless."[7] What this passage represents is the despairing view that the truth is not beautiful, that the beautiful is not true.

A few lines later, as Lewis elaborates his thinking at this period of his life, he writes about how the world of nature appeared to his senses.

> I chewed endlessly on the problem: "How can it be so beautiful and also so cruel, wasteful, and futile?" Hence at this time I could have almost said with Santayana, "All that is good is imaginary; all that is real is evil." In one sense nothing less like a "flight from reality" could be conceived. I was so far from wishful thinking that I hardly thought anything true unless it contradicted my wishes.

Again, we see a fragmentation among Truth, Beauty and Goodness. He fears that the good is imaginary, and hence not true. Where Beauty obviously resides, Goodness seems absent.

During this period of his life, he seemed committed to following the Truth, even if that meant abandoning the reality of Goodness and Beauty. Indeed, the period during which he was most focused on the goal of becoming a philosopher was one in which he thought the honest pursuit of Truth would cost him what he cared about most deeply. As Alan Jacobs has shown, during these years of his life, his imagination had died. Jacobs pointedly remarks that "Jack had gone a long way toward turning himself into someone who wouldn't even read books such as the Narnia stories, much less write them."[8]

As is well known, it was his conversion to Christianity that allowed Jack to bring the two hemispheres of his mind together. It was in Christianity that he discovered a true myth, a beautiful story that not only spoke to our imaginations and longing for goodness and meaning, but was also rooted in real history. In short, Christianity provided a way to hold together Truth, Goodness and Beauty.

His conversion also opened the door to a far larger and more exciting world to be explored philosophically as well as experientially. Now his reason led him past the shallow limits of rationalism to a world of reality that reason alone could never capture. His reason led him to see that Ultimate Reason is the best

---

[7] C. S. Lewis, *Surprised by Joy: The Shape of My Early Life* (New York: Harcourt, Brace & World, 1955), p. 170.
[8] Jacobs, *The Narnian*, p. 102.

explanation of why we can reason at all. It led him to see that ultimate goodness in the form of objective morality is at least as real as the world of nature that is beautiful, but marred by cruelty and waste. And if objective good is real, then there must be a solution to the problem of pain.

If it is true that the Chronicles represented a significant turning point in Lewis's literary career and that he could convey things in fantasy literature that he could never show in philosophical argument, the nature of the turn should not be exaggerated. It is beyond dispute that the stories could depict the beauty of truth in a way even the most elegant propositions never could.[9] But if we are to take a true measure of Lewis the philosopher, we must ever keep in mind that the same man who wrote the enchanting stories wrote the elegant propositions that framed the suggestive arguments. Otherwise we will pry apart the assembly of Truth, Beauty and Goodness that Lewis held together.

The essays below celebrate Lewis the philosopher by engaging him seriously as a thinker who has much to teach us about these three great ideals. It is our hope that they will not only honor his philosophical contributions but also enable us in our day to show the power and glory of Truth, Beauty and Goodness and the splendor of the One in whom they are perfectly joined.

---

[9]The stories are also rich with philosophical themes and suggestions. See the essays in Bassham and Walls, *The Chronicles of Narnia and Philosophy.*

Part One

TRUTH

1

Lewis's Philosophy of Truth, Goodness and Beauty

Peter Kreeft

THE THREE TRANSCENDENTALS

There are three things that will never die: truth, goodness and beauty. These are the three things we all need, and need absolutely, and know we need, and know we need absolutely. Our minds want not only some truth and some falsehood, but all truth, without limit. Our wills want not only some good and some evil, but all good, without limit. Our desires, imaginations, feelings or hearts want not just some beauty and some ugliness, but all beauty, without limit.

For these are the only three things that we never get bored with, and never will, for all eternity, because they are three attributes of God, and therefore of all God's creation: three transcendental or absolutely universal properties of all reality. All that exists is true, the proper object of mind. All that exists is good, the proper object of the will. All that exists is beautiful, the proper object of the heart, or feelings, or desires, or sensibilities, or imagination. (This third area is more difficult to define than the first two.)

Every culture seeks these three things too, for man makes culture before culture makes man. Some cultures, however, like some individuals, specialize in one of the three transcendentals. In the Orient, India has specialized in the love of truth, of ultimate mystical and metaphysical truth; China has specialized in the love of the good, the practical human good, whether Confucian or Taoist or even Communist; and Japan has specialized in the love of beauty, especially the beauty of the arts. In the modern West, German culture, as distinct from German politics, has specialized in truth, especially philosophical and scientific truth; American culture in the practical human good; and English culture in beauty. Small islands like Japan and England seem to respond especially to the love of beauty, perhaps because of the sea and perhaps because of the appreciation of limits.

God revealed these three attributes of his nature to all humankind: truth especially through the philosophers, good especially through the prophets and moralists, and beauty through the poets, artists, musicians, and mythmakers. He chose the Jewish people, especially Moses and the prophets, to be revealers of the infallible law of goodness. Yet many of the fathers of the church saw the Greek philosophers as fallible but also divinely inspired searchers for the truth, the word, the logos, who in Christ incarnated and fulfilled the Greek as well as the Jewish messianic hopes.

The two greatest Christian writers and thinkers of the twentieth century completed this scheme by seeing ancient pagan mythology in the same messianic way, in the more obscure area of the human heart that responds to beauty: G. K. Chesterton in *The Everlasting Man* and C. S. Lewis in the essay "Myth Become Fact" and in the novels *Till We Have Faces* and *Perelandra*. Lewis calls pagan myths "gleams of celestial strength and beauty falling on jungles of filth and imbecility," because they are "based on a solider reality than we dream, but are at an almost infinite distance removed from their base."[1]

God has not left himself without witness in any of the three distinctively human, more-than-animal powers of the soul, the three aspects of the image of God in us: the mind, which knows and understands the good; the will, which chooses and enforces it; and the emotions, which love and appreciate it. This threefold structure of the soul is also the reason why so many great classics in our literature have three protagonists corresponding to these three psychological faculties and social functions: prophet, king and priest. For instance, Gandalf, Aragorn and Frodo; Ivan, Dimitri and Alyosha Karamazov; Mr. Spock, Captain Kirk and Bones McCoy. And not only fictional trios. Within Christ's inner circle, we find John as the philosophical mystic; Peter as the rock, the leader; and James as the practical psychologist. The starship Soul, like the starship Enterprise, needs a science officer, a captain and a doctor. Every ship needs a knowledge of where it is going, the will and command to go there, and the sailor's work of bringing it there. Aristotle similarly divided up all human sciences into the theoretical, practical and productive. In Plato's terms, we are reason, "spirited part," and appetites. This is the psychological

---

[1] C. S. Lewis, *Perelandra* (New York: Simon & Schuster, 1996), p. 201.

basis for his natural division of society into philosophers, warriors and producers. In Freud's terms, we are superego, ego and id. We are head, hands and heart. We respond to truth, goodness and beauty.

We are this because we are images of God. Each of us is one person with three distinct powers. God is one God, but in three distinct persons. The Son, the Logos, is the mind of the Father and performs his good will in redeeming the world. The Spirit is the poet, who composes and choreographs the operatic love between the Father and the Son in both creating and redeeming, and so is the Sanctifier, the saint-maker—and the saint is the most beautiful thing on Earth. As the Spirit proceeds from Father and Son, children proceed from husband and wife, the holy family on Earth manifesting the holy trinitarian family of heaven, though very imperfectly and obscurely, through a glass darkly. And as the Son, though equal to the Father in all things, willingly and lovingly submits to the Father's good will, the loving wife lovingly submits to the loving husband's loving good will, though she is equal to him in all things. For this is not politics, but music; not equality, but harmony; not justice, but love.

The *order* of these three transcendentals of truth, goodness and beauty is ontologically founded. Truth is defined by Being, for truth is the effulgence of Being, the revelation of Being, the word of Being. Truth is not defined by consciousness, which conforms to Being in knowing it. Goodness is defined by truth, not by will, which is good only when it conforms to the truth of Being. And beauty is defined by goodness, objectively real goodness, not by subjective desire or pleasure or feeling or imagination, all of which should conform to it.

However, the psychological order is the reverse of the ontological order. As we know Being through first sensing appearances, so we are attracted to goodness first by its beauty, we are attracted to truth by its goodness, and we are attracted to Being by its truth. But ontologically, truth depends on Being, goodness on truth, and beauty on goodness. Truth is knowing *Being*. Goodness is *true* goodness. And the most beautiful thing in the world is perfect *goodness*. That is why the most beautiful movie ever made was also the bloodiest one: *The Passion of the Christ*.

According to Aquinas, beauty is "that which, being seen, pleases." Though beauty is derived from truth and goodness, it has the greatest power over our souls. This is why most addictions come from something that appears beautiful, whether Gollum's ring, a false "Precious," or a drug or alcohol high, which is a false mystical experience, or a false love that apes married love but lacks its truth. And therefore the only effective cure for addiction must come from something that appears even more beautiful than the addiction. As Aquinas says, the only thing strong enough to overcome an evil passion is a more powerful good passion. The beauty of a sober saint, to which the alcoholic aspires, is a powerful cure for alcoholism. The beauty of the bloody love of Christ can overcome the beauty of the forbidden love of a beautiful body.

Augustine in his *Soliloquies* imagines God asking him, "What do you want to know?" And Augustine replies, "Only two things: Yourself and myself." That is not narrow; that is broad. For a self, or person, involves all three of the things we need and want infinitely: truth, goodness and beauty. So there really are six things we want to know in knowing these two, but the six are really three, since our three are reflections of God's three.

C. S. LEWIS AND TRUTH, GOODNESS AND BEAUTY

Now, how many writers can tell us more than C. S. Lewis about all three things, the only things we need to know? Not many. Hardly any other writer had more strings to his bow than Lewis. Can you think of one who excels in all three areas, who is more intelligent and reveals more truth, *and* is more saintly and reveals more goodness, *and* is more creative and writes more beautifully and stimulates more deep feelings in the reader? I know of no one since Augustine. Possibly Kierkegaard.

When I began to summarize and order Lewis's wisdom about each of these three transcendentals, I discovered that all three of them follow the same order. In all three, Lewis shows us seven things: first, their logic, or definition; second, their metaphysics, their objective reality; third, their theology, their divine source; fourth, their epistemology, how we know them; fifth, their practical psychology; sixth, their axiology, the ordered relationship of these values; and seventh, their mystical eschatology, their fulfillment in heaven.

LOGIC

First, the logic: Lewis's *definitions* of truth, goodness and beauty. Lewis defines truth as Aristotle and common sense do, as correspondence with reality. In "Myth Become Fact" he said, "Truth is always *about* something" and "Reality is that *about which* truth is."[2] This is denied by Deconstructionism.

---

[2]C. S. Lewis, "Myth Become Fact," in *God in the Dock* (Grand Rapids: Eerdmans, 1970), p. 66.

(*Everything* is denied by Deconstructionism!) But we all know what truth means, even though we argue about which ideas *have* truth. "What is truth?" is really the easiest question of all in philosophy. Pilate was an imbecile, or perhaps a Deconstructionist.

We also all know what goodness is. We all know the goodness of goodness and the badness of badness. We cannot not know it. We even know, by nature and not just by divine revelation, something of *God's* goodness. God's goodness differs from ours not as white differs from black, but as a perfect circle from a child's first attempt to draw a wheel, to use one of Lewis's familiar images. Lewis rejects what he calls the extreme Calvinism of the idea that we are so depraved that our ideas of goodness must count for nothing: he points out that if that were true, then we would have no motive for obeying God. At the same time, Lewis defines goodness relative to God, not God relative to goodness. The proper good of a creature is to surrender oneself to one's Creator, to enact intellectually, volitionally and emotionally (the three transcendentals) the relationship that results from the mere fact of being a creature.

So goodness, like truth, is relative to reality. I think the most fundamental and most universal of all moral principles is what I call the "Three R's Principle": Right Response to Reality.

The definition of beauty, like beauty itself, is more obscure and mysterious than either truth or goodness. But our perception of it is just as sharp and certain and objective, as Lewis shows in *The Abolition of Man* by the example of Coleridge and the two tourists at the waterfall. (Read that passage, and that whole prophetic little book, again. And again.)

METAPHYSICS

Our second point is the metaphysics of truth, goodness and beauty: that is, their objective reality. Lewis's polemic against deniers of objective truth, goodness and beauty is wonderfully simple and powerful. In the essay "De Futilitate," he says, "If our minds are totally alien to reality, then all our thoughts, including this thought, are worthless."[3] This shows the self-contradiction of both the old-fashioned skeptical scientific materialist and the newfangled postmodernist subjectivist relativist. The old kind of skeptic forbids us to claim that any idea is true or good or beautiful; the new kind forbids us to

---

[3]C. S. Lewis, "De Futilitate," in *Christian Reflections* (Grand Rapids: Eerdmans, 1987), p. 71.

claim that any idea is false or evil or ugly. It is the tyranny of tolerance, the absolutism of relativism. Lewis's polemic against both of these denials of our knowledge of objective truth, goodness and beauty is simply to let his opponents talk, to give them rope and watch them hang themselves.

This simple point that truth, goodness and beauty are objectively real is liberating. It liberates us from many silly questions and wastes of time. For instance, Lewis says in *Letters to Malcolm,* "What makes some theological works like sawdust to me is the way the authors can go on discussing how far certain positions are adjustable to contemporary thought, or beneficial in relation to social problems, or have a future before them, but never squarely ask what grounds we have for supposing them to be true. As if we were trying to make, rather than learn. Have we no Other to reckon with?"[4] Well, not if we are dreaming, or if we are pantheists, or if we are in hell.

If intellectual subjectivism is self-contradictory, and even insanity and dishonesty, what could be worse? Moral subjectivism. Lewis says this is a disease that "will certainly end our species and damn our souls" if it is not crushed. Please remember that Oxford dons are not prone to exaggeration.

Lewis's arguments prove two things: negatively, that intellectual and moral and aesthetic skepticism and subjectivism are false because they are self-contradictory; and positively, that therefore their opposites are true. So he concludes, "We must grant logic to reality. We must, if we are to grant it any standards, grant it to moral standards too. And there is really no reason why we should not do the same about standards of beauty."[5]

THEOLOGY

Third comes the theology of truth, goodness and beauty, their ultimate source. All three of the transcendentals are not abstract ideals; they are concrete facts, like the softness of my skin or the selfishness of my soul, because they are attributes of God, the supremely concrete reality. They are, so to speak, what God is made of.

First, as Arthur Holmes has eloquently said, "All truth is God's truth." In *Reflections on the Psalms,* Lewis writes, "Whatever was true in Akhenaton's creed came to him in some mode or other as all truth comes to men: from

[4]C. S. Lewis, *Letters to Malcolm* (New York: Harcourt, Brace & World, 1964), p. 104.
[5]Lewis, "De Futilitate," p. 71.

God."[6] In *Surprised by Joy*, he says, "I think that all things in their way reflect heavenly truth, the imagination not the least."[7]

Chapter five of *Miracles* offers the same argument about our ideas of goodness as chapter three offers about our ideas of truth. He concludes, "As the argument in the previous chapter led us to acknowledge a supernatural source for rational thought, so the argument of this leads us to acknowledge a supernatural source for our ideas of good and evil."[8] And not just for our *ideas* of goodness, but also for our actual goodness, for Christians know any good they do comes from the Christ-life inside them.

In *The Four Loves*, he writes, "We were made for God. Only by being in some respect like him, only by being a manifestation of his beauty and lovingkindness and wisdom and goodness, has any earthly beloved ever excited our love."[9] That clearly is the Augustinian wisdom: "Thou has made us for thyself, and therefore our hearts are restless until they rest in thee." But then Lewis goes on to correct Augustine's definition of evil as loving creatures too much, writing that it is not that we have loved them too much, but that we did not quite understand what we were loving.[10] When we see the face of God, we will know that we have always known it. In *A Grief Observed*, Lewis says of his wife's beauty, "Of her, and of every created thing I praise, I should say, 'In some way, in its unique way, it is like him who made it.'"[11]

EPISTEMOLOGY

Our fourth category is the epistemology of truth, goodness and beauty, how we know them. We know all three transcendentals immediately and intuitively, not by inference or argument. Even truth. Lewis writes that one cannot produce rational intuition of truth by argument because all argument depends on rational intuition. This rational intuition is literally indubitable, or self-evident. Lewis describes it as that which no honest man has ever dreamed of doubting. For instance, no one has ever imagined, much less written a story, even a bad one, about a world in which the law of noncontradiction was untrue.

---

[6]C. S. Lewis, *Reflections on the Psalms* (New York: Harcourt, Brace, Jovanovich, 1958), p. 86.

[7]C. S. Lewis, *Surprised by Joy: The Shape of My Early Life* (New York: Harcourt, Brace, Jovanovich, 1955), p. 167.

[8]C. S. Lewis, *Miracles* (New York: Macmillan, 1974), p. 38.

[9]C. S. Lewis, *The Four Loves* (New York: Harvest Book/Harcourt, Brace, Jovanovich, 1991), p. 139.

[10]See Lewis's powerful "Charity" chapter in *The Four Loves*.

[11]C. S. Lewis, *A Grief Observed* (New York: HarperSanFrancisco, 2001), p. 63.

We also directly know moral goodness. In *The Problem of Pain*, Lewis says, "The experiences expressed by the words 'I ought' or 'I ought not' cannot be logically deduced. The consciousness of a moral law, at once approved and disobeyed, is neither a logical nor illogical inference from the facts of experience. If we did not bring it to our experience, we could not find it there. It is either inexplicable illusion or else direct revelation."[12]

Beauty is also experienced directly and immediately, as Lewis describes his early childhood experience of Beatrix Potter's *Squirrel Nutkin* and later of Norse mythology and Wagner's music. When we speak of religion rather than theology—that is, about the relation between ourselves and God rather than about the eternal essence of God—aesthetics proves to be in some ways more, not less, adequate than intellectual or moral analogies. In *Letters to Malcolm*, Lewis explains why the analogy of the artist is more revealing of God's way with the world than either the analogy of God the scientist or philosopher who thinks in abstractions and generalizations, or the analogy of the king or political ruler who rules by causality. He says, "How should the true Creator work by general laws? To generalize is to be a finite mind."[13] And he also says, "Strictly causal thinking is inadequate when applied to the relation between God and man. It has led to the whole puzzle about grace and free will."[14] He also says, "Surely, a man of genius composing a poem or a symphony must be less unlike God than a ruler. . . . The course of events on earth is not governed like a state. It is created, like a work of art."[15] From God's eternal point of view, that act of creation is going on right now.

PRACTICAL PSYCHOLOGY

Fifth, some practical psychology. If goodness, truth and beauty are all objective, then we can err about them. If not, then not. If we can err, how can we avoid error? What practical tools or clues does Lewis offer for attaining these three greatest things in the world? Concerning truth, first, in the essay "Religion: Reality, or Substitute?" Lewis repeats the answer that was well known since Aristotle, especially in the Middle Ages, and forgotten or denied only in the twentieth century: "Authority, reason, experience: on these three, mixed in

---

[12]C. S. Lewis, *The Problem of Pain* (New York: Macmillan, 1944), p. 10.
[13]Lewis, *Letters to Malcolm*, p. 55.
[14]Ibid., p. 49.
[15]Ibid., pp. 54, 56.

varying proportions, all our knowledge depends."[16] (Lewis is often original by not trying to be original. He quotes George MacDonald's saying: "Our Lord was never original." In an age of rebellion against all tradition, the only rebellion left is orthodoxy.)

In our day the most popular answer to the question of how one knows the truth, at least among so-called educated people in our so-called universities, is feeling. Our guru is really Rousseau. Lewis demolishes this answer—that we know truth by feeling—very simply. He writes, "The value given to the testimony of any feeling must depend on our whole philosophy, not our whole philosophy on a feeling."[17]

Of these three ways of knowing—experience, reason and authority—authority has become the dreaded word. But Lewis points out that we go to authority because reason sends us to it. One of the things our reason tells us is that we ought to check the results of our own thinking by the opinions of the wise.

Experience counts too—but not any and all experience equally, but especially spiritual experience, and especially by spiritual and wise experiencers. Both in *Miracles* and in *The Problem of Pain*, Lewis quotes John 7:17: "Anyone who resolves to do the will of God will know whether the teaching is from God." That is, there are personal and moral qualifications for knowing the truth. The primary moral qualification is honesty, and therefore this is the primary virtue Satan fears and attacks. It is the one mentioned most often in *The Screwtape Letters*. Screwtape writes to his apprentice devil that the great thing is to make his patient value an opinion for some quality other than truth.

For instance, take "Man or Rabbit." This is the one essay I think Lewis would pick if he could force every single person in modern Western civilization to read only one thing he wrote. This essay reminds me of Pascal's *Pensées* on diversion, and I cannot resist shooting a few of its sentences like arrows at your heart. The question of the essay is, "Can't you lead a good life without believing in Christianity?" And Lewis immediately challenges the question instead of answering it, just as Jesus almost always does. He writes:

> This is the question on which I have been asked to write, and straightaway, before I begin trying to answer it, I have a comment to make. The question sounds as if it were asked by a person who said to himself, "I don't care if in fact whether

---

[16]C. S. Lewis, "Religion: Reality or Substitute?" in *Christian Reflections*, p. 41.
[17]Ibid., p. 41.

Christianity is true or not. I am going to choose beliefs not because I think them true, but because I find them helpful." Now frankly I find it hard to sympathize with this state of mind. One of the things that distinguishes man from the other animals is that he wants to know things, wants to find out what reality is like, simply for the sake of knowing. When that desire is completely quenched in anyone, I think he has become something less than human. That man is shirking. He is deliberately trying not to know whether Christianity is true or false, because he foresees endless trouble if it should turn out to be true. He is like the man who will not go to the doctor when he first feels a mysterious pain because he is afraid of what the doctor may tell him. The man who remains an unbeliever for such reasons is not in a state of honest error. He is in a state of dishonest error, and that dishonesty will spread through all his thoughts and actions. A certain shiftiness, a vague worry in the background, a blunting of his whole mental edge, will result. He has lost his intellectual virginity.[18]

Lewis's greatest compliment to his wife in *A Grief Observed* is that she wanted truth at any price.

If we are honest, one of the truest clues for finding the most important truths is surprise. The real world is strange, not simple. And if we are full of pride and prejudice, we will not explore the bushes where the best game hides. For instance, we will not explore the puzzling, repellent, or difficult passages in Scripture, as Lewis does so wonderfully in "The Weight of Glory." Nor will we marry women like Joy Davidman, who was gloriously other than Lewis, and not what he called one of his bachelor pipe dreams.

In his apologetics, Lewis constantly turns difficulties into advantages, objections into arguments. As he says in *Surprised by Joy*, if any message from the core of reality were to reach us, we should expect to find in it just that unexpectedness that we find in the Christian faith: the taste of reality, not made by us, but hitting us in the face. In *Mere Christianity*, Lewis says that it's no good asking for a simple religion. After all, real things are not simple. And besides being complicated, reality is usually very odd. "It is not neat, not obvious, not what you expect. . . . That is one of the reasons why I believe Christianity. It is a religion you could not have guessed."[19] It is not the sort of thing anyone would have made up. By the way, that is also a very old apologetic argument.

---

[18]C. S. Lewis, "Man or Rabbit," in *God in the Dock*, p. 108.
[19]C. S. Lewis, *Mere Christianity*, in *The Complete C. S. Lewis Signature Classics* (New York: HarperCollins, 2002), p. 31.

We find it in Tertullian, who said, "I believe because it is absurd." We find it in Kierkegaard, who called the incarnation "the absolute paradox."

The psychology of knowing the good is easier than the psychology of knowing the truth, because God has left much more knowledge of moral goodness to be innate in fallen man's soul than he has left innate knowledge of theological truth. And that is why the world's religions differ radically about theology but not about morality. It takes divine revelation to give us knowledge of God, but it takes only personal, natural, human honesty to give us knowledge of God's will, of moral goodness. It's a "need to know" thing.

Lewis explains that there is one qualification for knowing good: being good. When a man is getting better, he understands more and more clearly the evil that is still left in him. When a man is getting worse, he understands his own badness less and less. We understand sleep when we are awake, not when we are sleeping, drunkenness when we are sober.

As the understanding of goodness is more natural, more innate, more universal and more simple than the knowledge of truth, so the knowledge of beauty is even more natural, innate, universal and easy. We all experience something that moves our heart to wonder and to joy, whether it is Wagner or Gregorian chant. The beauty of God is even experienced through our bodies. Save for the body, one whole realm of God's glory, all that we receive through the senses, would go unpraised, for the beasts cannot appreciate it, and the angels are pure intelligences. The beauty of nature is a secret that God has shared with us alone, Lewis wrote. That may be one of the reasons why we were made, and why the resurrection of the body is so important.

VALUE THEORY

Sixth, the value theory, or axiology, of truth, goodness and beauty. The relations between these three values have some strange similarities to the doctrine of the interrelationship of the three Persons of the Trinity. Truth is good and beautiful; goodness is true and beautiful; beauty is true and good. But there is an ontological (not temporal) order: it flows from Being to truth, truth to goodness, and goodness to beauty. Truth is judged by Being, goodness by truth, and beauty by goodness. The psychological order of our experiencing of them is the reverse: we are moved to goodness by its beauty, to truth by its goodness, and to Being by its truth.

The three main points I find Lewis making about the value of these three

transcendentals are these: first, beauty is not the absolute but points beyond itself; second, the goodness that transcends beauty is still dependent on truth;
and third, truth is absolute only if it is the truth of Being. In "First and Second
Things," Lewis notes that beauty withers when we worship it as the absolute.
The point of that very simple and practical article is that if you put first things
first and second things second, both flourish. If you put second things first and
first things second, not only do you lose the first things but also the second. Art
for art's sake is not only idolatry, but also fatal to art, though art for money's
sake or fame's sake is even worse. Put good above beauty, and beauty flourishes.
This does not mean moralism, or allegory; it means following the pointing finger of beauty, as Lewis learned to do in *Surprised by Joy*. That wonderful little
distinction between "looking at" and "looking along" in the essay "Meditation
in a Toolshed" is really the key to the psychology of *Surprised by Joy*.

Lewis shocks us psychologistic moderns, us feeling-fondlers, by telling us,
as do all the saints, that feelings, the powers by which we become aware of and
attracted to beauty, are irrelevant and unimportant to moral goodness. He believes that it is by one's will alone that a person is good or bad, that feelings by
themselves are not of any importance. That is shocking to us; it was not shocking to our ancestors.

On the other hand, Lewis disagrees with Kant. Moral duty is not duty for
duty's sake. It leads yonder, taking beauty and joy with it. So all the saints are
full of joy, not of dour duty. It is one-year-olds in toilet training who must
learn to do their duty. The perfect human would never act from a sense of duty.
One would always love the right thing more than the wrong one. Lewis says
that duty exists to be transcended, that there is no morality in heaven; "the
road to the Promised Land leads past Mount Sinai." The more virtuous a person becomes, the more one enjoys virtuous actions. The Catholic Church will
not canonize a saint unless the ecclesiastics find in one's life all the fruits of the
Spirit, one of which is joy. A dour saint is an oxymoron.

When goodness flourishes, so does beauty. The most beautiful thing in the
world is a saint, and the most powerful argument. No one can resist Mother
Teresa, except a columnist at the *Times*. Lewis once wrote that holiness is irresistible; that if even 10 percent of the world's population had it, the whole
world would be converted and happy before the year's end. Holiness is not an
abstraction. Goodness means ultimately Christ himself, the most beautiful
sight human eyes have ever beheld, and also the bloodiest, since in Christ's day

there were also many columnists who worked for the *Times*.

The meaning of the word *good* is ultimately the Word of God: Christ. As Lewis put it in *Mere Christianity*, all true goodness is a kind of "good infection" from Christ, known or unknown. When he describes this good infection, Lewis is very realistic. He says the New Testament

> is always talking about putting on Christ, about Christ being formed in us, about our coming to have the mind of Christ. Please put out of your mind the idea that these are only fancy ways of saying that Christians are to read what Christ said and try to carry it out, as a man may read what Plato or Marx said and try to carry it out. They mean something much more than that. They mean that a real person, Christ, here and now, in that very room where you are saying your prayers, is doing things to you, really coming and interfering with your very self, killing the old self in you, and replacing it with the kind of self he has.[20]

(Lewis is wonderfully scary.)

As in the end of chapter eleven of *Miracles:* "There comes a moment when the children who have been playing at burglars hush suddenly. Was that a real footstep in the hall? There comes a moment when people who have been dabbling in religion ('man's search for God') suddenly draw back. Supposing we really found him? We never meant it to come to that!"[21] Elsewhere Lewis describes human's search for God as "the mouse's search for the cat."

Truth, if we are honest, must trump all forms of beauty, including what we like and what comforts us. Comfort, Lewis thinks, is the one thing you cannot get by looking for it. "If you look for truth, you may find comfort in the end. If you look for comfort, you will not get either comfort or truth, only wishful thinking to begin with and, in the end, despair."[22] Hence the principle of first and second things again.

In the preface to *Mere Christianity*, Lewis addresses the question of which Christian church or denomination to join, since "mere Christianity" is not a church or a denomination. It is not a door into a living room, but only a hallway. And his answer is, above all, that you must be asking which door is the true one, not which pleases you best.

Truth transcends not only the comfort of beauty or pleasure but also goodness of motive. We cannot prove that Christianity or any other truth claim is

---

[20]Ibid., pp. 102-3.
[21]Lewis, *Miracles*, pp. 96-97.
[22]Lewis, *Mere Christianity*, p. 25.

false or true by showing that the motives someone has for believing it are morally bad or good. We must first prove a belief is false before explaining it away by impugning the motives for believing the error.

ESCHATOLOGY

Truth, goodness and beauty are "patches of Godlight" here in "Shadowlands." Their home is Yonder. The form they will take there will dazzle us forever, for they are what God is made of. Far from being "escapism," this gives each of us the ultimate meaning of our individual existence in this world, for (as Lewis says in that little mystical masterpiece called the "Heaven" chapter in *The Problem of Pain*)

> each of the redeemed shall forever know and praise some one aspect of the divine beauty better than any other creature can. Why else were individuals created, but that God, loving all infinitely, should love each differently? . . . For doubtless the continually successful, yet never completed, attempt by each soul to communicate its unique vision of God to all others (and that by means whereof earthly art and philosophy are but clumsy imitations) is also among the ends for which the individual was created.[23]

---

[23]Lewis, *Pain*, p. 150.

2

From Atheism to Deism

A Conversation Between Antony Flew and Gary R. Habermas

This interview was a featured event at Oxbridge 2005, a triennial conference sponsored by the C. S. Lewis Foundation and held on the campuses of Oxford and Cambridge Universities. On July 29, in Oxford, Habermas interviewed Flew regarding his personal memories of C. S. Lewis, his early philosophical publications, and his "conversion" from atheism to deism. The interview was preceded by a dramatic reenactment of the famous debate between Lewis and Elizabeth Anscombe, featuring Robin Meredith as Lewis and Christine Way as Anscombe.

INTERVIEW

HABERMAS: Let's begin with any reminiscences that you may recall regarding the now-famous meeting of the Socratic Club on February 2, 1948, at which you were present. What thoughts do you have regarding the dialogue between C. S. Lewis and Elizabeth Anscombe?

FLEW: At the time, of course, I was certainly impressed immensely by Anscombe's argument. I had heard Lewis lecture, and afterward I read Lewis's later thoughts about the subject. But most of my memories of that evening are more clear regarding the scene after the conclusion of the dialogue. I was heading back across the Magdalen Bridge, walking immediately behind Elizabeth Anscombe. She was absolutely exultant. A little way in front of us were a few people who had gotten out of the meeting early. But on the far side of Magdalen Bridge was C. S. Lewis, and he was obviously unhappy about the exchange that evening. He was going back hastily to his room in Magdalen College. That's about all I can say about the event, but it did indicate the mood afterward. It was very clear that Lewis was depressed and equally clear that Elizabeth was triumphant.

HABERMAS: Tony, you attended the Socratic Club for a number of years.

FLEW: Yes, I was in Oxford for a couple of terms during the war, and while I did not attend every meeting of the Socratic Club, I went pretty frequently. As I recall, it met once a week during the term and C. S. Lewis was the president of the organization.

HABERMAS: How did you find Lewis's ability to reason and think through topics in philosophy and religion?

FLEW: Oh, I thought that Lewis was a fine man. He was of course a literary scholar rather than a philosopher. But during a discussion, Lewis's contribution would always be relevant and to the point. He was a first-class thinker.

HABERMAS: Did you ever dialogue with him yourself?

FLEW: I don't think I did other than, more obviously, when I participated in some more general discussions. I don't think I ever read a paper that opposed one of the doctrines that he believed. But I did read one or two papers to the society.

HABERMAS: You sure did. In fact, in 1950 Tony published what has been his most influential paper, if we can judge from the number of reprints. Just three pages long, "Theology and Falsification" was reproduced later in the book that he edited along with Alasdair MacIntyre.[1] We might say that this paper is the most influential item that Tony has written. It has been republished over forty times. . . .

FLEW: . . . in seven different languages, with two separate German translations, but interestingly, it has not yet been translated into French.

HABERMAS: This essay was published more than forty times and has been called one of the most widely read essays during the second half of the twentieth century. I would like to ask Tony something about this that many may

---

[1] Antony Flew, "Theology and Falsification," in *New Essays in Philosophical Theology*, ed. Antony Flew and Alasdair MacIntyre (London: SCM Press, 1955).

not know. Didn't you read an earlier version of this paper at the Socratic Club, prior to its 1950 publication?

FLEW: Actually, I'm not sure of all the exact details. But my paper was an attempt to shut up the readers of A. J. Ayer's influential little volume, *Language, Truth, and Logic*[2]—regarding what sort of statements had literal significance. My paper was deliberately intended to stop that discussion, and I think that it was totally successful.

HABERMAS: I quote from a letter that you sent to me on April 22, 2005. Regarding the earlier form of your essay, read at the Socratic Club, you said, "It was my paper refuting the dogmatical positivistic contention that theological utterances are without literal significance which effectively eliminated Logical Positivism from the Socratic Club." This is an important connection between your best-known essay and the meeting chaired by Lewis. Tell me about the earlier form of your article that was read at the Socratic Club.

FLEW: Well, as I said, the paper was intended to simply refute the positivistic stance against religious utterances. It succeeded in that, but then its influence spread outside of Oxford. As a matter of fact, I was asked if the essay might be published in a journal that appeared once or twice per term. I was delighted to do it. Two or three others joined the discussions, and it appeared in print.

HABERMAS: That was the journal *University*, right?

FLEW: That's it, yes.

HABERMAS: Anything else about the Socratic Club?

FLEW: It was a very good institution in its time. It was the only place where there was organized discussion on a whole lot of topics that ought to have been discussed by university students, and in the war years it was even more interesting, partly because there seemed to be a substantial supply of very able Jewish scholars who had devoted their entire lives to supporting their ideas. It was a very interesting time because nothing else was going on around Oxford except people's academic work and the aftermath of the war.

---

[2]A. J. Ayer, *Language, Truth, and Logic* (New York: Dover, 1936).

HABERMAS: In this context, perhaps you would like to say a few words about your father and his connection with Oxford University, and some of those influences on your childhood.

FLEW: Well, my father was very much an Oxford man and received a doctorate there. Of course, he expected that I would go and take a course of study there, too. He hoped that I would take the same courses that he did. He served as a pastor.

HABERMAS: Let me provide a little background for our next topic. The friendship between Tony and me goes back more than twenty years. We met at a series of debates between atheists and theists in Dallas, Texas, in 1985. Tony was part of a team of four atheistic philosophers who debated an equal number of Christian theists, including Alvin Plantinga. We met and had dinner together that weekend.

Three months later, Tony and I debated for the first time, on the subject of the resurrection of Jesus. It was later published by Harper and Row.[3] We've had two additional dialogues on the same subject since then, in 2000 and again in 2003. Debate two was also recently published.[4] Over the years, Tony and I also exchanged dozens of letters. In our many phone calls, we could just as easily discuss the British or American educational systems, or any number of other topics.

In 2003, shortly after our third dialogue on the resurrection, Tony told me that he was considering theism. About a year later, in January 2004, he told me that he had been reading Aristotle, along with some ideas from the intelligent design movement. Of the two, Tony said that Aristotle had presented weightier arguments for the existence of God. In his words, he decided to go where the evidence was leading, a phrase that he has since used often, and he realized that he now believed in God's existence.

Later, we recorded a lengthy conversation and had it transcribed. Throughout the year, we worked on the manuscript and edited it. It was accepted for publication. But about two weeks before the article was due to appear, all of a sudden, everything hit the news, featuring titles like "Atheist's Turn Toward

---

[3]Gary R. Habermas and Antony G. N. Flew, *Did Jesus Rise from the Dead? The Resurrection Debate*, ed. Terry L. Miethe (San Francisco: Harper & Row, 1987).
[4]Gary R. Habermas and Antony G. N. Flew, *Resurrected? An Atheist and Theist Dialogue*, ed. John F. Ankerberg (Lanham, Md.: Rowman & Littlefield, 2005). The 2003 debate was never published.

God Was a Four-Year Process, Friend Says"[5] and later, "Thinking Straighter: Why the World's Most Famous Atheist Now Believes in God."[6] My personal favorite was, "Flew the Coup," where Tony said, "My whole life has been guided by the principle of Plato's Socrates: . . . follow the evidence wherever it leads."[7] The story seemed to spread around the world in a matter of days. For a few weeks we were deluged with contacts. I would call Tony, and sometimes he would say things like, "I am worn out with the press. I didn't want this to be about me. I'm tired of these discussions."

Our own discussion was finally published in early 2005 with the title "My Pilgrimage from Atheism to Theism."[8] Tony, perhaps you can talk a little bit about all this.

FLEW: I think that the description of me as "atheist" was very misleading for some people. When we see one of these words beginning with the letter *a*, we must remember that they are taken from the Greek, and that they do not signify anything more than the negative. I was an "atheist" in the sense that I was not a believer in God. It did not mean what some people might think. They may hear that somebody is an atheist, and assume that I was terribly excited about this state and wanted the Lord to strike me down, as if he really existed and all that. I have only been an "a"-theist in the proper sense of the word, which is like that of atypical, asymmetrical, and all the other English, formerly Greek, terms beginning with an *a*.

Regarding my change of belief, it seems to me that there never should have been a great deal of excitement about this. For me, my belief in God is not belief in the Lord of Christianity or Islam. The Qur'an is not the sort of book you would be eager to read, I think, unless you had to for some reason. Roughly one-third of all the suras, or chapters, make reference to eternal torment. It's an absolutely central, fundamental idea that is going to happen to the opponents of the Prophet. I think more people should realize that. But my theory about God is the same sort of belief as Einstein expressed in the first edition of his book. Since that time, many Nobel Prize-winning

---

[5]David Roach, "Atheist's Turn Toward God Was a Four-Year Process, Friend says," *BP News*, December 22, 2004, reprint, pp. 1-4.

[6]James A. Beverley, "Thinking Straighter: Why the World's Most Famous Atheist Now Believes in God," *Christianity Today*, April 2005, pp. 80-83.

[7]Gene Edward Veith, "Flew the Coup," *World*, December 25, 2004, p. 22.

[8]Antony Flew and Gary Habermas, "My Pilgrimage From Atheism to Theism: A Discussion Between Antony Flew and Gary Habermas," *Philosophia Christi* 6, no. 2 (2004): 197-211.

physicists have agreed with Einstein that there is some sort of Intelligence behind the physical world. I follow Einstein in that. But following Aristotle's concept of God is a very different thing from believing in the God of Christianity or of Islam. One might suspect that Aristotle was speaking for Einstein here. And I think that the ideal form of life would be to engage in philosophical contemplation.

HABERMAS: Do you think that "deism" is a more accurate description of your position than "theism"?

FLEW: Well, yes, much more accurate.

HABERMAS: When we first started working on our 2004 dialogue, I recall you making the remark that we should use the term theism of your position, simply because not enough people understood the notion of deism. But as the story started breaking in December 2004, people seemed to understand the difference fairly quickly and started saying that it was much more accurate to call you a deist.

FLEW: Yes. Other than that, I don't think I have much to say about it.

HABERMAS: On the issue of miracles, would you be roughly where you were before you became a deist?

FLEW: Yes. Except that, in at least one of our dialogues on the subject, I simply went to pieces. Basically because I follow David Hume on this subject, I think that it is conceivable that there might be sufficient evidence for the occurrence of a miracle, although I do not think that any of the alleged miracles that people have been excited about have begun to meet Hume's requirements. Hume of course pursues this in his first *Enquiry*. I have written at length about this topic.

HABERMAS: Such as in *Hume's Philosophy of Belief*?[9]

FLEW: Yes, that's it. It was a standard book on Hume's position.

HABERMAS: You have recently begun to make the distinction between what it would take for an atheist, or in your case a deist, to believe in a miracle, as opposed to what it would take for a person who already accepted the con-

---

[9]Antony Flew, *Hume's Philosophy of Belief* (London: Routledge & Kegan Paul, 1961).

cept of God's revelation. I refer here to what would make sense for each, given their background information.

FLEW: I think that that is right. When I was a student at Oxford University, studying under Gilbert Ryle, several graduate students in philosophy tried to work out what would be absolutely, decisively the sort of thing that would constitute a miracle. We used to think of things where all the media were present and some great change occurred in the structure of things. It might be a divine voice that we all heard or something like that—you know, God speaking to us. Even the most determined unbeliever would not be able to get away from such a really direct, dramatic interference with the normal workings of the universe. That is the sort of miracle that you could not possibly go on denying while claiming to be an actual scientific person. This would signify a substantial change in the natural order. But we continued to go on not believing in the occurrence of miracles, accepting Hume's argument.

HABERMAS: Tony, what position do you hold at present regarding some of the classic arguments for God's existence? What is the force of those rational or empirical attempts?

FLEW: They are not going to get us to the God of any religious revelation. The only reason why people are excited about miracles is because of the possibility that they provide information of which you had better take notice concerning the management of the universe.

HABERMAS: As I recall, you are a bit critical of C. S. Lewis's Moral Argument.

FLEW: I don't think that the moral arguments for the existence of God carry much weight. After all, one of the things that causes unbelievers to continue in unbelief is being told that God is omnipotent and perfectly good. Aquinas dealt with this, as did Leibniz. They thought [that] goodness and being are the same thing. They follow an argument in Plato that the Form of the Good is the same as the Form of the Real. Taking this line, they think that goodness does not mean being a good chap, you know, by actually helping the unfortunate citizens of Niger. But that is not the philosophical meaning of goodness. They have somehow tried to reconcile their belief in the goodness of God with what unbelievers take as evidence against this goodness.

HABERMAS: What argument did you find most persuasive when you moved over to deism? Where did the evidence lead you?

FLEW: I think it was entirely the idea of intelligence, such as Spinoza's concept.

HABERMAS: And as you said earlier, Aristotle probably carried the most weight for you?

FLEW: Yes, I think so. It was Aristotle who pointed me in the direction of taking another look at Einstein. Einstein tries to ground some of his key ideas in philosophy.

HABERMAS: Where are you on the intelligent design issue?

FLEW: This is what Einstein was apparently thinking, but he seemed not to think that intelligence is somehow actively involved in making decisions about things.

HABERMAS: Do you have any comments regarding recent statements in defense of atheism by Richard Dawkins?

FLEW: His job is to inform students and others regarding developments in biology. But he fails to present the whole picture. The thing he ought to be saying is that the physicist's consensus about the age of the universe does not leave nearly enough time for a chance development of the first organisms from Darwin's puddle of chemical mud in a lake or ocean.

HABERMAS: In our dialogue that was published in *Philosophia Christi,* you talked about Jesus and Paul as careful thinkers, moral philosophers, and so on. Would you like to add anything?

FLEW: It seems to me that the difference between Christianity and Islam is simply enormous. Paul was a first-rate philosopher—a first-rate mind, and Jesus was the defining instance of a charismatic figure.

I've been keeping on the back burner my study that compares Islam and Christianity. I'm not going to publish that right now. I'm not worried, at my age, about risking being the object of a Fatwah. In fact, I'd rather like a quick death. The organization of which Paul Kurtz is a looming figure has published a great deal of basic literature about Islam, including some writings of some people who have abandoned it and have had to go underground because of it.

HABERMAS: I think you mean Prometheus Books?

FLEW: Yes, Prometheus has done an important job [of] publishing what would have been very difficult, if not impossible, to publish in Holland. It would have been very difficult to get any British publisher now to do it, either. This, again, makes me think about Islam. Let's face it, several Muslim organizations think that in the near future, the expansion of Islamic ideology will control the whole world. Much of their information about the Bible was mistaken. I'm not sure that there was any part of the Bible available in that area at all.

HABERMAS: Some have commented that the reason you are now more interested in religion is that, at your age, you are concerned about an afterlife. I know from our frequent communications over the years that this is not the case.

FLEW: I treat this very seriously. I have had the ambition of producing an argument about the possibility of a future life. While I was a graduate student, I said that if I were ever asked to become a Gifford Lecturer, that I would speak on the subject of mortality, and I did.[10] And I am thinking of trying to produce another edition of the same work.

HABERMAS: Tony, you may remember the details of C. S. Lewis's conversion. In Lewis's autobiography, *Surprised by Joy*, he addressed the process of his conversion in chapters like those he titled "Check" and "Checkmate."[11] Lewis describes his two-stage conversion. He first moved from atheism to theism, deciding finally between Hinduism and Christianity. He chose Christianity because it had a strong historical component, among other things. So he moved from a more general theism to Christianity. When people refer to our friendship, I am often asked about the chances that you could someday become a Christian. I explain that this was the same question that I asked you at the conclusion of the *Philosophia Christi* interview. Perhaps you could address this issue once again for those who are interested. Do you think there would ever be much of a likelihood that you, following Lewis's example, might take that second step to Christianity?

---

[10] Antony Flew, *The Logic of Mortality* (Oxford: Blackwell, 1987); cf. Antony Flew, ed., *Body, Mind, and Death* (New York: Macmillan, 1964).

[11] C. S. Lewis, *Surprised by Joy: The Shape of My Early Life* (New York: Harcourt, Brace, Jovanovich, 1955).

FLEW: Well, it's certainly more likely than that I might become a Hindu . . . or a Buddhist.

HABERMAS: Before today, the last time I'd seen Tony, we had just concluded our third dialogue for a Veritas Forum, at Cal Poly University in San Luis Obispo, California. We were walking to an elevator just off campus, heading for our hotel. I got off the elevator, but Tony was going to an upper floor in the hotel. We were teasing a bit about having another debate, and Tony said, "I don't think I'm going to debate again on the resurrection." And I retorted, "What? You don't want four debates on this subject?" As I said, we were doing a little teasing. Then there was sort of a surrealistic experience for me. As I got off the elevator, I thrust my hand back through the open door to shake his hand and said, "When you become a Christian, I want to be the first one to know." And he said, "I think you've earned that right."

Let me make something clear, by the way, and Tony can confirm this. I'm not implying that I am the only influence on Tony's recent decision. For example, Tony has indicated that Roy Varghese's book *The Wonder of the World* has been a very influential statement of the scientific evidence.[12] But Tony has caused me to do a lot of thinking regarding the role of friendship. We've been good friends for a long time, and I think there's something to be said for friendship between believers and unbelievers. Perhaps this is another side of the legacy of C. S. Lewis—that friends can dialogue and everyone does not have to agree as a precondition for mutual appreciation. This is an aspect of tolerance at its best, that good friends can discuss what's going on in the news, whether serious or not. Would you like to comment further here?

FLEW: I don't think that's necessary. I might say that I'm sure that C. S. Lewis was the sort of person who would have learned from more than one avenue.

HABERMAS: Well, I just want to state publicly that I really appreciate your friendship and have for a good many years. This man is not just a standard example of a first-rate philosophical mind, but someone who has been a good friend. While waiting for this interview to begin, so many folks came up to Tony and said things like, "I studied your works in graduate school. I had to

---

[12]Roy Abraham Varghese, *The Wonder of the World: A Journey from Modern Science to the Mind of God* (Fountain Hills, Ariz.: Tyr Publishing, 2003).

read *God and Philosophy* or 'Theology and Falsification.'" So many of your works have been required reading. There have been so many comments about this today. Tony is an exceptionally humble person, and to hear him respond, as he has today, further indicates this. I think it is fair to call him the foremost philosophical atheist during the past fifty years, judging from his philosophical publications, as compared to the writings of other well-known British philosophers such as Bertrand Russell, A. J. Ayer or J. L. Mackie. Perhaps he will have an entirely different sort of influence now that he thinks that belief in the existence of God is warranted by the data.

I'll just add briefly that, talking to his wife, Annis, from time to time has also been very nice. Some of the things that she says about Tony are cute. From what I can tell, they have a marvelous relationship. By the way, the latest edition of *God and Philosophy* is dedicated to Annis with these words, "Take them, Love, the book and me together."[13] That's from Browning?

FLEW: It is, yes.

HABERMAS: Is there anything you would like to add, about any of my comments, or about C. S. Lewis?

FLEW: Of course, the most important part of Lewis's academic life was his literary studies. There were also his fairy stories.

HABERMAS: Yes, the Narnia Chronicles.

FLEW: And there were several other literary friends of his with whom he spent a good deal of time at the pub and elsewhere.

HABERMAS: Like J. R. R. Tolkien.

FLEW: Yes, especially Tolkien. I think they all met rather regularly, very near my own college, on the other side of the railroad. One of the places was the pub that we irreverently called "The Bird and Baby."

HABERMAS: As I recall, that's in between here and your college, St. Johns.

FLEW: Yes!

HABERMAS: Okay. We are going to open the floor now to some questions.

---

[13] Antony Flew, *God and Philosophy* (Amherst, N.Y.: Prometheus, 2005).

QUESTIONS AND ANSWERS

QUESTION 1 (UNNAMED PERSON): I actually had a question for you, Gary. What would you say is the most convincing evidence or argument for the resurrection?

HABERMAS: As far I am concerned, the most persuasive argument for the resurrection comes from the method that I prefer. All three times that Tony and I have dialoged, this is the approach that I used. I would never argue that the resurrection happened because the Bible said that it occurred, or something of that nature. I would argue from what I term the minimal-facts method. It builds on the historical facts that are generally held in common by virtually all critical scholars, regardless of their other beliefs. I have surveyed most of what is in print on the subject, written in French, German and English and published between 1975 and the present. The vast majority of these scholars will allow certain historical facts. This even applies to very skeptical scholars such as Gerd Lüdemann and John Dominic Crossan. I will use this data for two reasons: (1) Each fact is confirmed for a variety of reasons, usually arrived at from more than one angle. Therefore, they are very difficult to deny. (2) Virtually all scholars who deal with this subject hold these data and recognize them as historical truths.

From these historical facts, almost all scholars agree that Jesus' early disciples thought that he had been raised from the dead, because they were utterly convinced that they had seen Jesus alive again after his death. Today it seems that the tables have turned and that a large number of these scholars also conclude not only that Jesus was raised from the dead, but also that he appeared bodily. That was not the case a few decades ago. Add to this that naturalistic theories that attempt to explain away the resurrection are refuted by these same historical facts. The majority of critical scholars agree here as well. So here's how we get Jesus' resurrection from these historical data: for a variety of very strong and persuasive reasons that I will not be able to mention here, the early disciples thought that they had seen the risen Jesus, and natural theories have not been able to disprove this. In short, the conclusion of Jesus' resurrection rests on the disciples' conviction that they had seen resurrection appearances, while viable alternative hypotheses have failed. To me, that's the strongest basis for Jesus' resurrection.

QUESTION 2 (UNNAMED PERSON): Dr. Flew, this is very relevant to this conference. You keep reiterating the fact that C. S. Lewis was a literary scholar. It strikes me as a bit ironic that, so often, we get into discussions about the legitimacy of Christianity by aligning it with science, when there is another scholar who has been made famous in literary studies, who has followed the same trajectory as you have. I wonder if anybody has made this comparison between you and Jacques Derrida, who in the development of deconstruction realized that as he follows it to its logical extension (and he defines deconstruction as openness to the other), he became increasingly aware that we need to be open even to the possibility of the transcendent Other. And he took a position very similar to the position that you are taking in that he acknowledges what he calls the impossible, which he calls God, and that as soon as we start putting God into language, we limit God. But he is open to the idea of the messianic, which is what he describes as institutional religions. This is what I hear you saying too. Does that sound possible? Has anyone ever made that comparison between your approach and that of Derrida?

FLEW: No. I must say that if anyone had compared me to Derrida, I would have been quite worried.

FOLLOW-UP COMMENT: Derrida changed a lot during the last twelve years of his life.

[At this point, Flew rolled his eyes, and much laughter ensued.]

QUESTION 3 (DAVID BAGGETT): Dr. Flew, as a Christian philosopher, I admit that what you have done for several years is to provide me with many thoughts to push against, against which I might argue. But I think that in the process, you have made all of us, as a community of Christian philosophers, better for it. By the way, there is something that is very inspiring about this friendship between you and Gary. I think that you two have been a model for philosophical dialogue at its best, and it is a wonderful thing to witness. I have a question about miracles, regarding this scenario that you have depicted, where God speaks in a voice that everyone the world over can hear. Surely, if God existed, he could do this. But do you have any thoughts on what Pascal might have said by way of the reasons why God would *not* want to do such a thing? It would be such overwhelming evidence, such a powerful illumination, as to simply overpower the mind with light. In such a case, the decision of belief would be practically coerced. Right? And you might say that this would not measure anything in the heart, but would only concern intellectual honesty, as something that you could not avoid. There might be a reason why Pascal would be right—in other words, it might be necessary that God retain a certain measure of divine hiddenness. So, if you are looking for that kind of absolutely spectacular divine revelation, wouldn't there be some good reasons why God would not do that? Do you have any thoughts on that?

FLEW: I think this is one of the things about which the doctrines about eternal torment are highly relevant. It seems to me if that is what is going on, not to give people an inescapably obvious, true warning is a deplorable way of behaving. I cannot think that this is a reason for respecting God, and it is a very good reason for causing fear.

HABERMAS: What do you think about why God might not want to make everything so obvious? Wouldn't that simply coerce belief? That would not seem to be the best way to obtain faith and inspire worship. So perhaps God provides enough evidence, without giving too much.

FLEW: I think that if the stakes are eternal torment, then to do anything that keeps people out of the danger of going to hell is imperative. This seems to make the Christian God uncomfortably like the God of Islam. If you ever look at the English translation of the Qur'an, you will find that there are insertions before most of the suras (chapters), that read, "In the Name of Allah, the Compassionate, the Merciful." I think that this is an editorial introduction. Anyway, I have yet to discover how Muslims justify this introduction. The idea that the God of Islam is compassionate and merciful is difficult to understand. It is not based on any text of the Qur'an. But this seems to be an oddity. I look forward to hearing the answer. Does it not sound rather curious?

QUESTION 4 (PETER KREEFT): Dr. Flew, I would like to reiterate what the previous questioner said. From your premises, let's begin with your rightful fear of what you think is the God of Islam. I'm not an Islamic expert, but the Qur'an states that God is supposed to be good, but deliberately wills people to suffer forever through no fault of their own. Let's start with that as a premise. Then let's also remember your anti-Platonic premise, that that which is and that which is good are not identical. What I think you mean by that is Kant's point that the true good is a good will, a moral good. Regarding ontological good, perhaps Plato was right there. But obviously, not everything that is ought to be, including human behaviors. So we have your rejection of Allah and your rejection of Plato. Now, if Kant is right that the supreme good is good will, and if good will is a will that wills good to the other, that is basically what Christians mean by love. Aquinas's definition of charity is the will for the other. Well, if love respects human freedom, why don't you accept Pascal's explanation for why God does not give us more evidence, as per Russell's question? Isn't it because he respects our freedom, the same way that you respected your wife's freedom when you asked her to marry you? You did not compel her with philosophical syllogisms. You said, "Jump into my arms of your own free will."

FLEW: I think that it is all very well for any ordinary human relationship. But it seems to me [that] if you are proposing to torture people, then it is not time to respect their will. That is the time to save them from this most appalling catastrophe.

FOLLOW-UP QUESTION: Suppose you subtract that last premise. Suppose your God does not propose to torture anyone.

FLEW: That is a different story, as the world of Catholic Christianity soon learns.

FOLLOW-UP COMMENT: Well, the God of C. S. Lewis doesn't torture anyone. He says in *The Problem of Pain* that God does not toss anybody into hell.

FLEW: Anglicans, the Church of England, as part of what I fear is its continuing decline, did recently abandon the doctrine of hell.

FOLLOW-UP QUESTION: Well, that's another thing altogether, isn't it?

QUESTION 5 (CHUCK COLSON): Dr. Flew, I wanted, first of all, to congratulate you for your intellectual integrity. I really admire the courage with which you have spoken on these views. I think we all appreciate that. I wanted to add something here, which you might think we have rehearsed, but we did not. I was converted by reading C. S. Lewis. I believed in Christ and have spent much of the last thirty years as a Christian, proving that the biblical worldview is better to live by than any other. That being one test of truth, does Christianity correspond to reality? When one lives its teachings, does it have an internal integrity? As a lawyer, I've come to the strong realization, the belief, that this is the case. I think that the biblical worldview is true. Since Christianity conforms to reality, its suppositions are correct. But that does not get me to love God and have faith, and that is what God wants. More than anything else, he wants my love. I realized that, if he did give me all of the evidence, I'd no longer have the capacity to love him. He wants our love, and he tells us that. So, if he were to absolutely prove it all, if you were ever able to put the final piece into place and philosophically prove that God is who he says he is, that his Bible is his message to the world, that Christ is exactly who he says he is, then as (I think) John Henry Newman once said, God would be like the tree outside my window, and I would take him for granted. Only a mystery where we cannot really be sure, and have to come to faith, allows us to love God. If we knew for certain that he were God, or if he took away our free will, then we would not have the capacity to love him. That is exactly why he created us. Do not think you will ever get past that point. If you ever do get past that point, you will have talked yourself out of the ability to love God.

[No response by Flew.]

QUESTION 6 (UNNAMED PERSON): I, too, have wrestled with the same issue about heaven and hell, just as you have done. One of my seminary professors said something that has helped me a lot. You might consider it, or at least I'd ask you to do so. My professor said that it is possible that we could mistake heaven for hell. If so, then we might not like God. For instance, if I love classical music, coming here to London and listening to the London Symphony Orchestra would be like heaven. But if I liked rap music, and I was made to sit and listen to the London Symphony Orchestra, I might find it eternal hell.

FLEW: Yes, being totally unmusical, I can understand this.

3

Defending the Dangerous Idea

An Update on Lewis's Argument from Reason

VICTOR REPPERT

While C. S. Lewis's argument against naturalism, found in the third chapter of *Miracles: A Preliminary Study,* has been interesting to me since I began reading Lewis at the age of eighteen, my participation in serious discussion of the argument began as a graduate student at the University of Illinois at Champaign-Urbana. Although this argument is widely thought to have been put out to pasture by Elizabeth Anscombe's criticisms—and indeed it is sometimes claimed that Lewis was put out to pasture as an apologist by this exchange—I readily reached the conclusion that an adequately reformulated version of the argument could surmount Anscombe's objections. I defended this claim for the first time in print in my paper "The Lewis-Anscombe Controversy: A Discussion of the Issues," which appeared in *Christian Scholar's Review* in 1989.[1]

My research into the Anscombe exchange shows rather clearly:

1. Anscombe provided some legitimate objections to the formulation of the argument against naturalism as found in the first edition of *Miracles.*

2. Lewis seems to have felt discouraged in the immediate aftermath of the exchange, as shown by comments he made to literary friends.

---

[1]Victor Reppert, "The Lewis-Anscombe Controversy: A Discussion of the Issues," *Christian Scholar's Review* 19 (September 1989): 32-48.

3. Lewis did not think that Anscombe's considerations put the naturalist in the clear; in fact, Lewis employs Anscombe's distinctions in the response that appears in the very issue of the Socratic Digest in which Anscombe's paper appeared.

4. Anscombe considered the revised argument much more serious than the first edition, although she did not endorse it.

5. Although Lewis published no more books about apologetics after the Anscombe exchange, he did write many articles devoted to apologetics, revising and expanding the controversial chapter of *Miracles* for the Fontana edition.

6. Attempts to identify the Green Witch in Narnia (who attempts to persuade the children that the Overworld does not exist) with Anscombe are complete and utter nonsense.[2]

However, is the argument itself defensible? In the exchanges I have had with opponents of the argument, I find that some of them use arguments that echo those of Anscombe, but most responses to it are very different from those that Anscombe used. In fact, some have told me, after I presented a paper showing that Lewis could effectively respond to Anscombe, that Anscombe's objections were not very interesting.

Nevertheless, I have concluded that arguments along the lines Lewis was suggesting are indeed defensible, and my doctoral dissertation at Illinois-Urbana was an attempt to defend this claim against the relentless objections of my dissertation advisor, Hugh Chandler.

I returned to the work of defending the argument from reason with a paper that appeared first on Internet Infidels and later in the Society of Humanist Philosophers journal *Philo*, which was titled "The Argument from Reason." I engaged in some cross-debate with Keith Parsons and Jim Lippard in a subsequent issue of that journal,[3] and then wrote a response to Parsons in

---

[2]Victor Reppert, "The Green Witch and the Great Debate," in *The Chronicles of Narnia and Philosophy* (Chicago: Open Court, 2005).

[3]Jim Lippard, "Historical but Indistinguishable Differences," *Philo* 2, no. 1 (1999); Keith Parsons, "Defending Objectivity, *Philo* 2, no. 1 (1999): 45-47; idem, "Further Reflections on the Argument from Reason," *Philo* 3, no. 1 (2000): 90-102; Victor Reppert, "The Argument from Reason," posted online at <http://www.infidels.org/library/modern/victor_reppert/reason.html>, later published in *Philo* 2, no. 1 (1999); idem, "Reply to Parsons and Lippard on the Argument from Reason," *Philo* 3, no. 1 (2000).

Philosophia Christi.[4] When I got my contract to write *C. S. Lewis's Dangerous Idea*, the editors at *Philosophia Christi* asked me to do a symposium on the Argument from Reason with Theodore Drange, Keith Parsons and William Hasker as my respondents.[5] So a good deal of what appears in chapters four and five of my book also appears in that exchange for *Philosophia Christi*.

Since that time the book has attracted a lot of response, including some comments by critics. Most notable of these has been Richard C. Carrier on Internet Infidels, whose critique of my book is about as long as the book itself.[6]

Although when I began writing about Lewis's argument I had thought that it was basically one argument—that naturalism is incompatible with the existence of rationally justified belief—I reached the conclusion that as one follows the threads suggested by Lewis's argument, one actually ends up with a number of different arguments. So in order to keep the tracks straight, I presented not one formulation of the argument from reason, but six: the argument from intentionality, the argument from truth, the argument from mental causation in virtue of propositional content, the argument from the psychological relevance of logical laws, the argument from the unity of consciousness, and the argument from the reliability of our rational faculties. This chapter will be devoted to a discussion of three of these arguments; as I go along, I respond to criticisms, mostly those of Carrier.

First, I need to clarify something about the scope and limits of my arguments. The necessary conditions of reason that I mention in my arguments seem impossible to reconcile with a materialist or naturalist worldview, and I believe this is precisely because they *are* impossible to reconcile with such a worldview. However, some philosophers seem to think that while there is no apparent way to reconcile, say, intentionality with physicalism, this is a function of the limits of our understanding, not evidence that naturalism is false. I must say that I am not a classical foundationalist. Therefore, I do not expect that in order for an argument to be a good one, it must be such that it ought to persuade every reasonable person. What I do maintain, however, is that the

---

[4]Victor Reppert, "Causal Closure, Mechanism, and Rational Inference," *Philosophia Christi*, 2nd ser., 3, no. 4 (2003): 473-84.

[5]Victor Reppert, "Several Formulations of the Argument from Reason," *Philosophia Christi*, 2nd ser., 5, no. 1 (2003): 9-33; idem, "Some Supernatural Reasons Why My Critics Are Wrong," *Philosophia Christi*, 2nd ser., 5, no. 1 (2003): 77-89.

[6]Richard C. Carrier, "Critical Review of Victor Reppert's Defense of the Argument from Reason" (2004) <http://www.infidels.org/library/modern/richard_carrier/reppert.html>.

features of our mental lives with which these arguments are concerned are features that make more sense on a theistic worldview than on a naturalistic one, and therefore they provide substantial reasons for preferring theism to naturalism. There are other worldviews, according to which the mental is fundamental to reality, but which are not naturalistic; and the arguments from reason do not attempt to refute these worldviews. C. S. Lewis himself embraced one such worldview when he came to accept the Argument from Reason; instead of becoming a theist, he became an Absolute Idealist, and his rejection of Absolute Idealism did not have anything to do with the Argument from Reason.

Second, in reflecting on all of this, I believe that the arguments from reason reflect what I perceive to be a general problem with a naturalistic view of the world. Viewing a phenomenon on materialistic terms means eliminating from the final analysis of it any normativity and any subjectivity. For example, let us take the moral good. There is prima facie reason to suppose that a less than fully realist account of the moral good will result if we restrict ourselves to the ontological limitations imposed by naturalism. In the case of the moral good, materialists often appeal to an "error theory" to account for moral phenomena. We think there are objective standards of moral value, but there really are none. The strength of the arguments from reason is that we can expect naturalists not to take refuge in error theories where the norms of rationality are concerned. Naturalists, after all, must maintain that scientists draw logical inferences, and that their own beliefs are better reasoned than those of their opponents.

I see a fundamental problem that is going to plague any naturalist account of the mind, and the arguments from reason point to a subspecies of that problem. Naturalists often piggyback the case for naturalism on the success of reductive analyses in science. However, let us take one of the most successful scientific reductions, the reduction of heat in a gas to the mean kinetic energy of that gas. From one perspective, this reduction appears to explain heat away, in particular the element of heat that feels warm. By knowing that the air molecules are moving faster, we can infer nothing about the fact that people are more likely to take their jackets off when that happens. They also feel warmer. However, says science, that is not an intrinsic feature of heat, but is rather what happens to human minds in the presence of heat. Siphoning off secondary qualities to the mind enables the mechanistic reduction of heat. But when

we get to the mind, we have no place to siphon off the "mental" properties.
Edward Feser writes:

> One result of this is that materialists have, in the view of their critics, a tendency
> to give accounts of mental phenomena that leave out everything essential to
> them: qualia, consciousness, thought and intentionality get redefined in physi-
> calistic terms, with the consequence that materialist analyses convey the impres-
> sion that the materialist has changed the subject, and failed genuinely to explain
> the phenomenon the analysis was supposed to account for. This is arguably the
> deep source of the difficulties that have plagued materialist philosophies of
> mind. If the materialist conception of explanation entails always stripping
> away[,] from the phenomena to be accounted for, anything that smacks of sub-
> jectivity, meaning or mind-dependence, then a materialist "explanation" of the
> mind itself will naturally seem to strip away the very essence of the phenomena
> to be explained. Being, at bottom, attempts to explain the mental in terms that
> are intrinsically non-mental, such would-be explanations [that] appear implic-
> itly to deny the mental; that is to say, they end up being disguised forms of elim-
> inative materialism. Some professedly non-eliminativist philosophers of mind
> come close to admitting this: Fodor, for instance, has famously written that "If
> aboutness (that is, intentionality) is real, it must really be something else."[7]

This results in an interesting phenomenon; materialist philosophers try to
give an account of some mental phenomenon. However, either they implicitly
bring in the very concepts they are trying to explain materialistically, or they
give an account of the mental phenomenon—an account in which the phenomenon to be explained is not recognizable.

THE ARGUMENT FROM INTENTIONALITY

The first of the arguments that I presented is the Argument from Intentionality. Physical states have physical characteristics, but how can something
about dogs Boots and Frisky, or about my late Uncle Stanley or even the number 2 be a characteristic of some physical state of my brain? Can we not describe my brain, and its activities, without having any clue as to what my
thoughts are about?

To begin all of this, I am going to start with William Hasker's simple description of the commonsense conception of mental states from his book *The
Emergent Self*:

---

[7]Edward Feser, *The Philosophy of Mind: A Short Introduction* (Oxford: Oneworld, 2005), pp. 172-73.

Let us begin with a modest proposal. There are intentional conscious experiences. There are, that is to say, such episodes as wondering whether it is going to rain, or believing that this has been an unusually cold winter, or deciding to let the credit card balance ride for another month. In typical cases such as these the intentional content of the experience, what the experience is about, is something distinct from the experience itself, something that could exist or obtain (or fail to exist or obtain) regardless of whether or not the experience occurred. These episodes are consciously experienced; when we have them we are aware of having them, and there is "something it is like" to have them.[8]

This relation between a state of mind and some purported state of affairs is called intentionality, or about-ness. There is a relationship between some conscious state of myself and some putative state of the world, a relation to an object that may or may not exist, and that relation is intentionality. It is quite true that some accounts of intentionality do not require consciousness, but what I am talking about here is a conscious state of mind that is about something else, and is recognized by the subject as being about what it is about.

It is important to draw a further distinction, a distinction between *original* intentionality, which is intrinsic to the person possessing the intentional state, and *derived* or *borrowed* intentionality, which we find in maps, words or computers. Maps, for example, have the meaning that they have, not in themselves, but in relation to other things that possess original intentionality, such as human persons. There can be no question that physical systems possess derived intentionality. However, if they possess derived intentionality in virtue of other things that may or may not be physical systems, this does not really solve the materialist's problem.

John Searle presents the problem facing a physicalist account of intentionality very forcefully:

> Any attempt to reduce intentionality to something nonmental will always fail because it leaves out intentionality. Suppose for example that you had a perfect causal account of the belief that water is wet. This account is given by stating the set of causal relations in which a system stands to water and to wetness and these relations are entirely specified without any mental component. The problem is obvious: a system could have all those relations and still not believe that water is wet. This is just an extension of the Chinese Room argument, but the moral it points to is general: You cannot reduce intentional content (or pains, or "qualia")

---

[8]William Hasker, *The Emergent Self* (Ithaca, N.Y.: Cornell University Press, 2001).

to something else, because if you did they would be something else, and it is not something else.[9]

Admittedly, this is merely an assertion of something that needs to be brought out with further analysis. It seems to me that intentionality, as I understand it, requires consciousness. There are systems that behave in ways such that, in order to predict their behavior, it behooves us to act as if they were intentional systems. If I am playing chess against a computer, and I am trying to figure out what to expect it to play, then I am probably going to look for the moves I think are good and expect the computer to play those. I act as if the computer were conscious, even though I know that it has no more consciousness than a tin can. Similarly, we can look at the bee dances and describe them in intentional terms—the motions the bees engage in enable the other bees to go where the pollen is—but it does not seem plausible to attribute a conscious awareness of what information is being sent in the course of the bee dance. We can look at the bees as if they were consciously giving one another information, but the intentionality being discussed is "as-if" intentionality, not the kind of original intentionality we find in conscious agents. As Colin McGinn writes:

> I doubt that the self-same kind of content possessed by a conscious perceptual experience, say, could be possessed independently of consciousness; such content seems essentially conscious, shot through with subjectivity. This is because of the Janus-faced character of conscious content: it involves presence to the subject, and hence a subjective point of view. Remove the inward-looking face and you remove something integral—what the world seems like to the subject.[10]

If we ask what the content of a word is, the content of that word must be the content for some conscious agent: how that conscious agent understands the word. There may be other concepts of content, but those concepts, it seems to me, are parasitical on the concept of content that I use in referring to states of mind found in a conscious agent. Put another way, my paradigm for understanding these concepts is my life as a conscious agent. If we make these words refer to something that occurs without consciousness, it seems that we are using them by way of analogy with their use in connection with our conscious life.

---

[9]John Searle, *The Re-Discovery of the Mind* (Cambridge, Mass.: MIT Press, 1992), p. 51.
[10]Colin McGinn, *The Problem of Consciousness* (Oxford: Blackwell, 1991), p. 34.

The intentionality that I am immediately familiar with is my own intentional states. That's the only template, the only paradigm I have. I would not say that animals are not conscious, and if I found good evidence that animals could reason, it would not undermine my argument, since I've never been a materialist about animals to begin with. Creatures other than myself could have intentional states, and no doubt do have them, if the evidence suggests that what it is like to be in the intentional state they are in is similar to what it is like to be in the intentional state that I am in.

In reading Carrier's critique of my book, we find, in his response to the argument from intentionality, terms being used that make sense to me from the point of view of my life as a conscious subject, but I am not at all sure what to make of them when we start thinking of them as elements in the life of something that is not conscious. His main definition of "aboutness" is this:

> Cognitive science has established that the brain is a computer that constructs and runs virtual models. All conscious states of mind consist of or connect with one or more virtual models. The relation these virtual models have to the world is that of corresponding or not corresponding to actual systems in the world. Intentionality is an assignment (verbal or attentional) of a relation between the virtual models and the (hypothesized) real systems. Assignment of relation is a decision (conscious or not), and such decisions, as well as virtual models and actual systems, and patterns of correspondence between them, all can and do exist on naturalism, yet these four things are all that are needed for Proposition 1 (some states of mind are about other things) to be true.[11]

Carrier adds:

> Language is a tool—it is a convention invented by humans. Reality does not tell us what a word means. We decide what aspects of reality a word will refer to. Emphasis here: we decide. We create the meaning for words however we want. The universe has nothing to do with it—except in the trivial sense that we (as computational machines) are a part of the universe.[12]

Now simply consider the words *hypothesized* and *decide* that Carrier uses in these passages. I think I know what it means to decide something as a conscious agent. I am aware of choice 1 and choice 2, I deliberate about the matter, and then I consciously choose 1 as opposed to 2, or vice versa. All of this requires

---

[11]Carrier, "Critical Review of Victor Reppert's Defense."
[12]Ibid.

that I be a conscious agent who knows what my thoughts are about. That is why I have been rather puzzled by Carrier's explaining intentionality in terms like these; such terms mean something to me only if we know what our thoughts are about. The same thing goes for hypothesizing. I can form a hypothesis (such as "All the houses in this subdivision were built by the same builder") just in case I know what the terms of the hypothesis mean, in other words, only if I already possess intentionality. That is what these terms mean to me, and unless I'm really confused, this is what those terms mean to most people.

Again, we have to take a look at the idea of a model. What is a model? A model is something that is supposed to resemble something else. But if we explain "X is about Y" at least partially in terms of "X is a model for Y," I really do not think we have gotten anywhere. How can X be a model for Y if it is not about Y in the first place? As Angus Menuge pointed out to me in correspondence:

> The problem with defining intentionality as an assignment could not be more severe: assignment is an intentional activity! Furthermore if this assignment is a decision, then while it does seem to be something that an interpreter of a computer can do, I see no reason to suppose that the computer does it. Computers match patterns "syntactically," to use Searle's jargon, with no grasp of their meaning.[13]

The deepest problem in assigning intentionality to physical systems is, I think, that when we do that, norms of rationality are applied when we determine what intentional states exist, but normative truths are not entailed by physical facts. In the realm of ethics, add up all the physical, chemical, biological, psychological and sociological facts about a murder for hire, and nothing in that description will entail that it was a wrongful act. Similarly, scientific information about what is will not tell you what an agent ought to believe, but we need to know what an agent ought to believe in order to figure out what that person does believe. According to Searle, for example, intentionality cannot be found in natural selection, because intentional standards are inherently normative, but there is nothing normative about Darwinian evolution. So any attempt to naturalize intentionality will end up bringing intentionality in through the backdoor, just as Carrier's account does. When you encounter a new or unfamiliar attempt to account for intentionality naturalistically, look it over very

---

[13]Angus Menuge, personal correspondence.

carefully, and you should be able to find out where the bodies are buried.

It is quite true that one can be a physicalist and say that mental states do not reduce to physical states. In other words, one can try to defend a dualism of properties without accepting a dualism of substances. Nonreductionists, however, have a mystery on their hands in seeing how a materialist world can have nonmaterial properties, and an even more serious problem in showing that such properties can be causally relevant without violating the causal closure of the physical. So it is at least understandable for people like Carrier to try to come up with a reduction. The reduction Carrier offers is woefully inadequate, however, and I think all other reductions will be equally inadequate.

THE ARGUMENT FROM MENTAL CAUSATION

The third of my arguments is the Argument from Mental Causation. If naturalism is true, even if there are propositional states like beliefs, then these states have to be epiphenomenal, without a causal role. Now careful reflection on rational inference, if we think about it, commits us to the idea that one mental event causes another mental event by virtue of its propositional content.

Now, if events are caused in accordance with physical law, they cause one another by virtue of being a particular type of event. A ball breaks a window by virtue of being the weight, density and shape that it is in relation to the physical structure of the window. Even if it is the baseball that Luis Gonzalez hit against Mariano Rivera that won the 2001 World Series, its being that ball has nothing to do with whether or not it can break the window now.

So let us suppose that brain state A, which is token identical to the thought that all humans are mortal, and brain state B, which is token identical to the thought that Socrates is a human, together cause the belief that Socrates is mortal. It is not enough for rational inference that these events be those beliefs; it is also necessary that the causal transaction be in virtue of the content of those thoughts. If anything not in space and time makes these thoughts the thoughts that they are, and if naturalism is true, then the propositional content is irrelevant to the causal transaction that produces the conclusion, and we do not have a case of rational inference. In rational inference, as Lewis puts it, one thought causes another thought not by being, but by being seen to be, the ground for it. But causal transactions in the brain occur by virtue of the brain's being in a particular type of state that is relevant to physical causal transactions. Only that property of the brain can be relevant to what the brain does, according to a naturalistic account of causation.

What this means is that the forms of substance materialism that accept property dualism invariably render the "mental" properties epiphenomenal. If the physical properties are sufficient to produce the physical effect, then the mental properties are irrelevant unless they really are physical properties writ large, so to speak. And mental states that are epiphenomenal cannot participate in rational inference.

Carrier's account of mental causation clearly presupposes a reductive, rather than a nonreductive, materialism. He writes:

> Every meaningful proposition is the content or output of a virtual model (or rather: actual propositions, of actual models; potential propositions, of potential models). Propositions are formulated in a language as an aid to computation, but when they are not formulated, they merely define the content of a nonlinguistic computation of a virtual model. In either case, a brain computes degrees of confidence in any given proposition, by running its corresponding virtual model and comparing it and its output with observational data, or the output of other computations.[14]

Now *if* Carrier had successfully provided a physicalist reduction of intentional states, so that the intentional characteristics could be in causal connection, then perhaps this part of his argument would work. But since the reduction seems to be unsuccessful, the proposed solution to the problem of mental causation must also be a failure.

But more than that, here again we find Carrier explaining one kind of mental activity in terms of another mental activity and then explaining it "naturalistically" by saying "the brain" does it. My argument is, first and foremost, that something exists whose activities are to be fundamentally explained in intentional and teleological terms. In order for talk about the brain to play its proper role in a physicalistic (nonintentional and nonteleological in the final analysis) account of mental events, we have to be sure that we are describing a brain that is mechanistic and part of a causally closed physical world. What I have written in response to Keith Parsons applies here as well (Parsons had argued that we could simply take all the characteristics that I wanted to attribute to the nonphysical mind and attribute them to the brain):

> But we should be careful of exactly what is meant by the term "brain." The

---

[14]Carrier, "Critical Review of Victor Reppert's Defense."

"brain" is supposed to be "physical," and we also have to be careful about what we mean by "physical." If by physical we mean that it occupies space, then there is nothing in my argument that suggests that I need to deny this possibility. I would just prefer to call the part of the brain that does not function mechanistically the soul, since, as I understand it, there is more packed into the notion of the physical than just the occupation of space. If on the other hand, for something to be physical (hence part of the brain) it has to function mechanistically, that is, intentional and teleological considerations cannot be basic explanations for the activity of the brain, then Parsons' suggestion (and Carrier's as well) is incoherent.[15]

I think that many people fail to see the difficulties posed by the arguments from reason because they think they can just engage in some brain-talk (well, the brain does this, the brain does that, and so on) and call it done. I call that the Mr. Brain fallacy. The question should always be, "If we view the brain as a mechanistic system in the full sense, does it make sense to attribute this characteristic to the brain?" Otherwise, I am inclined to say in response, "Interesting fellow, Mr. Brain. Remarkable what he can do." Using brain-talk does not mean that the work of physicalistic analysis has really been done.

THE ARGUMENT FROM THE PSYCHOLOGICAL RELEVANCE OF LOGICAL LAWS

My fourth argument concerns the role of logical laws in mental causation. In order for mental causation to be what we ordinarily suppose it to be, it is not only necessary that mental states be causally efficacious in virtue of their content; it is also necessary that the laws of logic be relevant to the production of the conclusion. That is, if we conclude "Socrates is mortal" from "All humans are mortal" and "Socrates is a human," then not only must we understand the meanings of those expressions, and these meanings must play a central role in the performance of these inferences, but what Lewis called the "ground-and-consequent relationship" between the propositions must also play a central role in these rational inferences. We must know that the argument is structured in such a way that, in arguments of that form, the conclusion always follows from the premises. We do not simply know something that is the case at one moment in time, but we know something that must be true in all moments of time, in every possible world. But how could a physical brain, which stands in

---

[15]Reppert, "Causal Closure, Mechanism, and Rational Inference."

physical relations to other objects and whose activities are determined, insofar as they are determined at all, by the laws of physics and not the laws of logic, come to know, not merely that something is true, but could not fail to be true regardless of whatever else is true in the world?

We can certainly imagine a possible world in which the laws of physics are different from the way they are in the actual world. We can imagine, for example, that instead of living in a universe in which dead people tend to stay dead, we find them rising out of their graves on a regular basis on the third day after they are buried. But we cannot imagine a world in which, once we know which cat and which mat, it can possibly be the case that the cat is both on the mat and not on the mat. Now, can we imagine there being a world in which 2 + 2 is really 5 and not 4? I think not.

It is one thing to suggest that brains might be able to track states of affairs in the physical world. It is another thing to suggest that a physical system can be aware, not only that something is the case but also that it must be the case; not only that it is the case but that it could not fail to be the case. Brain states stand in physical relations to the rest of the world, and they are related to that world through cause and effect, responding to changes in the world around us. How can these brain states be knowings of what must be true in all possible worlds?

Consider again the difficulty of going from what is to what ought to be in ethics. Many philosophers have agreed that you can pile up the physical truths, and all other descriptive truths from chemistry, biology, psychology and sociology, as high as you like about, say, the killings of Nicole Brown Simpson and Ronald Goldman, and you could never, by any examination of these, come to the conclusion that these acts were really morally wrong (as opposed to being merely widely disapproved of and criminalized by the legal system). Even the atheist philosopher J. L. Mackie argued that if there were truths of moral necessity, these truths, and our ability to know those truths, do not fit well into the naturalistic worldview, and if they existed, they would support a theistic worldview.[16] Mackie could and did, of course, deny moral objectivity, but my claim is that objective logical truths present an even more serious problem for naturalism, because the naturalist, on pain of undermining the very natural science on which his worldview ostensibly rests, cannot simply say that they do not exist.

---

[16]J. L. Mackie, *The Miracle of Theism* (Oxford: Clarendon, 1982), pp. 115-18.

Arguing that such knowledge is trivial because it merely constitutes the "relations of ideas" and does not tell anything about the world outside our minds seems to be an inadequate response. If, for example, the laws of logic are about the relations of ideas, then not only are they about ideas that I have thought already, but they are also true of thoughts I have not yet had. If contradictions cannot be true because this is how my ideas relate to one another, and if it is a contingent fact that my ideas relate to one another in this way, then it is impossible to say that they will not relate differently tomorrow.

Carrier responds somewhat differently:

> For logical laws are just like physical laws, because physical laws describe the way the universe works, and logical laws describe the way reason works—or, to avoid begging the question, logical laws describe the way a truth-finding machine works, in the very same way that the laws of aerodynamics describe the way a flying-machine works, or the laws of ballistics describe the way guns shoot their targets. The only difference between logical laws and physical laws is the fact that physical laws describe physics and logical laws describe logic. But that is a difference both trivial and obvious.[17]

First of all, this conflates the laws of nature and what we ought to do given the fact that the laws of nature are the way they are. If there is gravity, and people tend to get hurt when their bodies are affected by a lot of gravitational force, then we ought to exit tall buildings through doors that lead by elevator or stair to the ground floor, as opposed to jumping out windows. But the fact that if you want a long life you should exit tall buildings in certain ways and not in others should not be regarded as a law of physics. The physics describes how things are; the application of physics tells us what we ought to do about it.

Carrier seems to be denying the absolute necessity of logic. If the laws of logic just tell us how truth-finding machines work, then if the world were different, a truth-finding machine would work differently. I would insist on a critical distinction between the truths of mathematics, which are true regardless of whether anybody thinks them or not, and laws governing how either a person or a computer ought to perform computations. I would ask, "What is it about reality that makes one set of computations correct and another set of computations incorrect?"

---

[17]Carrier, "Critical Review of Victor Reppert's Defense."

Logic, I maintain, picks out features of reality that must exist in any possible world. We know and have insight into these realities, and this is what permits us to think. A naturalistic view of the universe, according to which there is nothing in existence that is not in a particular time and a particular place, is hard-pressed to reconcile with the fact that some truths that we know are not only true in this world, but also in all possible worlds.

4

Aut Deus aut Malus Homo

A Defense of C. S. Lewis's "Shocking Alternative"

DAVID A. HORNER

One of C. S. Lewis's most popular and influential apologetic arguments[1] is his brief elucidation of the "shocking alternative" of Jesus' identity, which arises from his claims to deity: *aut Deus aut malus homo*—either God or a bad man.[2] In *C. S. Lewis and the Search for Rational Religion*, John Beversluis attacks the "shocking alternative" argument as logically unsound and emotionally inflammatory.[3] In this chapter I argue that Lewis's argument, although sometimes imprecise and underdeveloped, is sound, and that it is Beversluis's critique itself that is better characterized by the epithets he applies to Lewis.

THE ARGUMENT

In his popular-level introduction to the faith, *Mere Christianity* (hereafter,

---

[1]This is a modified version of a paper presented May 25, 1993, to the C. S. Lewis Society of Oxford University, in response to Beversluis's book and to a paper Beversluis presented to the Society on a previous occasion. I am grateful for comments on my original paper to John Beversluis, Linette Martin, Joe Martin, Philip Ryken, Christopher Shields and Patrick Richmond. I am grateful to the Overseas Research Student Award Scheme and to contributors to the "Oxford Project" for funding during initial work on this chapter.
[2]So C. S. Lewis characterizes the argument in "Christian Apologetics," "Rejoinder to Dr. Pittenger" and "What Are We to Make of Jesus Christ?" reprinted in *God in the Dock*, ed. Walter Hooper (Grand Rapids: Eerdmans, 1970), p. 101. He notes the same line of argument in G. K. Chesterton's *The Everlasting Man* (New York: Dodd, Mead, 1925).
[3]John Beversluis, *C. S. Lewis and the Search for Rational Religion* (Grand Rapids: Eerdmans, 1985).

MC),[4] C. S. Lewis argues that, when considered seriously, Jesus' claims about himself eliminate as a viable option what is probably the most common, unbelieving response to Jesus: to hold him in very high esteem as a *great moral teacher* (hereafter, GMT), while denying that he is God. Lewis concludes his brief argument with this famous paragraph:

> I am trying here to prevent anyone saying the really foolish thing that people often say about Him: "I'm ready to accept Jesus as a great moral teacher, but I don't accept His claim to be God." That is the one thing we must not say. A man who was merely a man and said the sort of things Jesus said would not be a great moral teacher. He would either be a lunatic—on a level with a man who says he is a poached egg—or else he would be the Devil of Hell. You must take your choice. Either this man was, and is, the Son of God: or else a madman or something worse. You can shut Him up for a fool, you can spit at Him and kill Him as a demon; or you can fall at His feet and call Him Lord and God. But let us not come with any patronising nonsense about His being a great human teacher. He has not left that open to us. He did not intend to.[5]

Beversluis, safe to say, is not persuaded. He concludes his critique:

> We must therefore emphatically reject the Lord-or-lunatic dilemma. Once its high-voltage psychological charge has been neutralized, it will no longer be able to jolt us into supposing that we can remain unorthodox only by reviling a universally revered sage. It is perfectly legitimate to suggest that Jesus was a great moral teacher even though he was not God. Because of the manner in which it denies this obvious fact, the Lord-or-lunatic dilemma is the most objectionable of Lewis's many attempts to confront us with false dilemmas and to formulate non-exhaustive sets of options in emotionally inflammatory ways.[6]

Before examining the merit of Beversluis's critique, we need to be clear about what Lewis's argument is. We may summarize it as a progression of exclusive disjunctions:

(1) Jesus claimed to be God.

(2) Jesus' claim to deity is either true or false.

(3) If his claim to deity is true, then Jesus is *Lord.*

---

[4]C. S. Lewis, *Mere Christianity* (New York: Macmillan, 1952). Following Beversluis, I shall focus on Lewis's account of the argument that is given in *MC*, because it is his most influential, and refer secondarily to his other discussions of it.
[5]*MC*, pp. 55-56.
[6]Beversluis, *C. S. Lewis and the Search*, p. 57.

(4) If his claim to deity is false, then either Jesus knew it to be false or he did not know it to be false.

(5) If he knew his claim to deity to be false, then Jesus was a *liar.*

(6) If he did not know his claim to deity to be false, then Jesus was a *lunatic.*

CONCLUSION: Either Jesus' claim to deity is true, and he is God; or his claim to deity is false, and Jesus was in fact either a liar or a lunatic, but not a good man, and a fortiori not a GMT. *Aut Deus aut malus homo.*

At the outset note that Lewis's fundamental assertion,

(1) that Jesus claimed to be God,

rests on two assumptions, both of which may be questioned. First, one may deny (1) by rejecting the historical reliability of the Gospel accounts, maintaining either that Jesus never existed, or that we have insufficient knowledge about him and his claims.[7] The Jesus of Lewis's argument is no more than a *legend,* and therefore Lewis's alternatives disappear. (Note, however, that strong skepticism about what we know of Jesus cuts in *every* direction: while it allows the historical skeptic to avoid Lewis's implications about Jesus' deity, it also precludes one from holding Jesus in esteem as a GMT.) Lewis simply assumes the general historicity and credibility of the Gospel records and the information they contain of Jesus' actions and claims.[8] More would be needed to defend the argument if it were challenged along these lines.

Second, even if one accepts the general historicity of the Gospel accounts, one may reject (1) by denying that in those records Jesus actually claims or understands himself to be God. On this view, what have traditionally been taken to be at least de facto claims by Jesus to deity (i.e., claims by Jesus to be or to do something that only God could be or do) should be interpreted in other ways.[9] Lewis's argument, then, also assumes that a traditional interpretation of at least some of the Gospel accounts is correct. Both of these

[7]E.g., A. N. Wilson, *Jesus* (London: Sinclair-Stevenson, 1992). For a response, see N. T. Wright, *Who Was Jesus?* (Grand Rapids: Eerdmans, 1992).

[8]Lewis argues against the legend objection in "What Are We to Make of Jesus Christ?" See also Craig Blomberg, *The Historical Reliability of the Gospels* (Downers Grove, Ill.: IVP Academic, 2007), esp. p. 22.

[9]In all, C. S. Lewis mentions a number of de facto deity claims of Christ. In *MC*, he lists three: Jesus' claims to have always existed, to be coming to judge the world at the end of time, and to be able to forgive sins. The only claim Lewis expounds, however, is the latter.

assumptions would need to be developed and defended if these historical and hermeneutical objections were raised.[10] In my view, Lewis's assumptions are plausible and defensible, but that is an argument for another time.[11]

These are two powerful objections to Lewis's argument—indeed, in my view, its strongest objections, albeit not finally successful. What is particularly interesting about Beversluis's critique of Lewis, however, is that *these are not his objections:* for the sake of discussion, he grants both of Lewis's assumptions.[12] His central objection, rather, is to the logic of the argument built upon them. Like Beversluis, I will here grant Lewis's assumptions and focus on defending the logic of Lewis's argument against Beversluis's critique.

Lewis's argument begins, we have seen, with Jesus' claim to be God (no. 1). The severely restricted alternatives of Jesus' identity follow from the significance of this claim. Hence, Lewis devotes the bulk of his discussion to spelling out this significance, emphasizing just how startling such a claim is—what a shocking thing it would be for someone to say what Jesus said, within the kind of theological and cultural context in which he said it. Lewis points out that

> among Pantheists, like the Indians, anyone might say that he was a part of God or one with God: there would be nothing very odd about it. But this man, since He was a Jew, could not mean that kind of God. God in their language, meant the Being outside the world Who had made it and was infinitely different from anything else. And when you have grasped that, you will see that what this man said was, quite simply, the most shocking thing that has ever been uttered by human lips.[13]

---

[10]Recently N. T. Wright has objected to facile assertions of "Jesus' claims to divinity" that characterize some appeals to "some form of the ['shocking alternative'] argument advanced by C. S. Lewis in many writings" (N. T. Wright, *The Challenge of Jesus: Rediscovering Who Jesus Was and Is* [Downers Grove, Ill.: InterVarsity Press, 1999], p. 98). Wright does not challenge the logic of the argument; his objection seems to aim chiefly at construals of Jesus' identity claims and self-understanding that are overly simplistic, both historically and theologically. Wright himself provides a detailed analysis of Jesus' self-understanding in the Gospels and reaches a conclusion that is more nuanced than Lewis's, but—for the purposes of the "shocking alternative" argument—is the same: that Jesus understood his vocation "to do and be, for Israel and the world, that which according to Scripture only YHWH himself could do and be" (p. 122). The "shocking alternative" argument may easily be reformulated along these lines.

[11]For recent philosophical critique and defense of Lewis's argument, see Daniel Howard-Snyder, "Was Jesus Mad, Bad, or God? . . . Or Merely Mistaken?" *Faith and Philosophy* 21 (2004): 456-79; and Stephen T. Davis, "The Mad/Bad/God Trilemma: A Reply to Daniel Howard-Snyder," *Faith and Philosophy* 21 (2004): 480-92.

[12]Although Beversluis does criticize Lewis for assuming "that Jesus' claims were so clear as to admit of one and only one interpretation" (*C. S. Lewis and the Search*, p. 54).

[13]*MC*, p. 44.

Lewis's comparison has more immediate currency today, since many Western people have also adopted pantheistic views and thus understand themselves to be divine. On this view, of course, there would be nothing particularly shocking about a claim to be God, since *everything* is God. Claims to deity, so understood, imply for the claimant no exalted—or even unique—status at all. In the context of first-century Jerusalem, however, it was a very different matter.

Suppose that I were to claim to be C. S. Lewis. No doubt there are many places where such a claim would be unsurprising, where no one knows enough about Lewis (for example, that he has been dead for over forty years) to question it. Possibly there is some place (such as a very highly literary mental hospital) where everyone thinks themselves to be C. S. Lewis, and thus where no one would think twice about my claim. There is one place, however, where I can be sure that there would be no mistaking exactly what I was claiming to be: the C. S. Lewis Society of Oxford University, which is made up of devotees, experts, and even some remaining friends and acquaintances of C. S. Lewis.[14] Claiming to be God in first-century Jerusalem would be something like claiming to be C. S. Lewis at the C. S. Lewis Society of Oxford.

What is shocking about Jesus, then, according to Lewis, is that he claimed—*and his hearers took him to be claiming*—to be none other than the one, true God of the biblical Scriptures. He understood himself to possess the status of one who is the Creator of the universe; the source of the existence of everything else that exists; the only wholly just, perfect, holy being; the almighty, eternal Sovereign, before whom the entire universe will one day submit in worship; the Judge who holds the eternal destinies of all other beings in his power. And so on. Understandably, Jesus' identity claim is generally considered, within the history of religions, to be unique. According to the British scholar of comparative religions, E. O. James: "Nowhere else had it ever been claimed that a historical founder of any religion was the one and only supreme deity."[15]

We have seen what, according to Lewis, follows from this unique claim:

(2) Jesus' claim to deity is either true or false.

---

[14]This chapter was originally presented as a paper to the C. S. Lewis Society (see source footnote at beginning of this chapter).

[15]E. O. James, *Christianity and Other Religions* (Philadelphia: Lippincott, 1968), p. 170. Cited in Jon A. Buell and O. Quentin Hyder, *Jesus: God, Ghost, or Guru?* (Grand Rapids: Zondervan/Probe, 1978), pp. 19-20.

(3) If his claim to deity is true, then Jesus is *Lord.*

(4) If his claim to deity is false, then either Jesus knew it to be false or he did not know it to be false.

From the question of Jesus' knowledge of the truth or falsity of his claim to deity, a *moral* implication follows, as reflected in Lewis's characterization of the alternatives.

First,

(5) If he knew his claim to deity to be false, then Jesus was a *liar.*

If Jesus knew that his claim to be God was false, then in making it he was in fact deliberately misrepresenting himself, making claims about himself that were not true. This makes him an imposter, a liar—one who is, we may say, a *moral failure.* The terms Lewis uses here to describe such a person are: "Devil of Hell," "demon," and "something worse"—terms of extreme moral disapprobation, denoting someone who is morally wicked. (The lunatic is not wicked; to make factually false claims because one is deluded or misinformed is not morally wrong.[16] To assert what one knows to be false, however, is wrong.) And on Lewis's view, for Jesus to be a liar in this context is for him to be monstrously wicked. This is because of the nature of the lie. For not only did Jesus deliberately misrepresent himself concerning his own identity and fundamental purpose (thus deceiving people about what was the very core and primary focus of his teaching); he also was in fact engaged in calling upon people to give up their livelihoods and follow him, even to entrust their very eternal destinies into his hand—all under false pretences. He was deliberately and callously misleading vulnerable people concerning what is of supreme importance.

Beversluis leaves Lewis's liar option out of his account entirely, characterizing the argument only as a "Lord-or-lunatic dilemma." I am unable here to explore more fully the reason for this; but it should be clear from this fact alone that Beversluis's account is an inadequate treatment of Lewis's actual view.[17]

On the other hand, according to Lewis,

(5) If he did not know his claim to deity to be false, then Jesus was a *lunatic.*

---

[16] Although Lewis does not explicitly use the word "liar" in the account in *MC*, it is clearly implicit in the logic of his argument and his characterization of the alternatives, as we have just seen. In "What Are We to Make of Jesus Christ?" he makes it explicit that the two alternatives to Christ's deity are "lunacy and lies" (p. 160).

[17] See the next note below.

On this alternative, Jesus actually believed himself to be the creator of all things, but he was mistaken in that belief. Following Lewis, given the nature of such a belief, the kindest thing one would say of such a person is that he was deeply, seriously deluded, suffering what we may call the highest possible delusions of grandeur. In Lewis's terms, he was a "lunatic," "fool" or "madman." On this alternative, as we have seen, Jesus would not be as such a moral failure, for he did not deliberately deceive about his identity. However, he would be, we may say, a *psychological failure.*

Lewis's argument, then, is that if we take Jesus' claims to deity seriously, we are faced with only these three options as to his identity (Lord, liar, lunatic), and that the common view—that he was a great, but merely human, moral teacher (GMT)—is logically excluded. If we think that Jesus was indeed a GMT, then we are forced, on this argument, to take the further step and accept him also as Lord, since, should he fail to be God, the only remaining alternatives as to Jesus' identity fall far short of a GMT. So Lewis's conclusion does express a dilemma, although not the one Beversluis identifies (i.e., "Lord-or-lunatic"): either Jesus' claim to deity is true, and he is God; or his claim to deity is false, and he was either a liar or a lunatic, but not a good man, and a fortiori not a GMT. We can *either* affirm that Jesus is a GMT *or* we can deny his deity, but we cannot consistently do both. *Aut Deus aut malus homo.*

FIRST CRITIQUE: OTHER ALTERNATIVES

According to Beversluis, Lewis's "shocking alternative" poses a false dilemma. To show this he provides three general lines of critique.[18] I have space here to address two of them. First, he avoids Lewis's exclusive alternatives concerning Jesus' identity by adducing other alternatives. He asserts that Lewis, by constructing a false dilemma of Lord-or-lunatic, "deprives his readers of numerous alternate interpretations of Jesus that carry with them no such odious implications."[19] Just what these "numerous" interpretations are, Beversluis does

---

[18]Because of space constraints in this volume, I must omit the analysis of a third line of critique by Beversluis: that Lewis misconstrues the implications of Jesus' claims to forgive sins, producing not a philosophical argument but a "psychological spell" (*C. S. Lewis and the Search*, p. 56). It is Beversluis, however, who misconstrues Lewis, on the basis of a tendentious reading of a single sentence, and so misses entirely the logic of Lewis's analysis. This misreading, I think, is chiefly responsible for Beversluis's striking omission of the "liar" alternative from Lewis's argument. Thomas V. Morris analyzes a further aspect of Beversluis's account here, in his review in *Faith and Philosophy* 5 (1988): 322.

[19]Beversluis, *C. S. Lewis and the Search*, p. 56.

not say; he mentions only three. Two of them, however, the blasphemer and the imposter (do these alternatives really carry no "odious implications"?), we have already noted, are not alternative interpretations at all, but in fact fall under Lewis's "liar" category.

Beversluis's remaining and favored alternative is that Jesus was not a lunatic: rather, Jesus "sincerely believed" that he was God, although he was mistaken. It should be clear that Lewis would not consider the sincere-believer option as a genuine alternative to his scheme, either; indeed, such a person would probably exemplify most clearly just what Lewis *means* by a *lunatic*. However sincere this person may be, he has lost meaningful contact with reality.[20]

Beversluis, however, wonders what is so objectionable about one's mistakenly believing oneself to be God. For one thing, according to Beversluis, "the term *lunatic* simply clouds the issue with emotional rhetoric."[21] It is better to say "sincerely believes." But exactly what work is "sincerely" doing here, other than "clouding the issue with emotional rhetoric"? Indeed, it is unclear how one would *in*sincerely believe something. If I believe, for example, that I am a member of Oriel College, what is added in saying that I *sincerely* believe it? What exactly would be lost with regard to my epistemic state if I *in*sincerely believed it? Perhaps "I sincerely believe it" in this context is to be analyzed as "I *truly* believe it," as opposed to pretending that I believe it (say, trying to deceive myself or others with respect to my beliefs). Or perhaps it is to be analyzed as "I *strongly* believe it," as opposed to weakly or barely believing it. But surely Lewis's lunatic believes both truly and strongly that he is God; if he did not truly believe it, he would not be Lewis's lunatic, but Lewis's liar; and if he only weakly believed it, we would not call him a lunatic, just "confused."

Perhaps, on the other hand, we mean by one's sincerely believing something that one has no hidden agendas or bad motives for believing it. It is disputed whether one can believe something for a motive other than that it seems to one to be true. Can I believe that the earth is flat, say, simply because such a belief would enable me to seduce a beautiful woman? I can certainly *pretend* to believe it—but am I actually able to believe what I think is false? That is, can I actually believe what I *do not* believe—for any motive, whether good or bad? According to some accounts I may be able to acquire such a belief voluntarily over time, by

---

[20]Ibid., p. 55.
[21]Ibid.

putting myself into circumstances (e.g., joining the Flat Earth Society, writing articles defending the flat-earth view) which make it more likely that I will at some time come to believe it. Along these lines, perhaps a "sincere believer," in the case of one who claims to be God, would be understood as one who does not seek to acquire (or who has not acquired) his belief that he is identical to the creator of the universe for bad motives (e.g., money, power, seduction and so forth). But Lewis's lunatic is surely such a believer. I suspect that the actual function of "sincerely" in Beversluis's discussion is simply as an emotionally loaded term (no less than is "lunatic") that casts Jesus' extraordinary belief in a benign light. In any case, Beversluis's "sincere believer" does not provide a counterexample to Lewis's argument. The "shocking alternative" stands. *Aut Deus aut malus homo.*

SECOND CRITIQUE: "GREAT MORAL TEACHER"

Beversluis's second critique of Lewis's argument turns from the nature of the alternatives to the conclusion drawn from them. He questions why we should think that if Jesus were mistaken about being God, he would be thereby excluded from being a GMT. What "disastrous conclusion," Beversluis asks, is supposed to follow concerning his teachings if "certain factual claims Jesus made about himself were false"?

> Why should the mere fact that Jesus was mistaken about himself have any implications for the soundness and acceptability of his moral teachings? Did Lewis think that if Jesus were not God, there would no longer be any reason for believing that love is preferable to hate, humility to arrogance, charity to vindictiveness, meekness to oppressiveness, fidelity to adultery, [. . . etc.]? Lewis failed to realize that the question of whether Jesus' factual claims about himself are true is wholly separate from the question of whether his teachings are sound.[22]

Beversluis's critique here raises the important questions of what constitutes a GMT and what are the criteria for ascribing GMT status to someone. Unfortunately, Beversluis's own answers are inadequate, both in accounting for the uniqueness of Jesus and his claims, and in providing an adequate notion of GMT more generally. The sole criterion discernible in Beversluis's account for determining whether someone is a GMT, while being weak enough to make room in the GMT club to admit one who falsely believes himself to be the creator of the universe, is also too weak to exclude

---

[22]Ibid.

a host of other characters that clearly ought not to be there.

First, for Jesus mistakenly to believe himself to be the single, eternal source of all life and the ground of all truth is hardly characterized adequately as "certain factual claims Jesus made about himself were false." The factual claims in question are of cosmic, as well as of supreme personal and existential, consequence. If Jesus was whom he said, then God has visited this planet and salvation has come through him. If he was not, then these theological conclusions are false—but even in this case, Jesus' mistake would hardly be a "mere fact." If Fred were mistakenly to think that he were I, it would be true that, in one respect, his being mistaken about his own identity would be a "mere fact" (thinking that one is David Horner hardly constitutes delusions of grandeur). Still, Fred's delusions, albeit of minimal grandeur, are still delusions, and quite fundamental ones at that: simply the fact that Fred is actually convinced that he is someone other than he is—that fact would render him classifiable as seriously mentally ill. A fortiori, one's factual mistake about being Almighty God could never be a mere fact—it is a maximal fact, if there ever was one. What greater disparity could there possibly be between belief and reality?

Second, more generally, Beversluis's notion of what constitutes a GMT is too thin. He does not explicitly supply a criterion for determining someone's GMT status, but that there is one is implicit in his account. Beversluis argues that Jesus should not be excluded from GMT status solely because of his false beliefs about his personal identity, since the soundness or truth of his moral teaching remains and is independent of the truth status of Jesus' other beliefs. Put positively, on Beversluis's account, the truth of Jesus' moral teaching—the *content* of his teaching—would be sufficient for his being a GMT. To generalize, then, Beversluis's implicit GMT criterion is this (for any subject, *S*):

(G) If *S* propounds true moral propositions, then *S* is a GMT.

However, (G) is false. That the moral propositions that one teaches are true is a necessary condition for one's possessing GMT status, but it is hardly *sufficient,* as (G) maintains. Even with regard to Beversluis's specific point about identity beliefs, (G) is surely too weak. For on (G), as long as *S* propounded sound moral teaching, *S* would be a GMT. This is compatible with *S*'s believing (falsely), not only that *S* is God, but also that *S* is Fido, Adolf Hitler, or an order of fish and chips. Would *none* of these false identity beliefs disqualify one for GMT status, on Beversluis's view? Although one's "factual beliefs" about one's identity may be logically independent of the truth of one's moral teachings (e.g., that "love is preferable to hate"), they are surely not "wholly separate" from one's being a GMT—which is the question that is at issue here. Moreover, other factors obviously deeply relevant to being a GMT are missed by (G). On the basis of (G), we could count S as being a GMT, but simply drugged, brainwashed, or "programmed" to utter true moral propositions. Indeed, on this construal, S could be a computer or recording device, not an agent at all. Further, on the basis of (G), we could recognize S as being a moral wreck—a liar, rapist, or murderer—as long as S *taught* the right things. Indeed, in such a case, as long as S were sufficiently hypocritical—as long as S's words and S's actions were sufficiently incongruous—S would turn out to be a GMT. But then, such a person would be a paradigm of exactly what a GMT is *not*.[23]

The soundness of one's moral teaching, then, is necessary but not sufficient for one's being a GMT. Beversluis's notion of a GMT, one that allows a seriously deluded Jesus to qualify, is simply too thin to rule out these counterexamples, and thus it is not adequate. We need a more substantive conception for an adequate account of a GMT—but it is likely that such a conception will also rule out a deluded Jesus.

WHAT IS A GREAT MORAL TEACHER?

The problems with Beversluis's conception of a GMT point to what further is needed for an adequate conception: considerations of one's *character*, not just the *content* of one's teaching. Here I will not attempt a thorough account of what it is to be a GMT, but I will briefly describe the general shape of such an account and respond to some objections, in order to finish unpacking and defending the logic of Lewis's argument.

The counterexamples to (G) that we have considered indicate the role of character, broadly conceived, to one's being a GMT. Considerations that are relevant here are similar to those that have motivated the revival of an ethics of character or virtue in recent years. Beversluis's thin notion of a GMT suffers from the kind of "moral minimalism"[24] afflicting modern ethics: reducing the

---

[23]Note that even if Beversluis were to strengthen his criterion to

(G*) If S propounds *numerous* true moral propositions, then S is a GMT,

it would still fall to these considerations.

[24]See David L. Norton, "Moral Minimalism and the Development of Moral Character," *Midwest Studies in Philosophy*, vol. 13, *Ethical Character and Virtue*, ed. Peter A. French, Theodore E. Uehling Jr. and Howard K. Wettstein (Notre Dame, Ind.: University of Notre Dame Press, 1988), pp. 180-95.

scope of what is morally important to considerations of acts, rules, and consequences. A character-oriented view, by contrast, insists that what we think is
morally important is much broader, including all that falls under the concept
of "character": who one is as a person, and not just what one does—one's actions, to be sure, but also one's reactions, feelings, beliefs, desires, aspirations
and sustained patterns of motivation. On this view, the content of one's moral
beliefs (and thus of one's moral teaching if one teaches) is certainly important
in the determination of one's moral condition, but it is only one part of the total "package" of one's character. A sufficient moral evaluation depends upon
the entire package. I will not attempt a defense of this view of ethics here, although I think that it is manifestly plausible and preferable to the minimalist
view; but I do want to note the similar considerations that underlie the desid-
eratum—and the content—of a substantively adequate conception of a GMT.

In the case of a GMT, these considerations are even more important because here we are not simply interested in what is morally important or what
are the proper applications of moral predicates, but also in what is morally exemplary. By "GMT," we have in mind, at least, a substantive conception of
someone who not only verbalizes sound moral teachings, but who also is an
admirable person, who exhibits excellence in character—wisdom, integrity,
wholeness and so forth—and is an exemplar, whose teaching is clearly worth
following *because* the person's life is a moral inspiration. Obviously, this needs
to be spelled out much more fully, and the degree to which these virtues obtain
will vary somewhat between GMTs. But in every case, a GMT constitutes a
kind of *moral authority,* and for such an authority there is an intrinsic relation
between teaching and character that may not be essential to authorities in
other fields. One may qualify as an authority in physics, for example, or in
wastewater management, without an exemplary character—Beversluis's thin
conception is closer to this case. What matters more than anything else in such
fields is that the content of one's pronouncements be accurate.[25] The relation
between the authority's character and the content of one's teaching in such

---

[25]However, character is necessary to some extent in any instance of authority that depends not merely
upon power but upon credibility. Since it is essential to being a medical authority, for example, that
one truthfully, skillfully, and insightfully provide medical information, the character trait of truthfulness is necessary, as are character traits that are necessary to becoming skilled and insightful in such
matters (discipline, hard work, docility, patience, etc.). My point in the text about intrinsic and extrinsic relations to character is consistent with this observation and only strengthened by it. If character is in some ways necessary for all credible authorities, how much more so for moral authorities?

matters is essentially extrinsic. But this is not the case with a moral authority. As suggested above, a disjunction between content and character, as in the case of hypocrisy, is perhaps the central disqualifying factor for GMT status. Put positively, *integrity* is a necessary condition for being a GMT.

However, is it not the case that some persons are regarded as GMTs, while exhibiting considerable defects in certain areas of character? For example, Dr. Martin Luther King is almost universally considered a GMT,[26] despite evidence of his sexual infidelities. Does this not suggest that the concept of GMT is elastic—perhaps enough to include someone who is maximally confused as to his identity?

This example does point to an important relativity between individual instances of GMTs. For this reason we need to take seriously both what is an adequate general conception of a GMT and also its specific application to Jesus. Clearly, one need not be morally perfect to be a GMT, generally speaking, or the class would be rather small. What, then, is necessary? Why is it that we consider Dr. King a moral authority, despite his moral imperfections? Part of the answer, surely, has to do with the importance of what he said. The truths he expressed concerning human dignity were much "bigger" than he was, so to speak, and his infidelities do not cast doubt upon them. So far, this is consistent with Beversluis's analysis. But, of course, anyone—including Adolf Hitler—could have *said* those things, could have articulated those same propositions. What is it that made Dr. King a GMT, and not merely a conduit or reporter of significant moral truths? A necessary, core condition, I submit, is a special case of what I am defending here, and that is integrity, which expresses the coherence or intrinsic relation between content and character. We consider Dr. King a GMT, despite his lack of complete moral integrity, partly because he never claimed to possess the latter, and partly because there was coherence between what he *did* claim and how he lived. He uttered profound truths about liberty and racial equality, and he lived consistently and with integrity with respect to them, to the point of being jailed, beaten, and ultimately killed. I dare say, however, that if his central message had been the importance of sexual fidelity (or if it had turned out that he was actually a secret informer for the Ku Klux Klan), he would not in fact today be considered a GMT—no matter how exalted his teaching had been in other respects.

---

[26]Beversluis's example, in discussion.

The coherence between content and character is especially important when we specifically consider the teaching of Jesus, since his central claims—unlike those of Dr. King—had to do precisely with his own identity, including his own moral character, which he portrayed as sinless. Although Dr. King freely admitted his own sinful status, Jesus never did. He admitted to no moral imperfection; at the same time he held forth the ideal of nothing short of moral perfection in both thought and deed: "Unless your righteousness exceeds that of the scribes and Pharisees, you will never enter the kingdom of heaven. . . . Be perfect, therefore, as your heavenly Father is perfect" (Matthew 5:20, 48). While calling for universal confession and repentance, Jesus himself confessed to no sin. He betrayed no need for forgiveness for himself, while offering forgiveness to all who have sinned, including, as Lewis points out, to those who have sinned against God. The comparison between Jesus and Martin Luther King, I suggest, only illumines the radical uniqueness of Jesus' claims for himself. The differences between the two are most striking. What is required for Jesus to qualify as a GMT is coherence between *his* character and the content of *his* teaching—and this would in fact be possible only for one who was morally perfect.

It might be objected that these considerations about integrity are solely moral concerns, which are relevant only to the case where Jesus knowingly misrepresented his own identity—Lewis's liar scenario. Granting that a lack of integrity between Jesus' content and character in that case would disqualify him from being a GMT, how does it follow that he would be disqualified from GMT status in the (more likely) scenario where he mistakenly believed himself to be God—the lunatic case? Admittedly, Jesus would be disqualified from GMT status if he were a moral failure, but how would his being a psychological failure disqualify him? This is the substance of Beversluis's third critique.

My response continues the appeal to a nonminimalist conception of character. Not being a moral *failure* is, of course, a necessary condition for being a GMT, but it is hardly sufficient. A substantive conception of one's being a GMT goes beyond simple avoidance of wickedness, such as lying; it includes, more broadly, positive character attributes that express an integrated, properly functioning personality—integrity in the most basic sense of being "whole" or "one" with respect to the entirety of one's character and orientation to the world. Obviously a completely integrated personality is an ideal rather than a minimal condition for being a GMT. But even at a minimal level—and a fortiori for Jesus, whose GMT status, even among unbelievers, is widely considered to be the highest of anyone who has ever lived—there is a necessary integrity or wholeness that goes far beyond simply not being a moral failure.

Once we admit substantive considerations of character such as these into our notion of a GMT, we abandon Beversluis's contention that the truthfulness of Jesus' factual claims about his identity is "wholly separate" from the soundness of his moral teaching (where "soundness" here refers to more than simply the truth-status of the propositions he uttered), for substantive considerations of character are related to one's self-perception and grip on reality. No doubt one could be a GMT while being mistaken about "certain factual" issues; indeed, aside from Jesus, on a Christian understanding, all GMTs have been so mistaken. It is another thing entirely, however, to be seriously mistaken about one's very identity, and a fortiori, to mistake oneself for Almighty God.

Someone with delusions as severe as those attributable to Jesus on this view would indicate a personality that is so *dis*integrated—one that falls so far outside a realistic boundary of sufficient psychological wholeness—as to be excluded from anything approaching the kind of exalted GMT status that Jesus is generally held to possess, even by those who deny his deity. And this is not unrelated to moral considerations. Although Jesus, on the lunatic scenario, would not be positively morally *wicked*, it does not follow that he would not be morally *deficient* for failing to exemplify a properly functioning moral character—and a fortiori in relation to being a moral exemplar and authority, a GMT. Someone in his state, for example, would lack humility in as serious a way as possible. Perhaps we would not exclude someone from possessing GMT status for having, say, a modestly "inflated" view of his own importance. But believing oneself to be the sole Perfect Being in the cosmos surely puts one out of the realm of mere "inflation" considerations altogether. In the case of Jesus, moreover, this raises an additional coherence problem: humility as a virtue was not only an emphasis of Jesus' moral teaching, but also one that, it is generally recognized, particularly sets him and his teaching apart from other ancient moral teachers.

Further, central components of a substantive conception of a GMT become simply unhinged in the case of a "GMT" who is massively deluded. For Jesus falsely to believe himself to be the eternal source of all life would put him out of touch with reality to such a degree that it should be open to serious question whether he in fact shared our moral world at all—much less whether he could be a moral authority for us; still less an ideal or exemplar. One's martyrdom is not so admirable if one has little grip on reality, and not so inspiring if one does not remotely view and value one's life as others do.[27] Without implying that Jesus on the lunatic scenario was morally blameworthy or reprehensible, we can recognize that the delusions attributable to him on this view would render him unsuitable for the moral requirements of a GMT, on any reasonably substantive conception.

Lewis's conclusion is even stronger, however. He claims not merely that, if Jesus were not God, he would fail to be a GMT, but that he would be a *malus homo*, a bad man. In the case of the moral failure, of course, this is obvious. In the case of the psychological failure, however, is this not far too strong? While the lunatic may not be regarded as a GMT, it surely seems too severe to call him "bad."

In response, it is evident that Lewis trades on more than one sense of "bad man" here.[28] The liar is a bad man in the sense of being positively morally wicked. The lunatic, however, may also be considered a "bad man" in the sense I have just described: as being unsuitable (including being morally deficient) for the status of a GMT. While there are important moral differences between these two senses of "bad man" (culpability and blame attach only to the former), we need to remember that the contrast Lewis is drawing here is to the GMT, not merely to basic moral goodness or decency. Lewis's opponent wants to deny Christ's deity, while affirming him as a GMT, a moral authority and exemplar (a status that goes beyond the question of mere moral nonculpability, to concerns of moral credibility and admirability). Lewis's argument is that, *with respect to a GMT,* both nondivine alternatives as to who Jesus is are morally unsuitable; they fail to make the moral grade: they are "bad" men, albeit in different senses.

Of course, one may argue with Lewis's terminology. If one wishes to reserve the term "bad" for "morally wicked" only, one may jettison Lewis's talk of *"malus" homo* altogether. The conclusion of importance, to Lewis, however— that Jesus could not be a *great moral teacher* without also being divine— remains. If Jesus is not God, he also cannot be what most who reject his divinity believe him to be.

---

[27]Thanks to Patrick Richmond for insights here.

[28]Of course, Lewis inherits the *malus homo* terminology from the Christian tradition, and he does not use it in all of his discussions of this argument (including his primary discussion in *MC*). So its use should not be pressed too far in his case.

CONCLUSION

Beversluis provides no good reason to reject Lewis's "shocking alternative" argument. He fails to show that Lewis's is a false dilemma, and despite the promise of "numerous alternate interpretations" of Jesus in the offing, he provides none that satisfy the description. Granting Lewis's historical and hermeneutical assumptions, the dilemma stands. *Aut Deus aut malus homo.*

Lewis's "shocking alternative" argument starkly demarcates the disjunctive options confronting one who considers the identity of Christ. How does one proceed from here? Which of the options is most likely to be true? Lewis construes the different options as constituting different explanatory hypotheses that are to be evaluated in terms of their ability to explain the data of the life and teachings of Jesus:

> The question is, I suppose, whether any hypothesis covers the facts so well as the Christian hypothesis. That hypothesis is that God has come down into the created universe, down to manhood—and come up again, pulling it up with Him. The alternative hypothesis is not legend, nor exaggeration, nor the apparitions of a ghost. It is either lunacy or lies. Unless one can take the second alternative (and I cannot), one turns to the Christian theory.[29]

Lewis's Christian apologetic takes one this far. Beyond this, as he says, "You must make your choice."[30]

---

[29]Lewis, "What Are We to Make of Jesus Christ?" pp. 159-60.
[30]*MC*, p. 56.

5

The Abolition of Man

C. S. Lewis's Prescience Concerning Things to Come

JEAN BETHKE ELSHTAIN

I suspect[1] that all of us know that the average reader of *The New York Times Magazine* prefers to choose the "humane," not the "barbaric," alternative. And the humane course, it turns out, is the one that favors infanticide if the correct procedures are followed. Euthanasia of babies under such circumstances is the way of "reason." Those who cry, "No, we must not cross that line," advance the way of "sentiment," also known as unreason.

The author of an essay on the topic, Jim Holt, a "frequent contributor to the magazine," asks his readers to imagine a heated dining room table argument about such matters. The way of "reason" requires "unflinching honesty." By contrast, moral "sentiments" are inertial, resisting "the force of moral reasons." The essay concludes in this way:

> Just quote Verhagen's [the Dutch doctor who identifies himself as a pro-infant euthanasia practitioner] description of the medically induced infant deaths over which he has presided—"It's beautiful in a way... It is after they die that you see them relaxed for the first time"—and even the most spirited dinner-table debate

---

[1] This essay was written originally for oral delivery. I have knowingly worked to preserve the forthright-ness and informality of a talk. In March 2005, the prestigious *New England Journal of Medicine* published an essay on the topic of euthanasia for newborns, printing the "Groningen Protocol" for such procedures. *The New York Times Magazine*, July 10, 2005, reprinted those protocols under the heading: "Euthanasia for Babies?" going on to ask: "Is this humane or barbaric?" This way of presenting alternatives, in the guise of neutrality, is typical of much "enlightened" opinion.

over moral progress will, for a moment, fall silent.[2]

The essayist obviously wants us to imagine the hushed atmosphere as one in which diners are overwhelmed by the vision of peace-at-last for congenitally deformed infants. I suspect that most of us would indeed fall silent from the sheer horror of it all: "Let's give these perturbed little spirits some peace at last; let's kill them."

Holt apparently believes that brutal candor about such matters is the ethically preferred route ("Yes, I'm killing them, and that's the right thing to do"), rather than the muddling through that may involve permitting multiple handicapped infants to die rather than using sustained heroic measures to keep them alive, for example. The latter is presented as "casuistic" confusion. So any course that reflects our moral uneasiness is dishonest; any course that candidly makes it easier for medical personnel to kill is honest and reasoned.

Does anyone doubt what C. S. Lewis might say about this—about the way in which healers become killers and all the rest? Those of you somewhat familiar with my work will know that these are issues that have long troubled me. I have worried in print that, in the name of "enlightenment," we are eliminating whole categories of persons. For example: So overwhelming is our animus against the less-than-perfect that nearly 90 percent of pregnancies that test positive for Down syndrome are aborted in the United States today, all under the rubric of "choice." In the name of expanding choice and eliminating "suffering," we are narrowing our definition of humanity and, along the way, our felt responsibility to create welcoming environments for all children. Indeed, because of the more "sophisticated" tests now available, medical experts now argue that *all* pregnant women, not just those in at-risk categories, should be routinely tested for Down-syndrome fetuses so that they might be aborted at an earlier stage in pregnancy.

When we aim to eliminate—whether through euthanasia or systematic, selective aborting of "flawed" fetuses—one version of humanity, perhaps suffer-

---

[2]Jim Holt, "Euthanasia for Babies? Dutch Doctors Have Proposed a Procedure for Infant Mercy Killing. Is This Humane or Barbaric?" *The New York Times Magazine*, July 10, 2005, pp. 11-12, 14, esp. p. 14. Notice, too, that the euphemism "medically induced deaths" is used rather than intentional killing. Holt also criticizes the American discussion of these matters, claiming that our way of doing it is shrouded in "casuistry." This is, of course, an attack on Catholic moral theology—anytime "casuistry" is condemned one knows that wariness of Catholic thought lurks nearby—but also on the fact that Americans spend so much time discussing moral issues. For Holt this in itself seems to be a problem.

ing humanity but nonetheless humanity—we dangerously constrict the boundaries of the moral community. In his posthumously published *Ethics,* the anti-Nazi theologian Dietrich Bonhoeffer insisted that the most radical excision of the integrity and right of natural life is "arbitrary killing," the deliberate destruction of "innocent life." "The right to live is a matter of the essence," "not of any socially imposed or constructed values," Bonhoeffer proclaimed. For even "the most wretched life" is "worth living before God."[3]

As with Bonhoeffer, so also Lewis was writing under the shadows of Nazism and Stalinism. His essay *The Abolition of Man,* published in 1944 and subtitled *Or, Reflections on Education with Special Reference to the Teaching of English in the Upper Forms of Schools,* would seem at first glance to have little to do with the grave matters with which I have begun. Not so. Lewis sees pernicious tendencies in, of all places, elementary textbooks. At first puzzling, this quickly makes sense. The general cultural milieu, a culture's mores, its "habits of the heart," as the great observer of the American democracy, Alexis de Tocqueville put it, are always embedded and embodied in the books we require our children to read, the books we use to teach them.

What on earth was going on with English textbooks such that C. S. Lewis would take note of them? First, he detects an embrace of subjectivism—which means, speaking epistemologically, the embrace of both positivism and emotivism. In 1944 and the immediate postwar decades came the heyday of this approach, and it had clearly made its way into elementary schools even as it was the dominant approach to the teaching of philosophy at Great Britain's elite institutions of higher learning.

The reduction of values to subjective "feelings"—the "sentiment" opposed to "reason" of which *The New York Times* piece speaks—leads to the embrace, or is itself a fruit of the embrace, of two interlocked propositions, summarized by Lewis thus: "firstly, that all sentences containing a predicate of values are statements about the emotional state of the speaker, and, secondly, that all such statements are unimportant."[4] One need not refer to the general philosophy at work "that all values are subjective and trivial" in order to promulgate this philosophy.[5]

Indeed, many textbook authors probably do not recognize what they are

---

[3]Dietrich Bonhoeffer, *Ethics* (New York: Simon & Schuster, 1955), pp. 142-85.
[4]C. S. Lewis, *The Abolition of Man* (New York: Simon & Schuster, 1996), p. 19.
[5]Ibid., p. 20.

doing to the schoolchild, suggests Lewis. Certainly the schoolchild "cannot know what is being done to [him]."[6] And in this way another "little portion of the human heritage has been quietly taken from them [schoolchildren] before they were old enough to understand."[7]

Let me provide an illustration of this from my own experience. When our daughter, Jenny, was in fifth grade in a progressive public school in the town where we then lived—one of those bucolic New England college towns in which university students outnumber permanent residents—she was required to complete a work sheet on distinguishing fact from value. "Values" were of course defined as subjective opinions having no cognitive status, and hence no defensible truth warrants: pure positivism. She read aloud as she did this, and as she was trying to figure things out. Her mother, myself, became a bit agitated, as I tend to do when confronted with this sort of thing in the guise of education. To help her understand, I said, "Well, Jenny, if I say something is 'wrong,' does that mean I am stating a fact or a value?" Values, to repeat, were supposed to be the things that we all have, and moreover, one cannot distinguish between them since they all come out of the same subjectivist stew.

Predictably, Jenny answered that it would be a value. I continued: "Well, Martin Luther King said slavery was wrong. Suppose there is someone who says slavery is good and we should bring it back. Couldn't we say he is wrong and Martin Luther King is right and that slavery is bad? Period." Jenny was stumped for a moment—and troubled—and then she said: "Well, I think slavery is wrong, too, but that is just my opinion." Our discussion did not end there, but this experience reinforces Lewis's claim concerning the pervasiveness of the sorts of teachings he indicts in his essay.

For Lewis, when "ordinary human feelings" are set up as "contrary to reason," we are on dangerous ground indeed, for a botched treatment of "some basic human emotion" is not only bad literature but is moral treachery to boot. "By starving the sensibility of our pupils, we only make them easier prey to the propagandist when he comes."[8] Lewis insists that in Platonic, Aristotelian, Stoic, Christian, and some Eastern religions, one finds in common "the doctrine of objective value, the belief that certain attitudes are really true, and others really

---

[6] Ibid.
[7] Ibid., p. 25.
[8] Ibid., p. 27.

false, to the kind of thing the universe is and the kind of things we are."[9] He refers to this simply as "the Tao"—certain transcultural, universal claims.[10]

Thus emotional states can be "reasonable or unreasonable," for one must not traffic in the false distinction between reason and emotion, rationality and sentiment. In the regnant positivism, by contrast, the world of facts, without one trace of value; and the world of feelings, without one trace of truth or falsehood, justice or injustice—these facts and feelings confront one another, and no rapprochement is possible. It is all a "ghastly simplicity."

Another example is drawn from experience. When I was a graduate student in the late 1960s and early 1970s, this "ghastly simplicity" was the reigning epistemology. I never quite "got it," I must say, and when I tried to argue the point with my professors, having had no formal training in epistemology, it was a nonstarter. It was clear that positivism was not up for debate; rather, it was assumed, taken for granted. This no doubt is one reason I wound up as a political theorist, for in a world in which a "scientific" approach allegedly dictates the severance of fact from value, political theorists and philosophers are seen as a strange breed apart, who specialize in "normative claims" or "evaluation."[11]

For a time, I believed, overoptimistically as it turned out, that the decisive critique of positivism mounted by philosophers such as Charles Taylor and Alasdair MacIntyre, among others, had pounded the nails into the coffin of positivism in the human sciences. Not so, as it turns out. This orientation reappeared with gusto in the current regnant epistemology in the social sciences—so-called rational choice theory.

Now is not the time to unpack rational choice—or "rat choice," as some of us prefer to call it—in any detail. Suffice it to say that, expanded to become a Weltanschauung rather than utilized as a relatively modest approach to a finite series of economic decision-making processes, rat choice trivializes all statements of value: they have no truth warrant or claim; they are "externalities."

---

[9]Ibid., p. 31.

[10]Of course, this assimilation of faith traditions is controversial but defensible in context, I would suggest. There are times when we want to clarify distinctions and differences; other times when we want to make the strongest case we can that a core or cluster of shared recognitions persists. Writing this particular essay *(Abolition),* Lewis took the latter tack.

[11]I should note that "real scientists" today do not work with such a simplistic severance of "description" and "evaluation" and other modalities of the positivistic approach. But that seems not to have made much of a dent on its practitioners in the social sciences.

Further, rat choice enshrines a reductive view of the human person as the sum total of one's preferences, one's calculations of marginal utility, for one cannot make substantive distinctions between different "utilities," between polishing one's Porsche or working in a hospice.

Within a universe limned by "rat choice," everything, in principle, can be commodified. Everything, in principle, has a "price" rather than a value. Any restrictions societies draw on where human "preferences" might take us are arbitrary. There are no intrinsic goods or evils at all. Nothing is valued for its own sake. True, we may "value" babies in a certain way. This is an ancient sentiment. But it has no rational content. Instead, every "value" is reducible to a "preference" and describable in the language of maximizing utilities.[12]

Let me illustrate. Years ago, when I was teaching at a particular university, an eager candidate for a political science position gave his job talk. To him, everything was a "preference." There was no other way to talk about politics or the moral life. When he had finished, I asked: "It is a curious thing, is it not? When Martin Luther King delivered his great speech, he cried, 'I have a dream,' not 'I have a preference.' How do you explain this? Is there a difference?" The somewhat flustered young man indicated that what King was calling a dream was at base just another preference, and so that was no different *in principle* from, say, debating marginal alterations in the price of commodities. This way of thinking makes hash of our moral sentiments, of our God-given capacity to reason about what is good, as Lewis asserts.

This, surely, is what he feared in 1944: that something precious and irreparable was being lost. Those debunking the normative status and truth warrants of claims of value, whether then or now, are tacitly promoting values of their own. Writes Lewis: "A great many of those who 'debunk' traditional or (as they would say) 'sentimental' values have in the background values of their own which they believe to be immune from the debunking process."[13] One thinks here of the fundamentalist skeptic who is skeptical of everything save his skepticism. Or the proclaimer of moral relativism who relativizes everything save his claim to moral relativism. Lewis feared this in his era; we should fear it in ours. Then and now, at least increasingly, what seems to matter is not the dignity of each and every human life but, rather, goals like "the preservation of the species" (or "maximiz-

---

[12]For an extensive critical unpacking of these issues, see Jean Bethke Elshtain, *Who Are We? Critical Reflections and Hopeful Possibilities* (Grand Rapids: Eerdmans, 2000).
[13]Lewis, *Abolition*, p. 43.

ing reproductive capacities"[14]) in their "optimal" form—and tragically deformed or mortally ill newborns will never maximize their reproductive potential. So they are without value. Too, they will never contribute to production. They would be worthless on the marketplace (so to speak), so they are without value. We might attach value to them arbitrarily, but this is emotive and not reasoned.

It is interesting—and troubling—that we are in an age of human rights par excellence, and yet there are forces at work in our world that undermine the ontological claims of human dignity that must ground a robust regime of human rights. At present some excisions of our humanity are obvious and in the headlines, such as Osama bin-Laden's claim that "Americans, Jews and infidels" should be slaughtered whenever and wherever they are to be found, whether men, women and children, armed or unarmed. We see the problem immediately: categories of humanity stripped of all rights rhetorically and in the actual practice of terrorists inflamed by this rhetoric.

But there are other forces at work undermining the ground of human dignity by eroding the full force of our humanity, whether whole or broken, "normal" or "abnormal," young or old. Totalizing the population biology or the econometric perspectives are two of the ways we have devised to do this. These approaches—utilitarian at base—have worked their way into medical thought and practice, including the field of "medical ethics."

I appreciate that many who share the view that seriously deformed infants should be euthanized, whether in furtherance of a particular approach or agenda or for a more generalized antipathy toward the "deformed," will no doubt be horrified by my remarks. They are being decent and humane, they will insist. They are trying to prevent "useless suffering"—an odd locution when you think of it. What distinguishes "useless" from "useful" human suffering? One implies the other, does it not?

Those of us working to counter the pressures at work in this matter should acknowledge these urgencies. The people one opposes are not monsters, for the most part, though there are surely some who wield the needles bearing death who are, like the notorious Dr. Jack Kevorkian, "Dr. Death," with his necrophiliac obsessions and admiration of Nazi experimentation with helpless death-camp inmates. Yes, the vast majority want to do the "right" thing. Lewis

---

[14]Some critics now write of "genetic fundamentalism" to characterize the new eugenics now spreading in the West and the East.

understood this, understood that various ideologies—including the contemporary "right to die"—are "arbitrarily wrenched from their context in the whole"—here his reference point is to those fundamental truths he calls "the Tao"—and "then swollen to madness in their isolation." In this way, fundamental claims to human value as such are weakened, reduced to superstitions. For "the Nietzschean ethic can be accepted only if we are ready to scrap traditional morals as a mere error and then to put ourselves in a position where we can find no ground for any value judgments at all."[15]

At this point in his essay, Lewis turns explicitly to "man's conquest of Nature," the way people in his era heralded a coming age of human triumph over nature's "arbitrariness." His examples of this power-over were the airplane, the wireless, and the contraceptive. I appreciate how hopelessly archaic such concerns sound to our contemporary ears. One has to probe deeply to make sense of it all rather than to dismiss it as the crankiness of a fuddy-duddy. Let's take contraception as an example for closer examination: the living deny existence to the not-yet-living through this method, argues Lewis, and we come to believe we can engage in "selective breeding" with "Nature as its instrument."

Harsh words, you might think. But consider. This exercise of power or, perhaps better put, the way this power is or can be exercised, implies "the power to make its descendants what it pleases."[16] For "each new power won by man is a power over man as well. . . . Each advance leaves him weaker as well as stronger. . . . The final stage is come when Man by eugenics, by pre-natal conditioning, and by an education and propaganda based on a perfect applied psychology, has obtained full control over himself. *Human* nature will be the last part of Nature to surrender to Man."[17]

Lewis held out hope that the obstinacy of "real mothers, real nurses, and (above all) real children"[18] might preserve "the human race in such sanity as it still possesses. But the man-moulders [*sic*] of the new age will be armed with the powers of an omnicompetent state and an irresistible scientific technique: we shall get at last a race of conditioners who really can cut out all posterity in what shape they please."[19] At the time, the reference point Lewis's readers

---

[15]Lewis, *Abolition*, p. 57.
[16]Ibid., p. 68.
[17]Ibid., p. 69.
[18]Ibid., p. 70.
[19]Ibid., p. 71.

could point to was National Socialist Germany, with its cruelly enforced eugenics, and this surely was what was in Lewis's mind. I doubt that many suspected that their own societies might one day enter into this danger zone, not under the banner of totalitarianism but, rather, under the rubric of human choice and freedom. As Lewis fretted about posthumanity, a bleak future indeed, we have our own apostles of the posthuman and transhuman future.[20]

When C. S. Lewis in 1944 wrote of "the abolition of man," he meant the end of humanity as we know it—brought about by humanity itself and our inability to stem what Augustine of Hippo called the *libido dominandi*. This can take such obviously disgusting and evil forms as gulags and death camps. But it can also appear in other guises and in the name of doing good. Mind you, I am not trafficking in moral equivalences here. I am not saying that contemporary "positive eugenics," as it is called, is identical to the intentional slaughter of millions of people because of their allegedly "underhuman [*Untermenschen*]" status. But I am alerting us to the very real dangers in our world at the moment.

Current projects of self-overcoming are tricky to probe critically precisely because they are not so manifestly hideous as the horrors of the twentieth century; because they present themselves to us in the dominant language of our culture— choice, consent, control; and because they promise an escape from the human condition into a realm of near mastery. We are beguiled with the promise of a new self. Consider, then, that we are in the throes of a structure of biological obsession that undermines recognition of the fullness and the limitations of human embodiment. A premise and promise driving the Human Genome Project was that we might one day soon intervene decisively in order to promote better if not perfect human products. Promoters of these developments ran—and run—to the ecstatic, as in a 1986 pronouncement by a geneticist that the genome project "is the grail of human genetics, . . . the ultimate answer to the commandment to 'know thyself.'"[21]

The "social imaginary" declares the human body a construction, something we make, unmake, and remake at will. We are loathe to grant the status of

---

[20]The literature on all this is vast. The interested reader might just search for "transhuman" on the Internet and amaze—and horrify—oneself by the celebration of various plans and possibilities for creating a nonhuman future—created by human beings themselves, of course. Nazi eugenics, or a version of eugenics, had infected nearly all Western societies in the 1920s and 1930s, with laws being put on the books to coercively sterilize the "unfit" and, in other ways, to prevent the "burden" on society represented by the "mentally deficient." I discuss this in detail in the forthcoming book based upon my Gifford lectures, *Sovereignties: God, State, Self* (New York: Basic Books, forthcoming in 2008).

[21]I go over this in detail in *Who Are We?* and in a number of essays.

givenness to any aspect of ourselves, despite the fact that human babies are wriggling, complex little bodies preprogrammed with all sorts of delicately calibrated reactions to the human relationships "nature" presumes will be the matrix of child nurture. If we think of bodies concretely in this way, we are then propelled to ask ourselves questions about the world that little bodies enter: is it welcoming, warm, responsive? But if we tilt in the direction of genetic fundamentalism, one in which the body is raw material to be worked on or worked over, the surroundings in which bodies are situated fades as The Body gets enshrined as a kind of messianic project.

It is unsurprising, therefore, that certain experts declare as a matter of fact—the point, for them, is not even worth arguing—that "we must inevitably start to choose our descendants." We do so now in "permitting or preventing the birth of our own children according to their medical prognosis, thus selecting the lives to come." So long as society does not cramp our freedom of action, we will stay on the road of progress and exercise sovereign choice over birth by consigning to death those with a less-than-stellar potential for a life not "marred by an excess of pain or disability."

What C. S. Lewis called the "extreme rationality" (not to be confused with reason as such) that consigns to the dustbin of history all claims of intrinsic value—since claims embracing such truths cannot, allegedly, meet certain standards of a rationalistic defense of these values—winds up promoting a subjectivism of values that it believes is somehow more honest. When this happens, those whose "values" triumph will be those possessed of the most overwhelming will-to-power. By contrast, "a dogmatic belief in objective value," Lewis writes, "is necessary to the very idea of a rule which is not tyranny or an obedience which is not slavery."[22]

Here we seem to have moved rather far from consideration of the real-world drama of a disabled newborn being intentionally euthanized, but I hope that the reader finds this not to be the case. I hope that in the establishment and

---

[22]Lewis, *Abolition*, p. 81. This statement, with its echoes of medieval Thomism, is worth rereading several times since it runs so counter to the dogma of our time. An essayist recently commented that Lewis adhered firmly "to an objectivist account of the world. Things are as they are, however I feel about them; the world is thus, and within and throughout and beside the world is God, and his historical dealings with human beings." Whether, therefore, our own inclinations chime with Christian understanding is "quite beside the point. How I feel about the incarnation or the moral law can no more affect its reality than my chafings against (say) the operations of gravity will permit me to fly unaided." See Raymond Edwards, "Fantasy Founded on Belief: Narnia Revisited," *The Tablet*, December 17/24, 2005, p. 22.

even celebration of deliberate infanticide as the only courageous and truly humane thing to do, as what reason rather than unreason dictates, we recognize the sort of thing Lewis warned us against in 1944. Why can we not love a helpless being in the time God has given that baby? What can this profoundly disabled newborn teach us about grace and beauty and goodness? About caritas? Why can we not ameliorate pain and discomfort without believing we must either use extraordinary measures to "keep alive" or else boldly kill?

In 2003, the eighteen-year-old son of one of my cousins died. He was "supposed" to have died when he was an infant. He was born anencephalic. He could never speak or feed himself or crawl or walk or do any of the normal things human beings generally do or learn to do. According to the doctors, there was no "there" there. Aaron was definitely a prime candidate for euthanizing or, as the moral theorist Peter Singer candidly puts it (in approval), infanticide. But to anyone who met him, Aaron was a beautiful child with the biggest blue eyes and the most striking dark eyelashes imaginable. He stared out at the world, making no apparent distinctions, until his mother came into view. Then his face would "beam" or "light up"—there is no other way to put it. He knew her and he loved her, and I defy anyone to claim otherwise. Her love and care and devotion kept him going for eighteen years. And when he died, an entire family—parents, sibling, grandparents, aunts, uncles, cousins—and an entire community mourned their loss.

My cousin Paula Jean did not bemoan her fate. Nor did she curse God or wonder "what might have been." This had been given to her, and she would do her job joyfully. The story of Aaron and Paula Jean is a story of human endurance and receipt of the gift of grace. I ask you to contrast it to the vision of "peace" promulgated by the euthanasia doctor who extols how "beautiful" are the handicapped newborns who have been intentionally killed. These are two contrasting visions of our shared human future, one in which human beings will write the decisive chapter on whether we will abolish humanity—obliterate that which is truly human—or, by contrast, remember how to love and cherish our humanity, however wretched, however broken.

6

C. S. Lewis and Emotional Doubt

Insights from the Philosophy of Psychology

GARY R. HABERMAS

Both as an atheist and later as a Christian, C. S. Lewis was a veteran religious doubter. Besides his initial factual questions, Lewis's more painful struggles seem to have been largely emotional in nature. To those who have trekked these same paths, Lewis's language may sound quite natural—"Been there, done that," they will say, immediately identifying with his experience.

Amazingly, not only did Lewis encourage at least the beginnings of an initial, thoughtful (though unsystematic) response to unruly emotions, but he did so even a decade or two before the work of the most influential cognitive and cognitive-behavioral psychological therapists. Thus, looking backward through the lens of these exceptionally influential psychological ideas, we can see that, at some key points, Lewis's thinking is strikingly similar to theirs.

In this chapter, we will view Lewis's identification of religious doubt that is emotional in nature, as well as his proposed remedy. This will be followed by an overview of select ideas by the most philosophical of contemporary psychotherapists, Albert Ellis. The comparison, I hope, will do two things: make explicit a theoretical framework in which to view Lewis's earlier ideas, as well as provide practical measures to calm the worst ills of what can be a very painful species of religious doubt.

C. S. LEWIS ON EMOTIONAL DOUBT

We will begin on a personal note. It is clear that C. S. Lewis was writing about a subject with which he was quite intimately familiar. His are not the comments of one speaking from a distance, having observed these processes in others alone, but rather those of someone who draws from his personal, painful experience.

For example, he recalls that doubt had assailed him both during his unbelieving, atheistic days, as well as after his conversion to Christianity. He says, "Now that I am a Christian, I do have moods in which the whole thing looks very improbable; but when I was an atheist, I had moods in which Christianity looked terribly probable."[1] So whichever worldview we embrace, "mere feelings will continue to assault our conviction." While at present the spiritual world may seem far away at times, "so, as I well remember, the atheist too has his moments of shuddering misgiving, of an all but irresistible suspicion that old tales may after all be true."[2]

Well known for his brilliant use of illustrations and analogies, seldom does Lewis reach the heights that he does when observing his own struggles with doubt. For instance, he likens his religious uncertainty to having an operation. Though he has good reasons to trust physicians and their methods, "when they have me down on the table and clamp their horrible mask over my face, a mere childish panic begins inside me."[3] Or again, "I find that mere change of scene always has a tendency to decrease my faith at first—God is less credible when I pray in a hotel bedroom than when I am in College."[4] And unless we learn how to deal with our emotions, our chances of holding on to our beliefs are about the same "as a snowflake has of retaining its consistency in the mouth of a blast furnace."[5] These picturesque remarks are quite helpful in laying some of the groundwork for our religious struggles.

In my own work on this subject, I have delineated three species of doubt—

---

[1] C. S. Lewis, *Mere Christianity*, rev. ed. (New York: Macmillan, 1952), p. 123 (hereafter, *MC*).

[2] C. S. Lewis, "Religion: Reality or Substitute?" in *Christian Reflections*, ed. Walter Hooper (Grand Rapids: Eerdmans, 1967), p. 41.

[3] *MC*, p. 122. Interestingly, in his Space Trilogy, Lewis attributes very similar words to his main character, Ransom, who likewise distinguishes between his beliefs and his imagination. See *Perelandra: A Novel* (New York: Macmillan, 1944), p. 27.

[4] Lewis, "Religion: Reality or Substitute?" p. 42.

[5] Ibid., p. 43.

factual, emotional and volitional.[6] Lewis is clearly aware of the differences between at least the first two. He thinks that when any "real" problems arise regarding the substance of Christian belief, then these must be met in a much
different manner.[7] And his remedy is to face squarely the philosophical, historical or other problems, presumably as he has modeled in many of his works.
Elsewhere, Lewis ventures with equal understanding and insight into the area
of volitional issues, where he argues that Christian belief must be based on a
firm foundation; but after that, our level of commitment to these data are "no
longer proportioned to every fluctuation."[8]

Thus, while being aware of different types of uncertainty, it is also clear that
Lewis is chiefly thinking in terms of emotional doubt. Words and phrases
above such as "moods," "mere feelings," "shuddering misgiving," "childish
panic" and "blast furnace" paint quite nicely what he has in mind: emotional
assaults that establish beachheads in our lives.[9] Human reason may fight back,
but apart from a disciplined approach that puts our feelings in their proper
place, we will never gain the victory.

What is Lewis's remedy for these unruly emotions? He thinks it is necessary for us to "train the habit of Faith." Without developing his answer in
much detail, he suggests a couple steps. First, we should begin by recognizing
the role of our moods and feelings. They can change on a daily basis and color
how we view our beliefs. Second, we must daily practice the classical disciplines, like prayer, inspirational reading and church worship, in order to be reminded of Christian doctrine.[10] We must constantly review and keep what we
believe before us.

Lewis realizes that changing our thinking will not simply occur overnight.
"Only the *practice* of Faith resulting in the *habit* of Faith will *gradually* do
that."[11] So we must work constantly, countering the powerful influence of our
emotions on our thinking.

---

[6]For a discussion of these and other details, see Gary Habermas, *Dealing with Doubt* (Chicago:
Moody Press, 1990); idem, *The Thomas Factor: Using Your Doubts to Grow Closer to God* (Nashville:
Broadman & Holman, 1999). Both volumes are available without charge on my website at <http://
www.garyhabermas.com/books/books.htm>.
[7]*MC*, p. 123.
[8]C. S. Lewis, "On Obstinacy in Belief," in *The World's Last Night and Other Essays* (New York: Harcourt Brace Jovanovich, 1960), p. 29.
[9]*MC*, pp. 123-24.
[10]*MC*, p. 124.
[11]Lewis, "Religion: Reality or Substitute?" pp. 41-42, emphasis added.

Lewis takes pains to emphasize that training the habit of faith is not a matter of talking ourselves into something that we know is untrue. Actually, the opposite is the case: the key is to bring our emotions and feelings into line with what our intellect has judged true on good grounds. He wishes to "make it clear that . . . feeling must depend on our whole philosophy, not our whole philosophy on a feeling."[12] It is a matter of our reason being opposed by our emotions, with the latter attacking our rational foundations. We should hold our established beliefs "in spite of our changing moods."[13]

Recall that religious persons are no different in this regard than atheists. Everyone experiences this personal battle, whether or not they are religious. And these struggles concern not only the realm of faith but also our secular beliefs.[14] In many areas, if we are perceptive, we can see moods carrying out their warfare against our best reasons.

ALBERT ELLIS AND RATIONAL EMOTIVE BEHAVIOR THERAPY

Developed in the 1950s by Albert Ellis, Rational Emotive Behavior Therapy (REBT) grew out of Ellis's dissatisfaction with his own training as a clinical psychologist in the psychoanalytic tradition. He was frustrated by the seeming inability of many of his patients to work through their problems and rid themselves of their painful symptoms. Ellis concluded that the chief reason they were unable to do so was that they readily accepted a number of irrational beliefs. They may have acquired these erroneous thoughts initially during their childhood, and then added further, similar errors throughout their lives.

When Ellis taught his patients to identify and then dispute these irrational beliefs, they often were able to adjust and move beyond these issues. The application of his techniques even to recalcitrant patients often produced strikingly helpful results.

Over the years, many other practitioners came to similar conclusions and rigorously tested their techniques. Rather astoundingly, Ellis reported years ago that several hundred research studies had already confirmed his theory, indicating that people could change their thoughts, emotions, and behavior. In significant ways they could deal with various sorts of painful maladies like anx-

---

[12]Ibid., p. 41.
[13]*MC*, p. 123. Cf. also Lewis, "On Obstinacy in Belief," pp. 17, 25-29.
[14]Lewis, "Religion: Reality or Substitute?" pp. 41-42; *MC*, pp. 123-24.

iety and depression, along with a host of other psychological issues. As with other techniques, not all persons were helped significantly. But Ellis asserts that the list of issues that REBT can handle effectively is much longer than the sorts of problems that are not treated well.[15] He argues that REBT is widely applicable and more effective than other psychotherapies.

The chief idea in REBT is that emotional upsets and pain are usually caused not by external factors, as is commonly held, but by the irrational beliefs that we accept and reinforce. It may be best known for its *A-B-C* doctrine. Although what happens to us (the *A*s, or "activating events" in our lives) can cause some pain and difficulty, the *primary* cause of our emotional suffering is our own belief system (the *B*s). Irrational beliefs (bad or negative *B*s) often cause painful consequences (the *C*s), while rational beliefs (good or positive *B*s) cause positive consequences. As Ellis says of irrational thoughts, "When these beliefs are effectively disputed (at point *D*), by challenging them rationally and behaviorally, the disturbed consequences become minimal and largely cease to recur."[16]

Therefore, the primary concern of REBT is to teach people how to locate their irrational misbeliefs and argue against them, thereby eliminating those beliefs and replacing them with rational ones. This disputing technique is at the center of REBT and is the method that most frequently brings healing.

Although it might seem as if rationally disputing our irrational thoughts, thereby healing our painful emotions, might seem to favor an exclusively rational process, Ellis and his supporters emphasize that REBT is quite multimodal. We are whole, integrated beings, and we work on issues from a variety of angles. Further, people differ from one another and prefer various applications. Thus, besides reason, REBT affirms and makes use of good emotions, cognitive imaging (both positive and negative), as well as reinforcing behavior, including in vivo desensitization, diet and exercise.[17] These elements mutually interact and influence each other as well.

In addition to its psychological dimensions, the philosophical basis for REBT is also frequently emphasized. Ellis often discusses his interest in phi-

---

[15] Albert Ellis, "Rational-Emotive Therapy," in *Current Psychotherapies*, ed. by Raymond J. Corsini and Danny Wedding, 4th ed. (Itasca, Ill.: Peacock, 1989), esp. pp. 197, 203-4, 222-23, 230.

[16] Ellis, "Rational-Emotive Therapy," p. 197; see also pp. 199, 207.

[17] Albert Ellis, "Special Features of Rational-Emotive Therapy," in Windy Dryden and Raymond DiGiuseppe, *A Primer on Rational-Emotive Therapy* (Champaign, Ill.: Research Press, 1990), pp. 79-80, 85-87, 90-93.

losophy and the philosophical basis for his system. He mentions the many influences on his views, citing a wide spectrum of thinkers ranging from Confucius, Lao-Tsu, Gautama Buddha, Epictetus and Marcus Aurelius to modern and contemporary philosophers like David Hume, Immanuel Kant, Ralph Waldo Emerson, Henry David Thoreau, John Dewey, Jean Paul Sartre and Bertrand Russell. He is especially indebted to the writings of the logical positivists and postmodernist thinkers like Richard Rorty. Intriguingly, Ellis even writes that he originally created REBT on the basis of logical positivism. He refers to his "passion for philosophy, and especially for the philosophy of happiness."[18] As Susan Walen, Raymond DiGiuseppe and Windy Dryden begin their volume, "Perhaps more than any other system of psychotherapy, RET [*sic*] grows out of and actively utilizes strong philosophical underpinnings."[19]

One other prominent matter in the philosophy of psychology might be briefly mentioned here as highly relevant to this discussion: the objectivist/constructivist debate. Although different nuances have been given, the objectivist outlook is sometimes aligned with more modernist epistemologies like that of logical positivism. This view is more prone to making claims about the nature of reality and claims that the consistent applications of empirical methodologies have not only produced meaningful results, but also can be known with a great amount of objective assurance.

In contrast, constructivism relies on the insights of Kant and many other philosophers, who emphasize that persons construct various models of reality based on how we view and order our own worlds. In this sense, we interpret the real world differently, seeing it through our own glasses, whether rose-colored or otherwise. For the most part, what we primarily know is our own interpretations of reality rather than objective reality itself.

In certain postmodernist writers, constructivism can take on a more radical spirit, moving further away from objectivism and coming closer to questioning the very existence of knowable reality. Here, more chastened, corrigible epistemic claims are much preferred to those that are overly dogmatic in their proclamations regarding knowledge.

---

[18]Esp. Albert Ellis, *Reason and Emotion in Psychotherapy: A Comprehensive Method of Treating Human Disturbances*, rev. ed. (New York: Carol Publishing, 1994), pp. 290-91, 385-86, 405-6. Ellis's quote above is from pp. 385-86 of this text. Also, Ellis, "Rational-Emotive Therapy," p. 202; Ellis, "Special Features of Rational-Emotive Therapy," p. 92.

[19]Susan R. Walen, Raymond DiGiuseppe and Windy Dryden, *A Practitioner's Guide to Rational-Emotive Therapy* (New York: Oxford University Press, 1992), p. 3.

Though psychologists wade less frequently into this more philosophical discussion, the prevalent psychological view at present appears to be some version of constructivism.[20] Intriguingly, REBT commentators exhibit tendencies that seem to invoke both objectivist and constructivist strands.

For example, Ellis states that REBT accepts a constructivist view, applied to reality as it is interpreted.[21] Further, he insists that REBT follows certain postmodern philosophical emphases and professes "no objective standpoint" for absolute truth. All theories are "human constructions," although "some are probably better than others."[22] This certainly has a constructivist flavor.

Yet, when Ellis developed REBT, he based it on the tenets of logical positivism. His system remains "logically consistent and fact-based (that is, has empirical or realistic referents)"[23] and embraces the scientific method. On the other hand, it is irrational thinking that is "unrealistic, antiempirical, and illogical."[24] This emphasis sounds more objectivist.

Dryden and DiGiuseppe are even clearer on the latter. Like Ellis, irrational beliefs are "inconsistent with reality." REBT is "reality-based" and corresponds to "confirmable reality." But surprisingly, given the more recent, constructivist flavor, "your client's descriptions of *A* can be confirmed as accurate by neutral observers."[25] As crucial here, even the client's *descriptions,* the very items that Ellis states are human constructions, are so demonstrable that they can be strictly verified in a neutral, empirical fashion. This seems to entail quite strongly an objectivist angle.

It is difficult, then, to know more precisely where REBT stands with regard to this philosophical question of whether we must conform our rational thinking to a knowable reality, or to our private, interpreted notions of reality. Ellis

---

[20]For some of the psychological discussion, see Donald Meichenbaum and Deborah Fitzpatrick, "A Constructivist Narrative Perspective on Stress and Coping: Stress Inoculation Applications," in *Handbook of Stress: Theoretical and Clinical Aspects,* ed. Leo Goldberger and Schlomo Breznitz, 2nd ed. (New York: Free Press, 1993), pp. 706-23; M. J. Mahoney and W. J. Lyddon, "Recent Developments in Cognitive Approaches to Counseling and Psychotherapy," *The Counseling Psychologist* 16 (1988): 190-234; R. Neimeyer and G. Felixas, "Constructivist Contributions to Psychotherapy Integration," *Journal of Integrative and Eclectic Psychotherapy* 9 (1990): 4-20.

[21]Ellis, *Reason and Emotion,* p. 83.

[22]Ibid., pp. 405-6.

[23]Ibid., p. 160.

[24]Ellis, "Special Features of Rational-Emotive Therapy," pp. 82-83.

[25]Dryden and DiGiuseppe, *Primer on Rational-Emotive Therapy,* pp. 3-4, 23, 25, 41-44, 69, 70, 72. Though Dryden and DiGiuseppe do not have to agree with Ellis, they are his former students, and Ellis contributed an essay to this book.

himself seems to have migrated over the years in his own position, moving from a more positivistic stance to a more postmodernist one. Yet he also appears to have kept some elements of both, holding them in tension.

Nevertheless, cognitive therapists who espouse the constructivist position seldom hold that our interpretations are groundless, false, or pertain to an unknowable reality. It is perhaps even likely that the majority position among cognitive constructivists is that we can usually be fairly or even quite sure that we know certain "facts," but that our knowledge of them is more probabilistic, chastened and corrigible. This may be the sense in which, as just seen, Ellis also describes REBT as factual and empirical.

Therefore, even though some practitioners of REBT theory may fluctuate on this more-theoretical question, the straightforward way to interpret them would seem to be that our beliefs (*B*s) should conform to reality, which can be known more-or-less clearly, according to the scholar and/or the specific situation. At any rate, some interpretations are simply better than others, so we should never embrace ideas that are altogether ungrounded. That is why the latter are treated as misbeliefs.[26] This seems to be Ellis's point even in his comments about following postmodern epistemologies.

FRAMING LEWIS IN REBT TERMS

The REBT theory arguably belongs within the camp of cognitive or cognitive behavioral psychotherapies. This broad methodological grouping contains several quite influential theorists and their ideas. Besides Ellis, other examples include especially Aaron Beck's more strictly cognitive therapy[27] and Donald Meichenbaum's cognitive-behavioral therapy.[28] At many crucial points, Arnold Lazarus's multimodal approach also employs major cognitive insights.[29]

It seems that casting C. S. Lewis's ideas on emotional doubt in terms that

---

[26]Ellis, *Reason and Emotion*, p. 406.

[27]Aaron T. Beck and Marjorie E. Weishaar, "Cognitive Therapy," in Corsini and Wedding, *Current Psychotherapies*, ed. by Raymond J. Corsini and Danny Wedding, 4th ed. (Itasca, Ill.: Peacock, 1989), pp. 284-320; Aaron T. Beck, *Cognitive Therapy and the Emotional Disorders* (New York: International Universities Press, 1976).

[28]Donald Meichenbaum, *Cognitive Behavior Modification: An Integrative Approach* (New York: Plenum, 1977).

[29]Arnold A. Lazarus, "Multimodal Therapies," in Corsini and Wedding, *Current Psychotherapies*, ed. by Raymond J. Corsini and Danny Wedding, 4th ed. (Itasca, Ill.: Peacock, 1989), pp. 502-44. For one of his more cognitive publications, see Arnold A. Lazarus, Clifford Lazarus and Allen Fay, *Don't Believe It for a Minute! Forty Toxic Ideas That Are Driving You Crazy* (San Luis Obispo, Calif.: Impact, 1993).

approximate at least a loosely REBT theoretical structure is a natural fit. However, this is not to single out REBT as the only form of cognitive therapy with which this could be accomplished. Similar comparisons might be made between Lewis's treatment and other cognitive systems as well.

Admittedly, this will involve some minor systematizing of Lewis's thoughts. But two caveats may keep this from being a serious intrusion. Lewis is seldom systematic in his writings, so comparing his ideas with more structured scholars might likewise require arranging Lewis's remarks more clearly. Further, as we will detail below, Lewis's ideas here predate the major cognitive therapists by at least a decade or two, so this at once means that his ideas are not derived from theirs, which makes a comparison all the more instructive.[30] But while his having less opportunity to rely on others for these explications might have made his treatment more original, it might also account for a bit more fluidity in his explanations.

Lewis distinguishes emotional doubt from its factual and volitional sisters. He clearly treats the former as by far the most bothersome of these varieties, although he seldom dwells on details of the emotional pain. Nonetheless, we can still assume that his references to being in a "trough of anxiety"[31] or to times when "a mere childish panic begins inside me"[32] depict emotionally painful situations. And when we try to assist others through their struggles, we may ask them to trust us "that what is painful will relieve their pain."[33]

So it seems clear that the relief that Lewis desires for both himself and others is a prescription that addresses these painful emotional moments. And while he acknowledges that this pain may afflict other areas of life as well, he is clearly interested in emotional assaults on the believer's faith.

What is the cause of this emotional pain? While not as clearly as the cognitive psychotherapists, Lewis still makes it plain that our improper beliefs often cause a great deal of our problems. For example, in his essay "On Obstinacy in Belief," Lewis begins by treating the false but common view that faith need not (or even should not) be grounded in evidence. Lewis's purpose is to show that this starting point will cause undue problems that need to be re-

---

[30] As we have already observed, there were various philosophical and psychological forerunners to cognitive and cognitive-behavioral therapies. However, it is chiefly practitioners like Ellis and Beck who formulated specific steps for countering emotional pain.

[31] Lewis, "Religion: Reality or Substitute?" p. 42.

[32] *MC*, p. 123.

[33] Lewis, "On Obstinacy in Belief," p. 23.

solved.[34] Elsewhere, he argues that those who think that all doubt is rational in nature fail to account for the often-prominent emotional element, thereby accepting a misdiagnosis.[35]

Like the cognitive psychotherapists, Lewis clearly and frequently repeats the claim that emotions are the biggest culprit here. The remedy is that reason must be brought to bear on the problem. In matters of faith, our feelings ought to be mistrusted.[36] And when the choice is between reason and emotions, we should always choose the former. These two forces regularly battle each other. Since reason is our clearest guide to the real world, we must keep emotions in their rightful place.[37] Though our feelings would like to have the upper hand, we must not allow it.

How do we correct our emotions and force them to take their rightful place? The answer is a disciplined, forceful use of our reason. His remedy consists of what today might be called applying a dose of self-talk. As Lewis asserts in one of his more brilliant lines, "Unless you teach your moods 'where they get off,' you can never be a sound Christian or even a sound atheist, but just a creature dithering to and fro, with its beliefs really dependent on the weather and the state of its digestion."[38]

Clearly then, one must take charge of the situation and act forcefully. No half-hearted attempt will work here. This is where Lewis initiates his plan to train faith, suggesting that the doubter must first learn that the fight is originating in his own emotions.[39] If we do not understand this, it is questionable whether we will take the proper steps. Next, faith must be reinforced by the regular study of theology and, presumably, the data that support these doctrines, the sort of data Lewis invokes throughout his writings. Then, our behavior is affected, too, as we practice on a regular basis such disciplines as prayer, devotional reading and worship.

In short, like the cognitive psychotherapists' analysis of emotional pain, Lewis thinks that emotional doubts readily cause pain. Misconceptions plague this topic. On many occasions Lewis clearly asserts that undisciplined emotions are at war with our reason and even with faith itself. The remedy is the

---

[34]Ibid., pp. 13-14.
[35]Lewis, "Religion: Reality or Substitute?" p. 42.
[36]Ibid., pp. 41-43.
[37]*MC*, pp. 122-23.
[38]Ibid., pp. 123-24; cf. Lewis, "On Obstinacy in Belief," p. 23.
[39]*MC*, p. 124.

application of strong reasons to our feelings, dictating to ourselves what is indicated by the evidence.

We have said that Ellis and many other psychotherapists are multimodal in their methodology, employing more paths than just reason alone for unruly emotions. Interestingly, Lewis agrees: our emotions may be dealt with in more than one way. He specifically mentions at least three paths for accomplishing this task. We can correct the problem in terms of authority, by citing the best experts; or by reason, as just mentioned; or we can solve the matter by first-hand experience. If, for instance, authority, reason and experience confirm the existence of a spiritual reality, then our emotions need to comply.[40]

Are there any parallels regarding the objectivist-constructivist discussion? Does Lewis favor one framework over the other? Are we conforming our reason to the world as it really is? Or does reason follow our configuration of the world?

On this subject, perhaps surprisingly for some, Lewis recognizes that there is something to be said for the constructivist account of knowledge. In one of his more technical volumes on English literature, Lewis argues that we can no longer say that our knowledge is some exact mental replica of reality. Neither does a particular worldview somehow capture reality as it actually exists. Rather, worldviews are human attempts to visualize various components of reality, yet from our own perspectives. Prevailing worldviews change from time to time, not simply because new evidence disproves the old model, but also for more subjective considerations; for instance, people may just be ready for a change. To be sure, real evidence will be involved, but the relevant evidence may have been recognized earlier too. So while evidence still plays a prominent role that influences our perspectives, we still conceptualize *about* reality.[41]

A bit more tantalizing is Lewis's depiction of many of these ideas in his works of fiction. In *Perelandra*, Ransom, the hero of the Space Trilogy, learns that we never fully observe things or persons as they really are. Rather, our perceptions of appearances are partially shaped by our perspective.[42] Only God observes reality as it actually exists. Of course, the belief that God exists and knows reality fully and perfectly profoundly distinguishes Lewis's view from

[40]Lewis, "Religion: Reality or Substitute?" pp. 40-41.

[41]C. S. Lewis, *The Discarded Image: An Introduction to Medieval and Renaissance Literature* (Cambridge: Cambridge University Press, 1964), epilogue, pp. 216-23.

[42]Lewis, *Perelandra*, esp. p. 202.

secular versions of constructivism that often deny objective truth and end up in relativism. On the other hand, *That Hideous Strength* provides almost a running critique of one-sided objectivist trends, including various aspects of logical positivism and related ideas.[43]

Therefore, it makes sense that when we change our thinking and use reason to keep our feelings in their proper place, Lewis intends us to understand that our use of evidence is not wholly objective in some mechanical sense. Rather, our worldview remains to some degree our conceptualizing about the nature of reality, which conforms to a greater or lesser degree to the world as it really exists. Just as we cautioned when speaking above about constructivism, it does not follow that Lewis rejects the existence of facts or evidences. It would be exceptionally difficult to see how anyone could glean this position from Lewis's writings. It is simply that there is not a one-to-one relation between reality and our conceptions of it.

It certainly appears that Lewis has some strong similarities to the cognitive psychotherapists, and perhaps REBT in particular, regarding the application of reason and other modalities to emotional issues. Of course, there are differences as well. The psychologists seldom address the subject of religious doubt, while that is Lewis's chief application (although he has other similar things to say about our emotions in general[44]). Further, the psychotherapists are more focused and forceful, and they present a wider variety of coping mechanisms. They also have an impressive number of empirical outcome studies that demonstrate the importance of rationally dictating to our emotions.

But this does not change the observation that Lewis predates them.[45] And he appears to have taken a related tack, accompanied by some quite similar, pertinent comments. I think that Lewis's advice on emotional doubt can be cast into a more systematized and empirical framework, and it would definitely benefit from such an exercise. In the next section, I will attempt such a reworking.

---

[43]C. S. Lewis, *That Hideous Strength* (New York: Macmillan, 1946), e.g., see esp. pp. 205, 255-59, 269, 353, 357-58.

[44]For a thoughtful application to the broader topic of the emotional "highs" of life, see *MC*, pp. 100-101.

[45]Ellis, arguably the earliest of the major cognitive psychotherapists, dates the origination of REBT to 1955 (Ellis, "Foreword," in Walen, DiGiuseppe and Dryden, *A Practitioner's Guide*, p. vii). But he does note the work of precursors such as Alfred Adler ("Rational-Emotive Therapy," p. 202). The respective works by Lewis date from years earlier than Ellis. For example, "Religion: Reality or Substitute?" was published in 1941, the particular portion of *MC (Christian Behaviour)* was published in 1943, and "On Obstinacy in Belief" was published later, also in 1955.

RECONSTRUCTING LEWIS IN REBT TERMS

Cognitive therapists emphasize different techniques for the actual application of their ideas. Dryden and DiGiuseppe suggest identifying one's irrational beliefs, challenging or disputing these troublesome thoughts, and changing them by replacing them with a different, more rational belief.[46] Christian psychologist William Backus and Christian counselor Marie Chapian employ a quite similar cognitive approach. They also suggest a three-step process for locating the misbeliefs that we tell ourselves, removing them by arguing against them, and replacing them with truth.[47] Another Christian psychologist, Chris Thurman, shortens the process to identifying our self-lies and replacing them with truth.[48]

How could advice like Lewis's be more rigorously cast in terms of an explicitly cognitive or cognitive-behavioral framework? Here we will try to outline a sample process that might be pursued in this regard.[49]

As Lewis rightly maintains, one must begin by recognizing that fluctuating, unruly feelings cause emotional doubt.[50] Since this specific form of uncertainty and its chief source of agitation are so easily confused with other species, to realize this is a crucial starting point. Working backward, these unruly emotions are themselves caused by our improper, untruthful thoughts. Like Ellis and Robert Harper remind us, our beliefs generally "take the form of *internalized sentences* or *self-talk*."[51] Thurman adds that most of our unhappiness and emotional pain are the result of telling ourselves things that are not true.[52] Lewis used the analogy of causing ourselves pain before undergoing surgery by telling ourselves that the anesthesia will smother us or that the doctors will begin operating before we are fully unconscious.[53] Therefore, to clean up our irrational thinking processes, we need to counter these private assertions.

So the emotional doubter might be telling oneself, "After all, maybe I am

---

[46]Dryden and DiGiuseppe, *Primer on Rational-Emotive Therapy*, pp. 44, 74.

[47]William Backus and Marie Chapian, *Telling Yourself the Truth* (Minneapolis: Bethany, 2000), chap. 1, esp. p. 15.

[48]Chris Thurman, *The Lies We Believe* (Nashville: Nelson, 1989), p. 22.

[49]There is no magic process or number of steps that must be utilized. Rather, such demarcations are better seen as methodological suggestions to be molded to individual needs.

[50]*MC*, p. 124; Lewis, "Religion: Reality or Substitute?" pp. 42-43.

[51]Albert Ellis and Robert A. Harper, *A Guide to Rational Living* (North Hollywood, Calif.: Wilshire, 1975), p. x.

[52]Thurman, *Lies We Believe*, pp. 22, 54.

[53]*MC*, p. 122.

really going to Hell," or "Perhaps I do not have enough faith," or something similar. Quite often, we express emotional doubt with the simple well-placed words, "What if . . . ?" Of course, we could ask this question about virtually anything! Since we can think much faster than we can speak, and because images or concepts can convey so much, a simple "Oh, no . . . " or "Here it comes again . . . " can even send a person into an emotional tail-spin.[54] We know what these self-statements imply, even without verbalizing the exact phrases. If we are really perceptive, we can trace a bad mood or painful moment precisely to such comments. It often happens mere moments after such a thought. When this occurs, we witness precisely what the cognitive psychotherapists are teaching.

The initial key here is to *identify* the troublesome misbeliefs. We begin by monitoring our thoughts and asking, "What did I just say [or think] to myself?" One helpful way to do this is to recognize that whenever our emotional alarm sounds and we begin hurting, for seemingly no reason at all, *that* is the time to decipher immediately what we just thought, being careful to recall images or concepts as well as the meaning that we attributed to them. The more we practice, the better we should become at picking out the offending misbeliefs.

Once we locate the troublesome idea(s), the second step is to *remove* it immediately. To change the mood and reduce the pain, we should argue with ourselves. The slogan is, "That's not true because . . . " Here we dispute the misbelief; whatever it is, we counter it. Lewis was right to say that we must basically tell our emotions to take a hike![55]

For example, if the doubt is, "What if I'm wrong?" we might simply counter, "Does asking 'What if?' automatically make something wrong? Anyone can 'What if?' *anything!* To the contrary, what if I'm right?"

Then we can continue: "And what *proves* that I am mistaken?" Now the emotional doubt is on the run! The question has been shifted from the original, ungrounded "What if?" scenario to one that requires a philosophical, scientific or historical response. The opportunity now exists to bring the discussion back to the real world. When truth or facts enter the picture, emotions are revealed for what they are: supposals that are often not based on reality!

Now the reinforcements need to arrive. The third step is to *replace* the orig-

---

[54]David Stoop, *You Are What You Think* (Grand Rapids: Revell, 1996), pp. 30-31.
[55]*MC*, pp. 123-24.

inal, offending thought with truthful comments. This can come in many forms, including developing a detailed statement or list as to *why* that particular kind of thinking is misplaced, or untrue. Memorizing Scripture for recall, worship, personal praise and thanksgiving, or reviewing doctrine along with the appropriate evidences is in line with Lewis's prescription for countering these emotional challenges.[56]

Behavioral techniques can work, too. For instance, one can divide a sheet of paper lengthwise into three sections. Misbeliefs should be recorded in the left column, with plenty of space after each one. In the middle section, across from the relevant untruth, several refutations should be given for each misstatement. Why is this particular misbelief false? In the third column, favorite Scripture verses, inspirational sayings or detailed evidences can be added that continue to make a case against the misbelief. This chart can be expanded periodically, providing a usable tool for those who may resort to these particular misbeliefs on other occasions.[57]

Basically, the chief idea is to confront the emotional doubt by locating the offending comment(s) or thought(s), followed by disputing its truth. When multiple reinforcements arrive, the uncertainty should be on the run. Practice is simply crucial, for the process often goes back and forth for a few rounds. But we must be resolved to weather the storms of uncertainty. The good news is that relief usually arrives when we repeatedly counter our feelings by employing the relevant facts. Proper thinking trumps undisciplined emotions.

CONCLUSION

C. S. Lewis was ahead of his time in several respects. One of these is his recognition, often borne from personal experience, that whether we are Christians or atheists, "mere feeling will continue to assault our conviction."[58] Elsewhere, he states that our "emotions will rise up and carry out a sort of blitz."[59] Few have stated these issues more graphically, complete with well-placed il-

---

[56]Ibid., p. 124; cf. Lewis, "Religion: Reality or Substitute?" pp. 41-42. In Habermas, *Thomas Factor*, esp. chaps. 7-8, I have listed more than a dozen cognitive and behavioral suggestions for replacing emotional doubt with truth.

[57]See Thurman, *Lies We Believe*, esp. appendixes A and B, where common lies are grouped together, along with lists of counterarguments. Until familiarity with the process has been achieved, Thurman's lists can be readily used to personalize, restate and adapt either to verbal application or to the charts just mentioned.

[58]Lewis, "Religion: Reality or Substitute?" p. 41.

[59]*MC*, p. 123.

lustrations and analogies that drive home the points, often augmented with a bit of humor. It is clear that Lewis was a veteran of these private wars.

Lewis was also perceptive enough to recognize that our feelings do not represent our truest selves, but chiefly reflect these momentary emotional struggles. To return to our true beliefs, then, we must counter our troubling feelings. Building on our strong philosophical and historical foundations, we must call ourselves back to reality. After all—and this is crucial—Lewis repeatedly makes it clear that he is not suggesting that we simply manipulate our emotions if we think that the evidence is against us.[60] But given a strong philosophical and evidential basis, we must recognize the source of the conflict and counter our misleading emotions. Constant practice restores our sanity.

Lewis's advice follows a lesser-known path, especially in his own time. But it is a welcome antidote that predates, while generally agreeing with, some of the most sophisticated recent psychological studies on dealing with emotional pain.

---

[60]See esp. *MC*, p. 123; Lewis, "On Obstinacy in Belief," p. 29; idem, "Religion: Reality or Substitute?" pp. 40-43.

Part Two

GOODNESS

7

Is Divine Iconoclast as Bad as Cosmic Sadist?

Lewis versus Beversluis

DAVID BAGGETT

An ardent critic of my writing (my mom) has repeatedly told me that I say in many and big words what can be said far more simply in a few. So allow me to boil down the central thesis of this essay into a succinct sentence: God is good.[1]

That says it all. It's all I'm saying.

Well, perhaps not *all*, since even if we delimit the topic to moral goodness, God is good in a way Mother Teresa was not—even though most of us who are not Christopher Hitchens do believe she was good. God, however, is maximally good, morally perfect; in God there is no darkness or even vulnerability to temptation. Moreover, since an atheist might affirm that God is good, in a sense similar to their affirmation that Santa Claus lives at the North Pole, I need to stress that the suggestion here is that God himself is essentially good. It's not merely that the idea of "God" has goodness as part of it. Philosophers more loquacious than I and not smarting from maternal criticism might point out that propositions about God's goodness are to be construed for present purposes *de re* (of the thing) and not merely *de dicto* (of the word).

[1]Thanks to Mike Peterson, Elton Higgs, Steve Patterson and Victor Reppert for offering insightful suggestions on earlier drafts of this chapter.

Beyond those qualifications is another, for divine and human goodness are not exactly the same. Presumably God has prerogatives that we do not have, has a perspective we lack, can redeem situations we cannot, and is not afflicted with our limitations. Since God's ways are above ours, God might command or allow something that, to our finite understanding, seems quite bad or radically wrong, yet he still may be good, even perfectly and essentially good. Just *how* different, though, can God's goodness be from standard human conceptions? For us to be justified in using the word *goodness* here at all, the goodness of God cannot be as different from our standards as night from day. If God's goodness bears inadequate resemblance to human goodness, our locution *good* concerning God is implicated in an irremediable equivocation.

When philosopher Immanuel Kant considered the "moral law within," he counted it as evidence for God; but when his predecessor David Hume had thought about implications of morality, he saw the world's suffering and counted that as moral evidence against the existence of a good and all-powerful God. Let us explore a bit whether the pain of this world poses a challenge to God's goodness.[2] But the more important and prior question to be explored is this: *Can* what God allows or commands pose an intractable challenge to the goodness of God? This chapter will explore C. S. Lewis's writing and life for insight into this question of perennial concern.

THE DIVINE VIVISECTIONIST

Richard Attenborough's beautiful 1994 film *Shadowlands* (based on a stage play written by William Nicholson) depicts Lewis's personal struggle with the problem of evil after the premature loss of his wife, Joy. After having written *The Problem of Pain* years earlier, a whole treatise on the problem of evil, Lewis encountered the problem of reconciling the evil in the world with a recognizably good God in an intensely personal way. After Joy's death, he kept a journal, later published as *A Grief Observed*, in which he chronicled the depth of his struggle. While still in the throes of grief, Lewis wrote: "Sooner or later I must face the question in plain language. What reason have we, except our own desperate wishes, to believe that God is, by any standard we can conceive, 'good'? Does not all the prima facie evidence suggest exactly the opposite?"[3]

---

[2] Explicit treatments of the problem of evil itself appear in Michael Peterson's and Philip Tallon's chapters (11-12) in this volume.

[3] C. S. Lewis, *A Grief Observed* (New York: Bantam, 1988), pp. 33-34.

So great was the struggle within Lewis that he wondered if God was really bad after all, the Divine Vivisectionist who treats us like rats in his laboratory. Having endured the anguish of unanswered prayer, and the agony of crushed hopes for his wife's recovery, Lewis faced head-on the question of whether or not God after all is good.

Central to Lewis's questions was God's goodness as *recognizable* goodness. This dimension of his quest comports with his earlier writings in which he had made clear his rejection of the idea that goodness is simply defined, or constituted, by divine fiat or arbitrary divine command. The Euthyphro Dilemma is a question posed by an early Socratic dialogue, and the question, put in monotheistic terms, is this: Is something moral because God commands it, or does God command it because it is moral? Lewis firmly embraced the "nonvoluntarist horn," according to which God commands something because it is moral. The contrary proposition—that the content of morality is just a function of whatever God happens to say—is one for which Lewis felt disdain. Such radical voluntarism raises the specter of a divine renegade invested with the authority to make whatever hideous deed he chooses morally permissible, even obligatory or morally good.[4]

In *Reflections on the Psalms,* for instance, Lewis wrote the following:

> There were in the eighteenth century terrible theologians who held that "God did not command certain things because they are right, but certain things are right because God commanded them." To make the position perfectly clear, one of them even said that though God has, as it happens, commanded us to love Him and one another, He might equally well have commanded us to hate Him and one another, and hatred would then have been right. It was apparently a mere toss-up which He decided on. Such a view in effect makes God a mere arbitrary tyrant. It would be better and less irreligious to have no ethics than to have such an ethics and such a theology as this.[5]

In *The Problem of Pain,* Lewis elaborated further:

> It has sometimes been asked whether God commands certain things because they are right, or whether certain things are right because God commands them. With Hooker, and against Dr. Johnson, I emphatically embrace the

---

[4]Depending on whether the theistic ethic in question is deontic or axiological in nature, God's commands are constitutive of moral obligation on the one hand, or moral goodness itself on the other, respectively.

[5]C. S. Lewis, *Reflections on the Psalms* (1940; reprint, London: Fontana, 1986), p. 54.

first alternative. The second might lead to the abominable conclusion (reached, I think, by Paley) that charity is good only because God arbitrarily commanded it—that He might equally well have commanded us to hate Him and one another and that hatred would then have been right. I believe, on the contrary, that "they err who think that of the will of God to do this or that there is no reason besides His will." God's will is determined by His wisdom which always perceives, and His goodness which always embraces, the intrinsically good.[6]

It seems clear, so far as Lewis was concerned, that there are objective standards of morality that God recognizes and cannot violate if he is meaningfully and recognizably good.[7] What can be said of moral constraints imposed on God's commands can be said similarly of what God allows. Certain immoral commands issued by God, and certain sufficiently bad states of affairs allowed by God, at least in principle, would preclude our rational ability to affirm his goodness. The sort of radical voluntarism represented historically by Paley or, even more so, by William of Ockham that recognizes no conditions for God to be good was not an option for Lewis.

Let us call this option he rejected "Ockhamism," or "radical voluntarism," and Lewis's preferred nonvoluntarism "Platonism," after Plato's view of morality as autonomous. Because Lewis was acutely aware that Ockhamism makes the attribution of divine goodness arbitrary if not vacuous, he was strongly opposed to the Ockhamistic thesis. Something is not morally acceptable simply by virtue of having been commanded by God or allowed by God. Despite the palpable difference in tone between, say, *The Problem of Pain* and the first half of *A Grief Observed*, both were written by a man who emphatically rejected Ockhamism. A grieving Lewis wanted to understand the suffering he and his wife had endured; he needed to reconcile such pain with standards of recognizable goodness if his reasonable faith in God's goodness was to survive.

---

[6]C. S. Lewis, *The Problem of Pain* (1954), in *The Complete C. S. Lewis Signature Classics* (New York: HarperCollins, 2002), p. 409.

[7]This understandably leads the Lewis critic John Beversluis, as we are about to see, to conclude that Lewis thought morality was ontologically independent of God. If the relevant moral standards are internal to God's nature, however, this is a mistake, and Lewis clearly thought that morality depends on God after all, just not in Ockham's sense, but rather more on God's reason and character than God's will. This chapter will not broach such issues, however, since it deals more with moral epistemology than moral ontology.

BEVERSLUIS'S CHARGE

In his book titled *C. S. Lewis and the Search for Rational Religion,* philosopher John Beversluis characterizes the questioning Lewis of the first two chapters of *A Grief Observed* as still committed to a realist understanding of goodness. By trying to make sense of the loss of Joy as consistent with his understanding of God's goodness, Lewis demonstrated his prior belief that what God commands or allows must be seen as compatible with constraints imposed by clear and autonomous moral standards. What frightened and tempted Lewis most, in the face of his excruciating loss when all his prayers met only a locked door, was not naturalism, but God as Cosmic Sadist, and us as mere rats in his laboratory.

As is well known, Lewis's crisis of faith in God's goodness would pass. He came to think of God as Sadist as too anthropomorphic. Such a God would not make a universe, or offer baits like love or laughter. How did Lewis reconcile God's goodness with his own painful episode of doubt? By his own account, Lewis came to recognize anew that a good God may subject his creations to pain, even intense pain, in order to remake them in his image. But "the terrible thing," Lewis wrote, "is that a perfectly good God is in this matter hardly less formidable than a Cosmic Sadist. The more we believe that God hurts only to heal, the less we can believe that there is any use in begging for tenderness; . . . the kinder and more conscientious he is, the more inexorably he will go on cutting."[8]

Here Lewis introduced his famous image of God as Divine Iconoclast: God knocking down false conceptions of himself and replacing them with more accurate ones. No gentle Grandfather in the sky willing to give us whatever we want and spare us from pain, God is rather the Divine Surgeon, who will do what he needs to do, short of violating our freedom, to ready us to inhabit a holy heaven, however painful a process it may be. Although such reflections helped salvage Lewis's faith and have served as a treasured source of comfort for many faith-filled mourners since, Beversluis argues that Lewis did not realize it, but his theological transition from Cosmic Sadist to Divine Iconoclast amounted to an admission of defeat. Beversluis claims it is simply tantamount to a "shift from Platonism to Ockhamism on the question of the connection between God and morality." For "the God who knocked down

---

[8]Lewis, *A Grief Observed,* p. 50.

Lewis's house of cards is not a Platonically conceived deity who is good in our sense, but rather an Ockhamistically conceived deity who is declared to be good *no matter what he does.*[9] Thus Beversluis's charge: Divine Iconoclast is just as bad as Cosmic Sadist.[10] A God whose goodness is unrecognizable and inscrutable is no different from a God who is actually bad.

Beversluis argues that if Lewis did not abandon the intuition that there are some things God cannot do, he did at least lose confidence in our ability as human beings ever to identify them. Calvinists may resonate with this stance attributed to Lewis, for they are notorious for refusing to privilege our moral intuitions or insights as standards to evaluate alleged divine behavior. They understandably insist that doing so would put us in the position of judging God. Such Calvinists may well reject the idea that God is liable to do just anything at all, since they refuse to believe that God, good as he is, would ever do something irremediably awful. They are nonetheless hesitant to insist that we could ever really judge any particular command issued (or state of affairs allowed) as something truly precluded morally. An important reason for their hesitancy, of course, is their firm belief in the ongoing effects of sin on our moral perspective. Our fallenness has warped our ability to discern good and evil. They insist that this should make us resist the notion that such finite and fallen creatures as ourselves could ever stand in the position of judging God. Moreover, there is no more ultimate vantage point from which to issue a moral assessment than what God himself provides, so any such attempt to pass judgment on the ground of all being is literally groundless.

Although we may wish to sympathize with this position, this attempt to deflect Beversluis's criticism or defend Lewis is inadequate. Using our best discernment to determine which alleged divine commands or actions are reconcilable with our deepest moral intuitions and considered reflections is not to place ourselves above God. Certainly the early Lewis would not have said that

---

[9]John Beversluis, *C. S. Lewis and the Search for Rational Religion* (Grand Rapids: Eerdmans, 1985), p. 151.

[10]Victor Reppert makes an excellent point against Beversluis: "If Lewis is open to the charge of Ockhamism in *A Grief Observed*, then he was an Ockhamist in *The Problem of Pain*. If Lewis can be acquitted of the charge of being an Ockhamist in *The Problem of Pain*, then the same arguments can be used to show that he was not an Ockhamist in *A Grief Observed*." Here Reppert is responding to the aspect of Beversluis's critique contrasting the Lewis of *The Problem of Pain* with the Lewis of *A Grief Observed*. See Reppert's delightful "The Ecumenical Apologist: Understanding C. S. Lewis's Defense of Christianity," in *C. S. Lewis: Life, Works, and Legacy*, 4 vols. (Westport, Conn.: Praeger, 2007).

such discernment is presumptuous, for he was notorious for saying that we should only believe in God and his goodness if that is where the evidence points. No, such sensitivity to the evidence and efforts of discernment are a responsible use of our God-given faculties for moral reflection, vital for determining which conception of God is the right one, and an important way of coming to love God with all of our minds. Our worship of God as good, to be meaningful rather than vacuous, has to be based on some determinate content, not acquiescence to inscrutable divine caprice diametrically opposed to our most cherished convictions. If nothing is identifiably beyond the range of possible commands God might issue or states of affairs God might allow, then our ascriptions of goodness to God are empty. They are as consistent with the command to visit widows in their affliction as with the command to snag live babies on the ends of burning pokers for the sport of it. Even if we are fallen creatures, we must still possess enough moral light and grace to determine that some commands are such that a good God could never issue them, any more than he could sin, commit suicide, or deny himself.

And so if we were to become convinced that God in fact *has* issued such an atrocious command, then we would be within our epistemic and moral rights to refuse to call such a God good.[11] For example, suppose we were in a position to know or be justified to believe that God has issued the command to torture innocent children for the fun of it. In that case, given the clarity with which we can see the moral impropriety involved, we would not be justified to continue calling God good. Such goodness would be so inscrutable as to be unrecognizable, and good sense and conversational clarity alone would demand that we stop using that term. More likely, of course, given the hiddenness of God, our current epistemic situation is more likely to be one in which we could not know or be justified to believe that God has issued such a command. It's more probable that we "missed God" than that he actually so commanded, a possibility we all wish certain zealous theists had more carefully considered on the morning of September 11, 2001.

---

[11]This thought experiment assumes that all else remains equal, including the strength and ingression of our core moral convictions, without necessarily assuming that such a stipulated scenario represents a genuine metaphysical possibility, and it is not meant to imply anything about the true ultimate connection or dependence relation that might exist between God and morality. Its import is to raise this question: What, counterfactually speaking, would we be rational to say about "God" in such a circumstance (a circumstance that may well be a counteressential: something in some sense conceivable but not actually possible)?

The point about morally abhorrent commands is parallel with the problem of evil, so there's something intuitive about what Beversluis is trying here. If a state of affairs God allows is so utterly and irredeemably horrible that it is completely beyond our ability to make sense of it, we would be justified to believe that a good God does not exist. Either there is no God at all, or God exists but is not good. Beversluis's logic in a sense is impeccable. His suggestion is that certain actions by God, if they were committed, would be so impossibly hard to square with our moral intuitions that their occurrence would provide good reason to reject God's goodness. If we continue attributing goodness to God, our ascriptions would be vacuous and arbitrary, motivated by a standard of goodness with no recognizable limits, and thus unable to attribute to God the determinate moral content they were traditionally thought to convey. They would be consistent with God's being what we normally consider barbaric and monstrous, so the ascriptions would pay no compliment.

Lewis himself either did not think we were so fallen as to lose our capacity to recognize the good, or thought that in our fallenness God had graciously restored our capacity for such recognitions, maintaining that this is why Scripture can appeal to the conscience even of unbelievers. In the second chapter of *A Grief Observed*, Lewis recognized that a sort of extreme Calvinism is a means of introducing the idea of a bad God "by the back door." He could see that if God in fact values the vices we abhor and it is only our own depravity that makes those values look wrong, there is little point in trying to think about God at all. "This knot comes undone when you try to pull it tight," he wrote.[12] Beversluis, however, would remind us that that reflection came early on, and stood at variance with the later chapters of Lewis's account containing his attempt at resolution. If he is right, then Lewis may later have embraced the Ockhamism he rejected early on. Lewis, the staunch critic of Calvinism, may himself have appropriated its spirit by smuggling in radical voluntarism. Is this what Lewis's Divine Iconoclast amounted to?

LOGICAL VERSUS PSYCHOLOGICAL

Beversluis's interpretation is certainly different from Lewis's own account of his recovery of faith. Lewis attributed his earlier doubts about God's goodness to inadequacies in his faith. He came to believe that the death of Joy had

---

[12]Lewis, *A Grief Observed*, p. 38.

added nothing essentially new to the problem of evil, and that his own faithlessness while drowning in a sea of sadness and grief was just a sign of his spiritual condition, not a philosophical problem. The issue was not logical, but psychological. The coherence of theism was less at stake than Lewis's mental and spiritual health.

Here Beversluis begs to differ, by arguing that what Lewis tried casting as a psychological, pastoral or existential problem was really a philosophical one after all. Beversluis makes his case not by denying that Lewis indeed underwent a profound personal struggle of faith. The real ground, though, of Lewis's doubts about God's goodness, Beversluis insists, was the intellectual challenge of reconciling God's goodness with the horrors God had allowed. Here Beversluis claims to be following Lewis's own criteria for genuine logical objections to Christianity. When theists find "that the arguments or reasons on which their faith depends no longer provide intellectually adequate answers, when they no longer enable them to deal adequately with contrary evidences," that is when their struggle is philosophical in nature. The struggle is merely psychological, in contrast, when "they feel that their religious beliefs are false while they fail to recognize that their arguments and reasons are as solid as ever."[13]

Why does Beversluis claim that Lewis's struggle was not merely psychological? Because Lewis could not find the answers he sought. Beversluis takes Lewis with the utmost seriousness when Lewis claimed, in the midst of his grief, that reality, looked at steadily, is unbearable; that there seems to be no evidence that God is good, only our own desperate desire that God be good. Lewis had prayed for Joy's healing and been bitterly disappointed, making God look for all the world like the consummate Cosmic Sadist. Lewis did not know why his wife had to die. He could not understand why he had been so happily drawn out of himself by her love only for death then so cruelly to snatch her away. He failed to comprehend why God would choose not to heal her when he so easily could have and seemed to have offered such strong signals of hope. For a season Lewis could not reconcile what had happened with a truly good God. According to Beversluis, this goes to show that Lewis's arguments on which his faith depended no longer provided intellectually adequate answers and were unable to contend successfully with contrary evidence.

---

[13]Beversluis, *C. S. Lewis and the Search*, p. 146.

God could no longer be described as good in the ordinary sense. So Lewis's attempt to change the rules of the game and affirm God's goodness by calling him Divine Iconoclast is really an effort to conform the meaning of goodness to whatever God happens to allow or command irrespective of how contrary to our intuitions and judgments about goodness it may be. Lewis thus salvaged his faith by embracing fideism (blind faith) and Ockhamistic theology.

Beversluis rightly holds that an important distinguishing feature of Ockhamism is that it renders moral discourse vacuous. Like rigid Calvinism's introduction of a bad God through the back door, it makes goodness a function of arbitrary divine fiat, leaving behind the "ordinary meaning" of moral terms. John Stuart Mill is well known for advocating the idea that meaningful discourse about God has to employ our ordinary conception of goodness. For a God who reverses our understandings of goodness altogether can hardly merit worship. "I will call no being good," Mill wrote, "who is not what I mean when I apply that epithet to my fellow-creatures; and if such a being can sentence me to hell for so calling him, then to hell will I go."[14]

Lewis, recall, had often expressed a similar sentiment, going so far to say that if God were to reverse our everyday meanings of good and bad, then he would be a devil. Yet by affirming God's iconoclastic nature, Beversluis suggests, Lewis was willing to believe that goodness is whatever God says, no matter what. What makes the thesis of Divine Iconoclast just as formidable as Cosmic Sadist, by Lewis's own admission, is the practical extent to which God can challenge our everyday intuitions about what a good God might allow or require. So Lewis unwittingly rendered himself unable to continue ascribing to God goodness traditionally construed, leaving Ockhamistic "goodness" his only option.

LEWIS VERSUS BEVERSLUIS

If Lewis is in one corner and Beversluis in the other, who wins? Let's have a face-off and see the result, one issue at a time.

To begin matters, Beversluis's argument fails to disambiguate two rather different notions. He seems to assume that Lewis's faith in God's goodness, *come what may,* was an affirmation of ongoing faith *no matter what, even in*

---

[14]John Stuart Mill, *An Examination of Sir William Hamilton's Philosophy* (1875; reprint, London: Routledge & Kegan Paul, 1979), pp. 102-3.

principle; versus come what may, *given the nature of a faithful and loving God.* Beversluis takes Lewis's suggestion that Divine Iconoclast is hardly less formidable than Cosmic Sadist to mean that there is no real difference in their behavior. Just as Cosmic Sadist might choose to inflict pointless suffering and untold harm on his creations, so might Divine Iconoclast. But surely Lewis would never have affirmed this. A good but unsafe Aslan is not the same, despite the surface similarities, as a malicious devil dressed up as a lion. In short, God as Divine Iconoclast is still worthy of worship and trust, whereas Cosmic Sadist is not. Lewis's faith in God was rooted in his personal trust of a good God, recognizing that God may need to deepen our understanding of what goodness is or allows or requires.

To put it another way, trusting God, "come what may," may mean trusting God while being willing to accept literally anything that God might even conceivably allow. This approach renders faith in God's goodness unfalsifiable in principle and thus vacuous. This is the sort of faith Beversluis claims Lewis adopted in the latter half of *A Grief Observed.* Lewis's tenacious faith, however, can instead be understood in a second way: as faith in a truly good God who would never do something that we cannot ultimately reconcile with our best, most nonnegotiable moral intuitions. Sure enough, in the throes of grief and suffering, our eyes might be blurred with tears, and we may have a hard time seeing God's goodness. This is not surprising. Before Lewis lost Joy, he had recognized such a possibility while writing "On Obstinacy of Belief": "If human life is in fact ordered by a beneficent being whose knowledge of our real needs and of the way in which they can be satisfied infinitely exceeds our own, we must expect a priori that His operations will often appear to us far from beneficent and far from wise, and that it will be our highest prudence to give Him our confidence in spite of this."[15] But *difficulty* in making sense of a divine action is different from the *impossibility* of doing so. Despite Lewis's argument for tenacity of faith, he wrote in that same essay, as Beversluis notes, that such faith is not entirely unconditional. In principle, conceivably at least, God could allow simply too much suffering (or issue a command impossible to reconcile with ineliminable moral intuitions). That Lewis came to believe that Joy's loss was not after all an instance of such irreconcilable suffering by no

---

[15]C. S. Lewis, "On Obstinacy in Belief," in *Philosophy of Religion: An Anthology,* ed. Louis Pojman (Belmont, Calif.: Wadsworth, 1987), p. 377.

means implies that nothing in principle could have functioned to undermine Lewis's faith or that his faith qualified as blind and Ockhamistic.

Beversluis constructs a false dilemma: Either Lewis must accept his grief-stricken perspective as ultimate, or Lewis must embrace radical voluntarism. Incidentally, Beversluis's book is rife with such false alternatives, which fail to exhaust the alternatives: Either be a Romantic or a rationalist; either follow your imagination or follow reason; choose between the way of feeling or the way of fact. The false alternatives at present are between accepting one's blurred, tear-filled perspective of grief when one's prayers seem to no avail, versus forfeiting all of one's ordinary understandings of goodness and affirming that goodness is a function of divine whim. But this is a patently false dichotomy, as Lewis himself recognized when he saw that some of our a priori intuitions about what goodness requires or allows can be mistaken.[16] *Some* does not mean *all*. That some of our intuitions are not sacrosanct does not mean that all are negotiable. To put the same point differently, the fact that some of what God does or allows is hard to understand does not mean that nothing God conceivably might do is impossible to square with his being good. The obvious truth that Lewis had a hard time losing Joy and eventually regaining his faith does not mean that he was committed to the view that God would be good even if, say, God were to command the torture of Tolkien for the fun of it. Lewis recognized that God might have to tinker with the paradigm of his faith, but that is not the same as God's replacing it altogether, substituting good for bad and bad for good.

Just as Beversluis presumes that Lewis's perspective during those grief-stricken moments of mourning was the final word, he also mistakenly assumes that since Lewis was left with unanswered questions, his theology was a failure. But does this really demonstrate the intellectual inadequacy of Lewis's faith? Only if those are questions to which Lewis was entitled to an answer. But that is just the question: Was Lewis entitled to know for sure why, say,

---

[16]Lewis likened legitimate discrepancies between our vision of the good and God's to that between a perfect circle and "a child's first attempt to draw a wheel" (*The Problem of Pain*, p. 39). Talk of "ordinary" moral standards is ambiguous between certain deficient though common cultural perspectives that don't comport with the dictates of reason, on the one hand, and core human convictions that are veridical insights into reality, on the other. The former can be replaced by God altogether, but not the latter; in fact, as James Petrick has argued, a Platonic account demands that the former be replaced. See his "In Defense of C. S. Lewis's Analysis of God's Goodness," in *International Journal for Philosophy of Religion* 36 (August 1994): 45-56.

God had not preserved Joy's life? In a word, no. In fact, it seems rather obvious that a good God may have reasons for doing or allowing certain things without being under any obligation to tell us why, and he may have excellent reasons not to. Moreover, if God's ways are above ours, we may not yet be in a position to hear, understand or appreciate those reasons. To insist that God must give us answers we are not meant yet to have is folly, and at worst a hubris-inspired denial of our epistemic limitations and realistic expectations.[17] We can trust a good God to provide all the answers we need all right, but that is quite different from insisting that God must answer any and every question we might like to ask.[18] As humans we are often quite notorious for asking the wrong questions, and silence on such questions may be what is best for us, until we learn to ask better ones or are better prepared to receive replies.

Beversluis wrongly criticizes Lewis for jettisoning his moral intuitions altogether; meanwhile Beversluis himself refuses to acknowledge any limitations at all in his own intuitions. On this score Lewis held the more defensible position. While rejecting a rigidly Calvinist paradigm, Lewis nonetheless acknowledged some real epistemic limits owing to our finite perspective: "Five senses; an incurably abstract intellect; a haphazardly selective memory; a set of preconceptions and assumptions so numerous that I can never examine more than a minority of them—never become even conscious of them all. How much of total reality can such an apparatus let through?"[19] Beversluis, on the other hand, acknowledges no limits to our intuitions, nor any human penchant for the idolatry of confusing our ideas for the realities to which they point. No: for him, if we have a hard time understanding God's ways, then we either have to abandon our belief or embrace Ockhamism. If God does not answer a question we ask, then our faith has encountered an intractable intellectual objection. Tenacity is not an option, contrary to Lewis's claim, echoing American philosopher William James, that if God is real, a logic of relationships trumps Cliffordian evidentialism.

Beversluis's simpleminded focus on "the evidence" not only assumes that every attempt at natural theology is a failure (not to mention that it ignores

---

[17]Or perhaps there are no specific reasons why God allowed Joy's death, and the only reasons that are relevant are more general considerations like the fact that as embodied beings in a fallen world, we are vulnerable to dying prematurely from disease, whether we are believers or not.

[18]As chapter six made clear, human beings are notorious for drawing the wrong sorts of inferences and asking the wrong questions.

[19]Lewis, *A Grief Observed*, p. 74.

the option of Reformed epistemology, which denies that rational belief requires discursive evidence); it also neglects the fact that what we see is often a partial function of who we are. He interprets the suggestion that our perspective might play a role in our perception of evidence as nothing but the lamentable suggestion that a cheery disposition rather than argument may have the last say. But live belief in the real world arises from a complex interdependence of many influences. To neglect these factors only creates a facade of doxastic responsibility that may allow subjectivity to continue to exercise a powerful and unregulated influence. The notion of a purely dispassionate judicial intellect producing its deliverances is a myth. Beversluis's appeals to evidence per se simply fails to do justice to the delicate idiosyncrasy and labyrinthine character of the intellectual life.[20]

Beversluis's inadequate epistemology is related to his equally problematic linguistic insistence that "goodness" be used univocally where God is concerned. As is his wont, he lays out two options that, though they may exhaust his readers, hardly exhaust the alternatives: Either we use "good" univocally or equivocally. Either God conforms to our every expectation and we then call him good; or if he does not and we continue calling him good, we thereby abandon our ordinary meaning of goodness altogether. The right response to Beversluis here almost goes without saying. Without delving into an elaborate explication or defense of analogical predication, we have to notice that the majority view throughout the history of Christianity has been that language predicating properties of God is to be understood neither univocally nor equivocally. The former is susceptible to anthropomorphism and a simplistic religious epistemology, and the latter subject to arbitrariness and vacuity. Rather, language about God is to be understood analogically, owing to differences in modes of being between, say, John Beversluis and God, while preserving the fact that it is in God's image that we have been created.

Once more, Lewis articulated the more defensible view. Before Lewis's death, Beversluis wrote Lewis and asked if he was prepared to call into question the moral propriety of such Old Testament narratives as Joshua's slaughtering of the Canaanites. Beversluis claims that Lewis's response confirmed his suspicions that, despite Lewis's Ockhamism by the end of *A Grief Ob-*

---

[20]Hunter Brown masterfully makes such points in his excellent *William James on Radical Empiricism and Religion* (Toronto: University of Toronto Press, 2000).

served, Lewis was not fully comfortable with such a stance after all. Lewis had responded by acknowledging "grave dangers" in calling Joshua's atrocities and treacheries into moral question. He nonetheless felt it to be even more dangerous to believe in a God "whom we cannot but regard as evil, and then, in mere terrified flattery calling Him 'good' and worshipping Him." Given an insuperable tension between the goodness of God and biblical inerrancy, Lewis counted the former as the more certain of the two. Then he reiterated that God commands something because it is good and not vice versa, according primacy to God's Reason over his will, but then he ended his letter by writing that we must apply his approach "with fear and trembling." For "some things which seem to us bad may be good. But we must not consult our consciences by trying to feel a thing good when it seems to us totally evil. We can only pray that *if* there is an invisible goodness hidden in such things, God, in His own good time will enable us to see it. If we need to. For perhaps sometimes God's answer might be 'What is that to thee?'"[21]

What Beversluis casts as a "curious view" here for an Ockhamist makes perfect sense if Lewis was never an Ockhamist in the first place. What's curious is Beversluis's neglect of that possibility! Notice the content of Lewis's letter: the primacy of our nonnegotiable moral commitments, the distinction between negotiable and nonnegotiable moral intuitions, epistemic humility and recognition that our limited perspective may need correction, a rejection of total Ockhamistic voluntarism, a connecting up of the ultimate good with the divine Reason, recognition that not all of our questions must be answered, and a predication of goodness to God that is neither univocal nor equivocal with our everyday usage. And all of these features are consistent with Lewis's settled views throughout his mature career. To interpret Lewis otherwise is to read him most uncharitably and with wooden literalness; and regrettably, that's just what Beversluis seems intent on doing, treating Lewis as though he cannot think his way out of a paper bag. It's actually Beversluis who overlooks principled distinctions Lewis makes and conflates what should not be synthesized.

In the battle of ideas here—from analogical predication, to subtle distinctions in Lewis's thought ignored by Beversluis, to false dichotomies constructed by Beversluis, to Beversluis's penchant for erecting straw men, to subtlety of epistemology—Lewis holds his own quite impressively. Although Joy's

---

[21]Quoted in Beversluis, *C. S. Lewis and the Search*, p. 157.

death did not disprove God's goodness, in principle some things would. As to examples of what those might be, perhaps a world with far more evil than good, or a divine command to torture children for fun. Or perhaps Lewis would suggest that Calvinism is a paradigmatic example of what could not be reconciled with a recognizably loving God, thus making it irrational to believe, but that argument will have to await another occasion.

That's all I'm saying.

8

Pursuing Moral Goodness

C. S. Lewis's Understanding of Faith

KEVIN KINGHORN

One of the wonderful qualities of C. S. Lewis's writings in the area of moral philosophy is that his comments typically strike us as so intuitively right. We read Lewis's analysis in *The Great Divorce* of the deep motivations of various characters, and we think to ourselves, "Yes, I know someone just like that!" Or we read Lewis's description in *The Abolition of Man* of our universal experience of the Tao, and we find ourselves saying, "Yes, that just *has* to be the way things are."

At the same time, Lewis occasionally makes a comment that strikes us as quite unexpected, if not shocking. It is not that we immediately think that the remark must surely be incorrect. Rather, the remark seems to cry out for further explanation. Here is one such remark, in which he challenges the neat distinction between "Christian" and "non-Christian."

> The world does not consist of 100 per cent Christians and 100 per cent non-Christians. There are people (a great many of them) who are slowly ceasing to be Christians but still call themselves by that name: some of them are clergymen. There are other people who are slowly becoming Christians though they do not yet call themselves so.[1]

Our immediate reaction to Lewis's remarks may be to think that something

---

[1] C. S. Lewis, *Mere Christianity* (New York: Macmillan, 1978), p. 176.

is surely amiss. After all, with respect to people's affiliations with the Christian religion, it seems natural to think of people as being in one of two categories: those who *are* Christians and those who *are not* Christians. Perhaps we might think of a person as slowly and thoughtfully considering *whether* to take the step of becoming a Christian. But Lewis is not making this claim. He is making the stronger, and more controversial, claim that some people are actually in a *process* of *becoming* Christians—even if they do not know it! Correspondingly, other people are slowly *ceasing to be* Christians—again, even though they do not realize it. Are we to conclude that a person's status as a Christian is somehow a matter of degree?

Without further explanation, Lewis's comments will probably remain very counterintuitive to many readers. The key to understanding these comments is to see how they fit into Lewis's overall understanding of the nature of faith. Unfortunately, Lewis did not provide a philosophically detailed definition of faith. He did not offer a systematic discussion of what it means for a person to "put one's faith in God."[2] So the best procedural avenue available to us is to ask the question: What account of faith does Lewis *need* to be committed to if his comments on "becoming a Christian" are to make sense? In the discussion that follows, I outline an account of the nature of faith that differs in some important respects from the understanding of faith popularly defended within many contemporary Christian circles.[3] I argue that this alternative account of faith is in a number of ways preferable to the more popular, contemporary account. And along the way we shall see how Lewis provides clues in his writings strongly suggesting that he meant to endorse an account of faith much along the lines of the one I outline.

FAITH IS NOT SIMPLY BELIEF

The first step in outlining our alternative account of faith is to see how it differs from *belief.* Historically, belief has been a central element of quite a num-

---

[2]The closest Lewis came to such a discussion was his theological reminder in *Mere Christianity,* book 3, chap. 12, that faith works hand in hand with serious moral effort. Lewis emphasizes that true faith can come only when one tries one's hardest to obey God's law, recognizing in the end that one's best efforts result in failure. However, in this chapter his discussion of faith does not address our question of what exactly a person decides *to do* when one decides to put one's faith in God—nor does it provide us the key for making sense of the original quotation from the previous paragraph.

[3]I have given a fuller discussion and analysis of this alternative account of faith in Kevin Kinghorn, *The Decision of Faith: Can Christian Beliefs Be Freely Chosen?* (London: T & T Clark, 2005).

ber of theologians' descriptions of faith. For example, at the beginning of the third century, Clement of Alexandria stated that faith is "the assent of piety. ... The exercise of faith directly becomes knowledge."[4] In the thirteenth century Thomas Aquinas defined the inward act of faith as the act of "believing" or "thinking with assent."[5] And in modern times it is common practice to refer to people of faith simply as "believers." However, if we equate *faith* with *belief,* we open the door to some very problematic scenarios.

Consider the example of Abraham from the Old Testament. When God stated to Abraham that his offspring would be as numerous as the stars, Abraham responded by following God's directions to uproot his family and move to a not-yet-identified foreign land. Abraham's response is extolled by the writer of the book of Hebrews—and by the Christian tradition throughout history—as the kind of response we should seek to emulate. But what exactly was the nature of Abraham's response?

As a way of answering this question, let us consider a thought experiment. Let us suppose (contrary to fact) that God, instead of appearing to Abraham, had instead appeared to someone named "Abruhum" and had made Abruhum the same promise that was made to Abraham. Let us also suppose the following background information about Abruhum. Abruhum had decided early in life that he was going to spend his life cheating people out of money. Thus we suppose that he is a perfect scoundrel. Upon hearing God's testimony to him, he might then have thought to himself, "I do *believe* that God will in fact give me many descendants, and this will greatly help in my goal of cheating people. For if my descendants are in places of power, I'll be less likely to be punished or held accountable for my unlawful acts!" In such a case, Abruhum, eager to cheat people in whatever land he finds himself, might have been happy to demonstrate *trust*—to act on the assumption that God's statement is true— following God's call to move to a not-yet-identified foreign land where his household will prosper.

What this thought experiment shows is that a person can have true beliefs about God and God's commands—and can even exhibit trust in God—and yet still be an absolute scoundrel. Why is the response of Abruhum not a vir-

---

[4]Clement of Alexandria *Stromata*, in *The Ante-Nicene Fathers*, ed. and trans. A. Roberts and J. Donaldson, vol. 2 (Albany, Ore.: Sage Software, 1996), book 2, chap. 2.
[5]Thomas Aquinas *Summa Theologica*, trans. Fathers of the English Dominican Province (New York: Benziger Bros., 1947), 2-2.2.1; 2-2.2.2. For Aquinas, the "outward" act of faith is confession.

tuous one? Well, in our thought experiment, the ultimate *purpose* we imagine Abruhum as seeking to achieve is not a virtuous one. His ultimate purpose, again, is to cheat people out of money. And this is certainly not the kind of purpose God invites people to join him in pursuing. We shall return to this issue of purposes in the next section. Let us first look at another biblical passage that touches on the nature of faith—this time from the New Testament.

The Gospel of Matthew records Jesus making reference to people who profess to perform acts of faith in his name but who do not, through these actions, participate in the kind of relationship into which God invites people.

> Not everyone who says to me, "Lord, Lord," will enter the kingdom of heaven, but only one who does the will of my Father in heaven. On that day many will say to me, "Lord, Lord, did we not prophesy in your name, and cast out demons in your name, and do many deeds of power in your name?" Then I will declare to them, "I never knew you; go away from me, you evildoers." (Matthew 7:21-23)

The people described here do use the name of Jesus when praying to God and when performing acts that they themselves no doubt consider to be acts of faith. Yet, Jesus does not consider their actions to be acts of virtuous faith. Why? Perhaps their ultimate purpose in prophesying in Jesus' name is to manipulate people. Perhaps their ultimate purpose in working to facilitate miraculous healing in others is to draw undue attention to themselves. There may be any number of reasons that account for the lack of virtuous faith on the part of these individuals who see themselves as doing acts of service in the name of Jesus. Yet, the reasons will all have to do with the *purposes* they ultimately seek to achieve. So again we find that the nature of the purposes one seeks to pursue—as opposed to the true beliefs one holds—seems key in determining whether one enters into a positive relationship with God (cf. James 2:19, "even the demons believe").

FAITH AND THE PURSUIT OF GODLY PURPOSES

At this point we should clarify exactly what it means to "pursue a purpose." Purposes are linked to goals. To pursue a purpose is to pursue a goal. Some purposes are consistent with the purposes Jesus pursued and encouraged others to pursue. Other purposes are not. For example, Jesus pursued the purposes of helping the poor, comforting those who mourn, extending mercy to others, promoting peace and so forth. He invited others to join him in these pursuits. On the alternative account of faith I am proposing, the exercise of faith is not at its heart the holding of certain true *beliefs about* God. Rather, it is more a matter of what *purposes* one chooses to pursue.

In the Chronicles of Narnia, Lewis addressed this very question of whether a virtuous response to God is primarily a matter of correct beliefs about God or, alternatively, the pursuit of godly purposes. In his stories about Narnia, Aslan represents the one true God. By contrast, Tash is the "false God" of the Calormenes, whose character is evil and of whom Aslan says, "We are opposites." In *The Last Battle*, Aslan adopts an attitude of approval and reconciliation toward a soldier in the Calormene army, explaining why the soldier's deeds have, in the final analysis, been deemed noble. He says of Tash:

> I and he are of such different kinds that no service which is vile can be done to me, and none which is not vile can be done to him. Therefore if any man swear by Tash and keep his oath for the oath's sake, it is by me that he has truly sworn, though he know it not, and it is I who reward him. And if any man do cruelty in my name, then, though he says the name Aslan, it is Tash whom he serves and by Tash his deed is accepted.[6]

Of course, there may be some poetic license within children's stories. Did Lewis himself ever explicitly endorse the view that deeds performed in the name of "another God" would be accepted by Jesus Christ? The answer is yes. In a 1952 letter to "Mrs. Ashton," Lewis writes:

> I think that every prayer which is sincerely made even to a false god or to a very imperfectly conceived true God, is accepted by the true God and that Christ saves many who do not think they know Him. . . . In the parable of the Sheep and the Goats [Matthew 25:31-46], . . . those who are saved do not seem to know that they have served Christ.[7]

When Lewis speaks of "keeping an oath for the oath's sake" and "sincerely making a prayer," he is talking (even though he does not explicitly use this expression) in terms of a person's *purposes*, or the goals one seeks to achieve. Lewis's point seems to be that faithfulness to one's promises and earnestly seeking after one's Creator are purposes that God wants us to pursue. And when we do pursue these purposes, we are following the one true God— whether we know it or not.

---

[6] C. S. Lewis, *The Last Battle*, in *The Complete Chronicles of Narnia* (New York: HarperCollins, 1998), chap. 15, p. 517.
[7] C. S. Lewis, *Letters of C. S. Lewis*, ed. W. H. Lewis and Walter Hooper (New York: Harcourt, Brace, 1993), p. 428.

At this point, Lewis's picture of faith stands in need of a bit of refinement. If by coincidence a person just happens to pursue the purposes God pursues, this does not automatically mean one is *following* God or establishing any kind of real *relationship* with God. What is needed in Lewis's line of reasoning is a further premise about how we come to have moral beliefs about what purposes we should pursue. The Christian tradition has always understood our conscience, especially when properly tuned, to yield moral beliefs that are somehow "put there" by God through the activity of the Holy Spirit. It is Jesus who is recorded in the Gospel of John as clarifying the Holy Spirit's role as the one who "will teach you everything, and remind you of all that I have said to you" (John 14:26). If certain moral beliefs, or "promptings," do come from God, then we can plausibly describe these beliefs as a form of divine communication to us. When we then follow the leading of our moral beliefs about helping the poor, extending mercy to others and the like, we are responding to the leading of God. While the Christian tradition has more commonly spoken in terms of God "writing his law on our hearts,"[8] it is open to us to redescribe this activity as God inviting us to join him in pursuing certain purposes.

This construal of moral beliefs as divine communication could readily be adopted by Lewis to strengthen the connection he (rightly) wants to make between pursuing godly purposes and following after God. Indeed, in Lewis's discussion of the Tao, we find the resources for explaining how all people have the opportunity to respond to God by pursuing godly purposes. Though Lewis uses the language of the "Law of Human Nature" or the "Moral Law," he emphasizes that our grasp of basic, objective moral values is common historically within all cultures. If we add the theological point that these basic moral values are a kind of divine communication to all people, then we have a way to explain how all people from all cultures have the opportunity to respond to the call of God.

CAN WE CHOOSE OUR BELIEFS?

In noting the universal opportunity for people to pursue godly purposes in accordance with their consciences, we are led to a very important advantage that

---

[8]This phrase follows the wording of biblical passages such as Jeremiah 31:33; Romans 2:15; Hebrews 8:10; 10:16.

our alternative account of faith has over more traditional accounts focusing on a person's beliefs. Most of the Christian tradition historically has stressed that the exercise of faith is a *voluntary* decision people make. And it is this decision (or the failure to make this decision) for which God will one day hold all people accountable.

In explaining how faith is voluntary, many Christian writers have assumed that the choice "to believe" is a viable choice people can freely make. For example, Augustine cited the apostle Paul as an example of one who "refused to believe" but was turned by Christ into a "willing believer."[9] Søren Kierkegaard, in referring to the religious beliefs central to being a Christian, declared that an individual "may believe if he wills it."[10] And Vatican II, following Aquinas,[11] described the person of faith as one who is "freely assenting to the truth revealed by [God]."[12]

But there is a major problem looming. On closer analysis we find that a logical contradiction exists in the idea of "choosing to believe" something. To see the problem, suppose I told you that page 55 of this book is written in a pink font color. You might take my word for it and believe that this is true. Thinking it would be quite something to own a book with a page bizarrely written in pink, you might also desire my statement to be true. Thus, as you turn to page 55, we imagine that you *believe* that it is written in pink, and you *desire* that the page be written in pink.

When you reach page 55, you see that the ink is black, just like every other page. I was only pulling your leg. What happens to your desire? Well, nothing. You can still *desire* that the page be written in pink ink. You can even choose to *imagine* that it is written in pink. But what you will not be able to do is *believe* it is written in ink—and this is because beliefs have a certain connection to the truth that our desires and imaginations do not. Our beliefs are *representational* in nature; they represent what we think is already true of the world. To hold a belief is to think that the propositional content of that belief repre-

---

[9] Augustine *On The Predestination of the Saints*, in *The Nicene and Post-Nicene Fathers*, ed. P. Schaff, trans. P. Holmes, R. E. Wallis and B.B. Warfield, 1st ser., vol. 5 (Albany, Ore.: Sage Software, 1996), chap. 4 (2).

[10] Søren Kierkegaard, *Concluding Unscientific Postscript*, ed. Walter Lowrie, trans. David Swenson (Princeton, N.J.: Princeton University Press, 1998), p. 190.

[11] See Thomas Aquinas *Summa Theologica* 2-1.4; 2-2.2.9; 2-2.5.2.

[12] *The Documents of Vatican II*, ed. Walter Abbott, trans. and ed. Joseph Gallagher (London: Geoffrey Chapman, 1996), p. 113.

sents some fact about the actual world.[13] Now, if I could somehow *choose* to believe something, I would realize that my belief stems from my own sovereign *choice*—and that the belief does not necessarily have any connection with facts about the actual world. But now we have a big problem. For, if I realize that my *belief* does not necessarily have any connection with what is true about the actual world, then it is not a belief in the first place!

Another way of making the point is to observe that our beliefs are our "maps" of the world. Just as a map represents what is true of the actual world, so, hopefully, do our beliefs. Imagine if a mapmaker were to *choose* where to put the borders of the fifty states. Suppose he said to himself, "I think I'll put Florida up here today, and I'll put Kansas on the East Coast, and I'll make Wyoming the shape of an oval." If a mapmaker realized that the map before him was simply the product of his own *choices,* and did not therefore necessarily represent the *actual* physical borders of the fifty states, then he could not consider it a genuine map. Similarly, if a person knows that his belief is merely the product of his own choice, then it simply cannot be an actual *belief.* So we have a logical contradiction in the idea of "choosing to believe" something.

The involuntary nature of our beliefs poses an enormous obstacle to anyone wishing to hold both that faith is voluntary and that faith is fundamentally about a person's decisions to believe the truth about God. Our alternate account of faith, however, does not face this obstacle. For on our alternate account, faith is not characterized in terms of what a person chooses to believe. Rather, the exercise of faith is more a matter of what purposes a person chooses to pursue, given what one believes. And there are no logical problems with the idea that people can freely choose to pursue one purpose over another purpose.

Lewis placed a great deal of emphasis on the voluntary nature of our response to God. He famously referred to the gates of hell as being "locked from the inside," explaining: "There are only two kinds of people in the end: those who say to God, 'Thy will be done,' and those to whom God says, in the end, 'Thy will be done.' All that are in Hell chose it."[14] If our philosophical arguments against "choosing to believe" are correct, then Lewis's emphasis on

---

[13] By "propositional content" I mean, roughly, a statement that begins with the word *that.* Thus, in describing the content of your beliefs, we refer to your beliefs *that* you are holding a book, *that* page 55 is written in black ink, *that* the earth is round, and so forth.

[14] C. S. Lewis, *The Great Divorce: A Dream* (New York: Macmillan, 1978), p. 72.

moral freedom gives him a significant reason for adopting an account of faith that emphasizes the pursuit of purposes over the holding of true beliefs.

Having recognized the advantage our alternative account of faith has in terms of preserving a role for voluntary choice in the exercise of faith, we should also deal with a couple possible objections to this account. First, one might object that, notwithstanding the philosophical arguments that belief is involuntary, we are commanded throughout the New Testament *to believe.* However, this objection makes an unwarranted assumption that the New Testament speaks of "belief." In point of fact, the New Testament texts, which were originally written in Greek, speak of *pistis.* The etymology of *pistis* is different from the English word "belief." Indeed, this Greek word is used in a wide variety of contexts throughout the New Testament to denote, in various places, belief, trust, obedience, commitment, faithfulness and a number of other concepts. Thus, we must be careful what we read into English translations of biblical passages stating that salvation awaits those who "call on the name of the Lord," or who "believe in him," or who "believe that Jesus is the Christ." The New Testament encourages us to have *pistis;* and we must not simply assume that the ancient Greek word *pistis* has the exact same meaning as the modern English word "belief." Unfortunately for our philosophical discussion, the New Testament writers were (understandably) more concerned with encouraging their readers to follow Christ than with providing a philosophically subtle account of what this "following" consists in. Our alternative account of faith construes this "following" in terms of joining God in pursuing the purposes he invites us to pursue with him. And this seems at least as plausible an interpretation of *pistis* as is an interpretation of *pistis* as "belief"—particularly in light of our previous discussion of Matthew 7, where Jesus rejects the response of some who profess belief in his name.

A second possible objection to our alternative account of faith is that it smacks of works righteousness. By linking faith with the pursuit of purposes, the objector might claim, faith ends up being something *we* do. Salvation thus becomes something we can *earn.* This objection, however, relies on an entirely mistaken understanding of the Christian view of heaven. For Christians, heaven is not understood to be a wondrous place because there are wonderful, external things like exotic foods or sexual pleasures available there. Rather, Christian doctrine is that we are created in the image of a trinitarian God and that our ultimate fulfillment comes only by being in proper *relationship* with

God and others. For Christians, what is so great about heaven is that our relationships with God and others are as they should be. So the objector is mistaken in thinking that our alternate account of faith makes salvation a reward
for something we do (pursue godly purposes). When we respond to God's invitation to join him in pursuing godly purposes, our response *is an act of relating* to God. Salvation and the attainment of heaven are not *additional rewards*
we earn because we have responded to God's invitation and thereby related to
him. Rather, the relationship is the reward. Heaven provides us a place where
this relationship can flourish for eternity.

In keeping with Christian doctrine, we can readily agree with our objector
on the point that God's initial invitation to a relationship with him is entirely
an unmerited offer. And we can agree that God's grace must renew our
thoughts and desires so that we are able to see his offer for the wonderful thing
it truly is. However, we should not concede to the objector that our salvation
is something *in addition to,* and *as a reward for,* the relationship we participate
in as we respond to God.

THE POSSIBILITY OF IMPLICIT FAITH

So far in our analysis of religious faith, we have provided a basis for C. S.
Lewis's claim that "the world does not consist of 100 per cent Christians and
100 per cent non-Christians." Unlike the either-or nature of *belief*—we either
believe that Jesus is the Christ or we do not—the pursuit of godly *purposes* is
something that happens in degrees. Christians do not (typically, at least) pursue with perfect consistency only those purposes that are godly and self-
giving. Even mature Christians can be prone to moments of stubbornness or
stinginess. So our alternative account of faith can make perfect sense of
Lewis's claim that the exercise of Christian faith is a matter of degree. Indeed,
Lewis *needs* something much like our alternative account if his affirmations
about people "becoming Christians" and "slowly ceasing to be Christians" are
to make sense.

I now want to focus on Lewis's claim that people can become Christians
"though they do not yet call themselves" Christians. Can a person become a
Christian without knowing it? Clearly, if faith is a matter of having true beliefs
about God, then such a scenario is impossible. However, as we shall see, we
have the resources in our alternative account of faith to make sense of Lewis's
claim here.

Perhaps the best way to begin is to think for a moment about the Old Testament patriarchs such as Abraham and Moses. The eleventh chapter of Hebrews extols these two figures as having the kind of faith toward which we should all strive. And the Christian tradition has always understood various Old Testament figures as having a place in heaven. Yet during their earthly lives these early people of faith did not know of the person and atoning work of Jesus Christ. So how do we reconcile the fate of the Old Testament patriarchs with the Christian doctrine that *all* people must explicitly plead the cross of Christ before full and final reconciliation with God can occur?

The church fathers gave much consideration to this question, and their consensus was that the Old Testament patriarchs learned the truth about the person and work of Jesus Christ sometime *after* their lives on earth. They were then able to explicitly plead the cross of Christ as atonement for their sins; and at that point—and only at that point—were they fully and finally reconciled to God. We should not think of Old Testament patriarchs as *wrestling* with this decision. Instead, their explicit decision to embrace Christ was inevitable, given the kinds of people they were. And their fixed, godly character was a product of their repeated decisions on earth to pursue certain purposes—purposes that, again, Hebrews 11 describes as exemplifying the exercise of virtuous faith. Admittedly, the Old Testament patriarchs did not in their earthly lives exercise *explicit* Christian faith. Without explicit beliefs about the person and work of Christ, this would have been impossible. Still, they were able to exercise what we might call *implicit* Christian faith.

The idea of implicit faith has a long history within the Christian tradition. Justin Martyr, a second-century church father, described Christ as "the Word (Logos) of whom all humankind partakes." In referring to those who came before Christ, Justin stated, "Those who lived by reason *(logos)* are Christians, even though they have been considered atheists: such as, among the Greeks, Socrates, Heraclitus and others like them."[15] Thomas Aquinas, in describing how our faith as Christians resembles the faith of those before Christ, commented that "whatever those who lived later have believed, was contained, albeit implicitly, in the faith of those Fathers who preceded them."[16] And John

---

[15]Justin Martyr *First Apology*, in *Fathers of the Early Church*, ed. Ludwig Schopp, trans. Thomas Falls, vol. 6 (New York: Christian Heritage, 1948). For Justin, living according to reason *(logos)* meant keeping the moral law that we recognize within the natural order.

[16]Thomas Aquinas *Summa Theologica* 2-2.1.7.

Calvin, while affirming that the piety of godly Old Testament characters "must have been the result of faith," explained that "their faith was not explicit either as to the person of Christ, or the power and office assigned him by the Father."[17]

Lewis would, I believe, have been very attracted to the idea that implicit faith involves *becoming the kind of person* who—like the Old Testament patriarchs—would explicitly plead the cross of Christ once the truth about Christ became known. Lewis put a great deal of emphasis on the continual moral transformation that Christ seeks to bring about in the life of each person.

> "Make no mistake," He says, "if you let me, I will make you perfect. The moment you put yourself in My hands, that is what you are in for. Nothing less, or other, than that. . . . Whatever suffering it may cost you in your earthly life, whatever inconceivable purification it may cost you after death, whatever it costs Me, I will never rest, nor let you rest, until you are literally perfect."[18]

Lewis's understanding of salvation as fundamentally a process of transformation gives us, I think, a decisive reason for thinking that he would prefer to think of faith as the pursuit of godly purposes rather than the holding of true beliefs. Think for a moment if God *were* to grant access to heaven to all those who simply held true beliefs about the person and work of Christ. For those in this group who did not pursue the godly purposes that the redeemed in heaven pursue, God would need to radically overhaul their moral character. Given the value that Lewis placed on moral freedom, he would surely find such a scenario deeply problematic. On the other hand, consider the person who already *does* pursue godly purposes, but who *does not* hold true beliefs about Christ. Once such a person comes to see the truth about Christ—and makes the inevitable, positive response to Christ—that person will naturally fit in quite well with the heavenly community. No radical reversal of one's moral direction and orientation will be needed. Thus, with Lewis's emphasis that a relationship with God involves ongoing moral transformation, he needs an account of faith in which faith is conceptually connected with moral transformation. And this is precisely what our alternative account of faith provides. To say that a person is pursuing godly purposes with increasing consistency is, after all, another way of saying that a person is growing toward Christian perfection.

---

[17]John Calvin *Institutes of the Christian Religion*, trans. Henry Beveridge (Albany, Ore.: Sage Software, 1996), 2.2.32.

[18]Lewis, *Mere Christianity*, p. 172.

Returning to the precedent of the Old Testament patriarchs, one important implication we draw from their situation is that people can become more and more Christlike in character—and can exercise a kind of implicit faith in Christ—without having explicit beliefs as to who Christ is. And so our account of faith allows us to make sense of Lewis's claim that people are often becoming Christians *without knowing it*. As people respond to their God-given moral intuitions, they respond to God's invitation to join him in the pursuit of loving, self-giving purposes. Though they may *not recognize* their moral beliefs as in fact a divine invitation to them, they nonetheless can exercise a kind of implicit faith in Christ when they respond positively to this invitation.

AN ENIGMA NO MORE

Let us end our discussion by again looking at the passage from Lewis with which we began.

> The world does not consist of 100 per cent Christians and 100 per cent non-Christians. There are people (a great many of them) who are slowly ceasing to be Christians but still call themselves by that name: some of them are clergymen. There are other people who are slowly becoming Christians though they do not yet call themselves so.

While initially enigmatic, every aspect of this quote becomes understandable once we assume an account of faith that centers on the pursuit of good purposes, rather than the holding of true beliefs. The extent to which Lewis himself thought through and meant to endorse our alternative account of faith is an open question. However, what is clear is that Lewis needs something akin to our account of faith if his overall moral and religious framework is to exhibit clarity and consistency.

9

"Belief" in the Writings of C. S. Lewis

David Rozema

Several years ago a conference of the C. S. Lewis and the Inklings Society had as its theme the question, "How did the Inklings define 'mere Christianity'?" A good question, but one for which the answer seemed easy: the unity of all Christians is the common virtue of faith in Jesus [the] Christ. What makes the question such a good one, however, is that giving the answer does not necessarily mean that we understand it fully. So what I propose to do in this chapter is what Wittgenstein said is the work of a philosopher: to "assemble reminders for a particular purpose."[1] My purpose is to clear away confusions about what it means for a Christian to "believe in God," assembling reminders mostly from C. S. Lewis, although Wittgenstein and Kierkegaard will have prominent cameos.

In his essay "On Obstinacy in Belief," Lewis addresses the charge often made against Christians: that their attitude toward belief is that it is "positively praiseworthy to believe without evidence, or in excess of the evidence, or to maintain belief unmodified in the teeth of steadily increasing evidence against it." The contrast to this attitude is the so-called scientific attitude, that one ought to "proportion the strength of his belief exactly to the evidence; to believe less as there is less evidence, and to withdraw belief altogether when re-

---

[1] Ludwig Wittgenstein, *Philosophical Investigations*, trans. G. E. M. Anscombe, 3rd ed. (New York: Macmillan, 1958), 50e.

liable adverse evidence turns up."[2] As Lewis says, this superficial description of the difference in attitude toward belief shows the need for some conceptual (and grammatical) investigation: "The sense in which scientists proportion their belief to the evidence, and the sense in which Christians do not, both need to be defined more closely." He thus begins his discussion with a review of the ways in which we actually use the word *belief.*

VARIETIES OF BELIEF

The most common use of the word *belief,* Lewis says, "expresses a very weak degree of opinion," as in "Tom is in London, I believe."[3] The negative form of this is also common: "I don't believe she is coming, so we may as well start without her." In contrast to these more common usages, Lewis points out two related "special usages," which, as he says, "may imply a conviction which in subjective certitude might be hard to distinguish from knowledge by experience." One such use is in the negative; for example, "Mrs. Jones has run off with the butler? I don't believe it!" Or the reaction of the hardened materialist who responds to the report of a miracle: "I don't believe it." The other special use, Lewis says, is the positive version of this negative use: "I believe" as uttered by the Christian. In both of these special usages, Lewis says, "we are speaking of belief and disbelief to the strongest degree, but not of knowledge. In this sense, belief seems to me to be assent to a proposition that we think so overwhelmingly probable that there is a psychological exclusion of doubt, though not a logical exclusion of dispute."

According to Lewis, then, Christian belief is no mere weakly held opinion, but a proposition strongly or even maximally held, involving an assent to something considered overwhelmingly probable.[4] There is conviction bordering on subjective certainty and difficult to distinguish from what characterizes the most certain kinds of knowledge, although there remains logical space for doubt. But, as his comparison with the sort of knowledge that scientists are after shows, Lewis is speaking of belief here in the *cognitive* sense. He is considering the beliefs of the Christian as *propositions,* or claims, capable of being

---

[2]Sometimes philosophers call this approach "Cliffordian evidentialism."

[3]All of the quotations in this paragraph are from C. S. Lewis, "On Obstinacy in Belief," in *The World's Last Night and Other Essays* (New York: Harcourt Brace Jovanovich, 1960), pp. 13-17.

[4]Kevin Kinghorn's chapter in this volume argues powerfully for a rather different Lewisian understanding of Christian faith.

judged as either true or false. Taken in this cognitive sense—as propositions—
the beliefs of the Christian, though perhaps held with subjective certainty,
cannot be shown to have anything like objective or Cartesian certainty.

Now as much as I value the distinctions that Lewis makes here, perhaps he
has not gone far enough. He is certainly right to point out these different uses
of *belief*, but did he consider the possibility that the "I believe" as uttered by
the Christian is actually a third use, different from both of these? To illustrate,
imagine two intelligent people who hold very strong but opposing beliefs regarding the existence of life on other planets. Both of them can give persuasive, convincing arguments and cite evidence in favor of their beliefs, yet because of the subjective strength of each one's convictions, they will not succeed
in making the other doubt what they believe. This would be a case of one person using "I believe" and the other one using "I don't believe" in the special
sense that Lewis is talking about.

But now imagine that the disagreement is not about the existence of life on
other planets, but about the existence of God or the truth of Christianity. In
the former example both persons have some idea about what would and what
would not count as evidence for the proposition that life exists on another
planet. And even though they might call into question the reliability or the relevance of any particular piece of evidence, they certainly do not disagree about
what sorts of things *would* or *could* count as evidence either way. But is there
such agreement in the religious debate? Do the opposing parties agree on what
sorts of things *would* or *could* count as evidence either way? We might think
that in principle there could be. For example, if the suffering in the world were
decidedly and obviously greater on balance than the good and pleasure in the
world, then perhaps many theists would admit the intractability of the problem of evil; or perhaps a Christian and a non-Christian would agree that finding the confirmed bones of Jesus would disconfirm Christianity.

Nevertheless, our epistemic limitations pose a particular difficulty for con-
firming that last piece of evidence. Bearing in mind those limitations, imagine
the following scenario: Let's say that one person sees the harmony and order
in nature as evidence of an intelligent creator. The second person also sees this
harmony and order—the same order and harmony and to the same degree—
as no evidence at all, perhaps even as evidence of the chaotic forces of nature
blindly working to produce this harmony and order over a very long period of
time. Is the believer more or less rational than the unbeliever? The disagree-

ment goes deeper than in the "life on other planets" case: believers not only disagree with unbelievers in their *beliefs;* they often also disagree on *what sorts of thing* can even be considered *as evidence for their beliefs.* In light of this sort of disagreement, on many occasions it hardly seems appropriate to ask who is more or less rational. On the one hand, there are obviously differing views about *what counts as evidence* for beliefs; on the other hand, these views obviously cannot be *based* on evidence. That would make these views "beliefs" of a different sort.

LEWIS, CRITICAL RATIONALISM AND REFORMED EPISTEMOLOGY

The difficulty, as I think Lewis knew, was in keeping this distinctive nature of religious belief before one's mind. We can hardly help but speak of belief in the cognitive sense (as propositional), and when we do, we are forced by the logic of propositions to make a judgment—true or false, warranted or unwarranted, rational or irrational. And as long as we see beliefs merely as propositions, we are forced—by the form of the language, as it were—to give an answer. So in religious debates that focus on beliefs as propositions, "hard rationalists" would argue that one side or the other of this debate must be irrational; that there is always some in-principle way to adjudicate such a question about what would count as solid evidence. "Critical rationalists" tend to disagree, leaving room for such in-principle disagreements about the relevance and power of certain kinds of evidence, and concluding that intelligent and equally rational people can disagree about, say, the rational status of belief in the existence of God or the truth claims of Christianity.

Lewis himself argued for various pieces of evidence that fit together to make a powerful cumulative case for the truth of Christianity: from his "Lord, Liar, Lunatic" argument,[5] to his argument from reason[6] and the moral argument, to name a few. But it is clear from what he says in the early sections of "Obstinacy" that he is a "critical rationalist," at least insofar as he regards Christian beliefs as merely cognitive and propositional. Note in particular the example he gives of a nontheological belief that implies "assent to a proposition which we think so overwhelmingly probable that there is a psychological

---

[5]See David Horner's chapter (4) for a contemporary defense of this argument.
[6]See Victor Reppert's chapter (3) for his responses to critiques of his contemporary formulation of this Lewisian argument.

exclusion of doubt, though not a logical exclusion of dispute." He says, "Most of my generation had a belief in the reality of the external world and of other people—if you prefer it, a disbelief in solipsism—far in excess of our strongest arguments."[7] Lewis's selection of this example is strategic and informative. Most nonphilosophers would scoff at the very question of solipsism, of course, but philosophy has an inimitable tendency to call into question our most basic of beliefs. When we are pressed to argue for the existence of other minds, for example, what epistemologists from around the time of the Enlightenment discovered was something altogether surprising: there are few, perhaps no, good noncircular reasons for believing in them! A strict evidentialist approach would probably be forced to conclude that belief in their existence is unjustifiable, because of our inability to provide decisive-enough evidence for their existence. A solipsist who upholds the most rigid of evidential standards here is one who indeed withholds belief in the existence of anyone beyond his own mind, and efforts to convince him otherwise are likely to fail so long as such standards are upheld.

The point is generalizable; as it happens, as Pascal noticed and Reformed epistemologists have recently stressed, other minds are just the start of first principles or axiomatic beliefs that cannot be well supported evidentially: from the reliability of our senses, to the deliverances of memory and induction, many of our most cherished convictions cannot meet the standards imposed by classical evidentialism. It would seem, given our failures to prove such things, that either we are bound to end up as radical skeptics if we retain the highest of evidential standards, or we need to allow for the possibility of some warranted beliefs that do not meet them. Pascal replied to Pyrrhonian skeptics after this manner, suggesting that it is better to acknowledge reason's limitations than to assume that reason is sacrosanct. Reason itself declares its limitations. What facts can prove our axioms so that we can be more certain of them than our first principles themselves?

The fact that Lewis referred to just such a case in the context of discussing Christian conviction raises the fascinating possibility that he saw reason's limitations in this arena. As important as evidence was for Lewis, he might have agreed with Pascal that the heart has its reasons of which the mind knows nothing, and with William James, who thought that we could have nondiscur-

---

[7]Lewis, "Obstinacy," p. 16.

sive reasons to believe in God's existence. Testing "the God hypothesis" is not a science experiment; deciding whether or not to believe in Jesus is no mere philosophical exercise. It is more a matter of the heart than the head, and perhaps by design; for as Pascal said, God could have chosen to illuminate the mind with revelation, but he wants to woo our hearts, not just enlighten the mind. He wants us to love him, not merely believe in his existence. He wants us to know him in the deepest of all possible senses: to have a vital, life-transforming relationship with him; not merely to affirm his existence as one more item in the inventory of reality. For if God is anything, he is not merely one more item.

LEWIS AND WITTGENSTEIN ON FAITH

There are plenty of intriguing indications that, despite Lewis's reputation as a formidable apologist who wants to give sufficient reasons for belief in God, he is aware of faith as a distinctive kind of belief—a belief not merely, or even essentially, propositional. For example, he writes, "And, in fact, the man who accepts Christianity always thinks he had good evidence; whether, like Dante, *fisici e metafisici argomenti* [physical and metaphysical arguments], or historical evidence, or the evidence of religious experience, or authority, or all these together. For of course authority, however we may value it in this or that particular instance, is a kind of evidence."[8] Note in particular his appeal here to *authority*.

Now surely Lewis is well aware of the philosophical misgivings against authority as a basis of belief. From the question Socrates posed to Euthyphro— "Is the pious loved by the gods because it is pious, or is it pious because it is loved by the gods?"[9]—to Kant's insistence on the autonomy of reason in discovering and legislating laws of nature and morality, to Peirce's critique that

---

[8]Ibid., p. 17.

[9]Lewis himself rejects Divine Command Theory because of its unpalatable implications that morality could be just anything at all, although he also affirms that morality is somehow rooted in God's nature. Although he sees the truth of both goodness and beauty as having their foundation in God, he does not deny the objective existence of such values; by rooting them in God's nature, he tries grounding that objectivity, not making their content malleable and subject to divine caprice. Theistic ethicists can evade the charge that according primacy to their own moral intuitions undermines God's rightful authority by, for example, telling a story according to which, though ontology might be a top-down matter, epistemology might be a bottom-up matter; that is, perhaps God has given us the faculties by which we can apprehend certain moral truths first, before the question ever arising as to their ultimate ontological foundations, truths that may well, on reflection, have for their best explanation God himself.

the "method of authority" amounts to intellectual slavery—in all these ways, philosophers have questioned authority as a basis for belief. Put simply, the problem with authority is this: How do you determine who is or is not an authority? If you just take the so-called authority's word for it, then you will be easily duped; but making your own determination of whether or not someone is an authority means that you yourself are more authoritative than the authority, for you have the authority to tell who is or is not an authority.

Now everyone recognizes that people do, in fact, rely on authorities for many of their beliefs—it is hardly avoidable from a practical standpoint—but this does not mean that they *ought* to do so. So when Lewis says that authority is a kind of evidence, he must know it can count as evidence only when the authority is genuine. And since in most cases we need evidence for that, he can only be thinking of the kind of case where it makes no sense to question authority or to ask for evidence that would warrant taking it to be an authority.

In the case of belief in God, if we believe that God is the authority, the *standard* of reliability, trustworthiness and goodness, then could it make sense to ask for evidence for this? If God himself is the ultimate first principle, as it were, might our acceptance or rejection of God be less a deliberation of the intellect and more reflective of something yet more fundamental to what and who we are? If so, then the choice in question—to believe or not to believe—might in an important sense transcend reason, might be reflective of something more ultimate than merely an expression of rationality or irrationality. If considered merely cognitively, there is enough evidence to show Christian faith is not irrational, as Lewis may have been arguing; but the question of faith is not mainly about intellectual honesty or how good we are as evidentialists. It is something more basic to our whole person. The separation of the wheat from the chaff is not a division between smart evidentialists and befuddled ones.

Lewis might have more quickly arrived at this analysis of belief if, instead of referring to the "'I believe' as uttered by the Christian," he had completed the expression by giving *the subject matter* of the Christian's belief. Something like the lines of the Apostles' Creed might do the trick: "I believe in God the Father Almighty, maker of heaven and earth." By not giving the subject of the belief, we are tempted by the illusion that this kind of belief—religious, and specifically Christian belief—is a matter only of reason. For without identifying the subject of the belief, we might fall under the illusion that what it means to "believe in God" is the same as what it means to "believe in" anything or anyone else. But can our belief be categorized as being merely reasonable or unreasonable if the person or object of our belief is the person or object that is the very manifestation of our ideal *standards* of trustworthiness, love, justice, goodness, reliability and strength? The question of whether such an ultimate standard is instantiated surely makes good coherent sense, but the means of answering the question, given its ultimate nature, may not be merely evidential or evidential as narrowly construed. And Lewis, Christian apologist extraordinaire, seems to have had a sense of this truth.

Interestingly, Wittgenstein reminds us of these same points regarding religious faith. About evidence he says,

> If I even vaguely remember what I was taught about God, I might say: "Whatever believing in God may be, it can't be believing in something we can test, or find means of testing." You might say: "This is nonsense, because people say they believe on *evidence* or say they believe on religious experiences." I would say: "The mere fact that someone says they believe on evidence doesn't tell me enough for me to be able to say now whether I can say of a sentence 'God exists' that your evidence is unsatisfactory or insufficient."

And with regard to God being spoken of as *both* the standard of goodness *and* as a person, Wittgenstein says,

> The word "God" is amongst the earliest learnt—pictures and catechisms, etc. But not [with] the same consequences as with pictures of aunts. I wasn't shown [that which the picture pictured]. . . . The word is used like a word representing a person. God sees, rewards, etc. . . . One said, had to say, that one *believed*, . . . and if one did not believe, this was regarded as something bad.[10]

Wittgenstein reminds us here of the uses—or, as he would say, the *grammar*—of the word God and expressions about God. These uses *show* what can or cannot be sensibly said about God. What theologians call "doctrines" are what Wittgenstein might call "grammatical remarks": reminders of what can and cannot be sensibly said about God and his relation to the world and to human beings. What an investigation of these uses reveals is that the word *God* is used in ways similar to both how we speak of a *standard* of truth, goodness and beauty, *and* how we speak of a *person*. So the reason it was regarded as some-

---

[10]Ludwig Wittgenstein, *Lectures and Conversations on Aesthetics, Psychology, and Religious Belief,* compiled from notes taken by Yorick Smythies, Rush Rhees and James Taylor, ed. Cyril Barrett (Berkeley: University of California Press, 1972), pp. 59-60.

thing bad if one did not believe in the existence of God is that this unbelief involves not only doubting the existence of a person, but also doubting the reality of a standard of trust, love, justice and power. It is this latter doubt that makes the unbelief "something bad," a moral fault, and not just an intellectual failure. Lewis was no thoroughgoing Wittgensteinian; but interestingly enough, there is a point of resonance here between Lewis's recognition of faith as essentially a relation of trust between two persons, one of whom is Goodness himself, and Wittgenstein's reminders of how a Christian uses the words—what one *means* by—*God* and *belief.*

To see this relational theme that trumps evidentialism, let us consider some additional selections from Lewis.

THAT HIDEOUS STRENGTH, THE CHRONICLES OF NARNIA AND *TILL WE HAVE FACES*

In *That Hideous Strength,* when Arthur and Camilla Denniston are trying to convince Jane Studdock to join the Pendragon (Dr. Ransom) and his band of followers, Arthur says to his wife, "You must see it from Mrs. Studdock's point of view, dear. You forget that she knows practically nothing at all about us. And that is the real difficulty. We can't tell her much until she has joined. We are in fact asking her to take a leap in the dark." "In that case it is rather difficult to see why one should take it at all," responds Jane. "I admit frankly," said Denniston, "that you can only take it on trust. It all depends really, I suppose, what impression the Dimbles and Grace and we two have made on you: and, of course, the Head himself, when you meet *Him.*"[11]

There are several examples also from the Chronicles of Narnia, where the children are asked to "take a leap in the dark," to simply believe, without anything we would ordinarily call proof: Lucy first returns from the wardrobe and asks the others to believe that she has been to another world *(The Lion, the Witch, and the Wardrobe)*. She again asks them to believe that she can see Aslan in the dark, and that he wants them to follow him down into the river gorge *(Prince Caspian)*. Eustace, in his dragon form, must believe that Aslan's tearing off of his dragon skin will not kill him but restore him *(The Voyage of the "Dawn Treader")*. And Jill and Eustace and Puddleglum must decide if the Black Knight, chained in the silver chair, is or is not really Prince Rilian *(The Silver Chair)*.

---

[11]C. S. Lewis, *That Hideous Strength* (New York: Macmillan, 1946), pp. 115-16.

In *Till We Have Faces,* after Psyche has been received and wed to the god of the Mountain, her sister Orual confronts her with the question of evidence that would show that he really is a god, or if a god, that he is good. Orual presents her arguments, which amount merely to an appeal to the opinions and guesses of herself and others as to the possible identity and nature of this so-called god: "There's your lover, child. Either a monster—shadow and monster in one, maybe, a ghostly, un-dead thing—or a salt villain whose lips, even on your feet or the hem of your robe, would be a stain to our blood." To which Psyche responds, "But what is all this to me? How should they know? I am his wife. I know." "How can you know if you have never seen him?" Orual asks. "Orual, how could you be so simple? I—could I not know?" "But how, Psyche?" "What am I to answer to such a question? It's not fitting." When Orual proposes that Psyche take a lamp and look upon the god's face in the night, Psyche tells her that she cannot do it. Orual then insinuates that Psyche is afraid to do it, afraid of what she will find. Psyche responds, "Oh, Orual, what evil you think! The reason I cannot look at him—least of all by such trickery as you would have me do—is that he has forbidden me." "I can think of one reason only for such a forbidding. And of one only for your obeying it," says Orual. Psyche answers, "Then you know little of love."[12]

It is clear from this passage that Psyche's ground for believing in the god is the love he has for her. She does not present what we would ordinarily call "evidence" for her belief and trust. And Orual, of course, knows that this is not hard, decisive evidence, for she knows that there are charlatans, seducers and villains in the world, and this so-called god may be one of them. But Orual does not present evidence either. For how will the lamp test help? Would not the result—*whatever it is*—fail to convince Orual that he is a god, and fail to persuade Psyche that he is not? Since Psyche's relationship of love and faith in the god of the Mountain is a picture of the Christian's relationship of love and faith in Christ, it is appropriate to be reminded that "if there were evidence, this would in fact spoil the whole business. Anything that I normally call evidence wouldn't in the slightest influence me."[13]

In *all* these cases there might seem to be a kind of "evidence," but it is all couched in relational terms: trust in someone who is reliable. The Christian

---

[12]C. S. Lewis, *Till We Have Faces* (New York: Harcourt Brace Jovanovich, 1956), pp. 161-62.
[13]Wittgenstein, *Lectures and Conversations*, p. 56.

leap of faith is not blind, which is an Enlightenment understanding of faith, quite at odds both with biblical faith and Lewis's understanding of faith. It has been said that Christian faith is a leap into the light: trust in God's character and faithfulness; and Lewis is convinced that God lets us see enough of him to trust him, just as Pascal said that there is enough light to convince those who are willing to be convinced (and enough darkness for those who prefer to live in darkness). Faith in this context is profoundly relational faith, trust in a person, not just faith in impersonal propositions; that is its most distinctive feature. But putting faith in a person is not something we do blindly. Relational faith is entitled to a tenacity to which scientific faith in a bad theory is not entitled. Trust in a person is simply not rightly understood in cold, dispassionate terms or according to the careful calculations of the Cliffordian evidentialist.

BELIEF IN, BELIEF THAT AND KIERKEGAARD

What finally convinces me that Lewis might share this insight in the culpability of unbelief that is more than an intellectual failure is this: Lewis's explicit awareness of how a person's reasoning that there *is* a God can easily lead to the illusion that "belief in God," or "having faith in God," is simply a matter of intellectual assent to the proposition that there exists such a standard, such a person.[14] *Such* a belief or unbelief is *not enough* for it to count as *faith;* believing *that there is a God* is not necessarily the same as *believing in God.* Faith is belief of a different sort (cf. James 2:19).

In connection with this last kind of mistake, Kierkegaard, under the pseudonymous voice of Johannes Climacus, says that "faith is a passion." In *The Point of View for My Work as an Author,* Kierkegaard says that "the whole of my work as an author is related to 'the problem of becoming a Christian,' . . . with the direct or indirect polemic against . . . the illusion that in such a land as ours all are Christians of a sort."[15] Kierkegaard sees his task as a writer to dispel the illusion that Christian faith is not essentially different from any other sort of faith; that the only difference is a difference in object—that faith in God is not essentially different from faith in oneself or in anyone or anything else. In his writing he tries to illustrate what Wittgenstein reminds us of, that faith in

---

[14]Bouwsma makes such a point in O. K. Bouwsma, *Without Proof or Evidence,* ed. J. L. Craft and R. E. Hustwit (Lincoln: University of Nebraska Press), pp. 12-13.

[15]Søren Kierkegaard, *The Point of View for My Work as an Author,* trans. Walter Lowrie (New York: Harper & Row, 1962), p. 5.

God—insofar as that is the same as belief in God—is essentially different from faith in anything else, precisely because it is faith *in God.*

But how can one dispel such an illusion? It is not sufficient to simply say, "Look, this is an illusion. Here is how it works. . . ." For the illusion is not an optical illusion, but an intellectual one. Mere argument will not dispel the illusion, for the illusion *consists* in thinking that mere rational assent to the conclusion of an argument for the existence of God or the reasonableness of believing in God *constitutes* being a "Christian of a sort." Since most of Kierkegaard's readers are living under this illusion, his method of demonstration must be indirect: he must do more *showing* than *saying.* He must *show* his readers where their thinking leads by presenting literary characters (including his pseudonymous authors) who say and think the sorts of things his readers might be made to say or think. Kierkegaard considered the dispelling of this illusion his calling, his task. And as such, he pursued it with all the passion of John the Baptist or an Old Testament prophet. For the illusion concerns the very nature of faith and what it means to "become a Christian." The illusion might be expressed this way: People think they understand Christianity and therefore live in the illusion that they are Christians. The illusion makes them impervious to, let us say, Jesus Christ. They keep on hearing and repeating what Jesus Christ said, and then, through mere repetitiveness, this language becomes a shield against understanding the Word. It is an illusion spawned by the easily made—but difficult to spot—confusion between what it means to understand a statement (or an assertion or a report or a theory), and what it means to understand a command (or an invitation or a request or a plea), especially when it comes from someone both authoritative and loving. If the latter kind of understanding is mistaken for the former, there is no radical change in a person's life, no transformation. But "becoming a Christian," says Kierkegaard, is a "qualitative leap" from one way of life—one "mode of existence"—to another. A Christian's testimony does not consist in testifying about an eternal happiness, but in transforming one's existence into a testimony concerning it.

But this confusion between different senses of understanding is just the root of the problem. The problem itself is not how to point out the confusion, but how to help effect *just such a transformation* as is described by Johannes Climacus. That is, not simply to lead people to see what it means to become a Christian, but to help them actually *become* Christians. To be of any help in doing the latter, Kierkegaard knew that he must not just tell: he must show.

For only by portraying the various possible ways of life (including the ways each form of life would understand Christianity itself) could he evoke the "pathos," or the type of felt suffering, that each form of life would entail. This is why Kierkegaard so often writes in parables, and why all of Kierkegaard's pseudonymous authors portray a certain "mode of existence" more or less similar to that of a true disciple of Christ. By portraying such ways of life, we are compelled to examine our own lives in relation to Christ.

For example, by having Johannes Climacus characterize religious faith as a *passion*, Kierkegaard forces his readers to judge the passion in terms of whom or what one's faith is *in*, rather than whom or what it is a belief *about*. Such a move also forces the reader to look at what the passion leads to, in terms of a person's actions and way of life, rather than merely in terms of intellectual assent. Furthermore, the pictures Kierkegaard paints with these pseudonymous authors and their stories also evokes in his readers the appropriate passions for the life of faith that they portray—a deep longing for such a life; an abiding desire to know such a Teacher as Christ; a spine-tingling wonder at the thought of that which cannot (merely) be thought: the God-Man, the Absolute Paradox; and a profound fear and trembling before the Father and the Son.

Kierkegaard is no more (and no less) a "subjectivist" than Aquinas or Augustine or Calvin or Luther or Lewis or Tolkien. Like them, he recognizes the unique nature of religious belief because he recognizes the unique nature of Christ. The idea in Christianity is that Jesus is the *divine standard* of human goodness, love, justice, hope and faith. A person must, if one knows what this means and accepts the idea, *subject* oneself to God, completely and absolutely. If a person does not do this, then one cannot truly be said to have faith or to believe in God. Such subjection implies passion; it simply *is not* submission— it simply *is not* faith—if it is cold and dispassionate. "To believe in the Invisible One is not only to believe that there is the Invisible but to be subject to the Invisible, to be haunted by, to be demanded of, to be touched by, accused by a man who had it in his power to make such a gift."[16]

---

[16]Bouwsma, *Without Proof or Evidence*, p. 39. Here I also emphasize a distinction Lewis drew in "Obstinacy," between *coming to* faith and *staying in* faith. Initially coming to faith should not be done apart from where the evidence points, but once committed, a Christian is entitled to tenacity, entitled to trust the character of God, which the believer has good reasons to think is altogether good. Kierkegaard's emphasis on radical commitment resonates with Lewis especially in terms of the committed believer, whose relationship with God means that a logic of relations has replaced a cold logic of evidence dispassionately considered.

CSL: CLIVE, SØREN AND LUDWIG

Lewis, too, is clear and eloquent about this essential nature of Christian faith. Speaking of his own conversion from atheism to theism (and then to Christianity), Lewis describes his call to faith in similar terms. In his autobiographical *Surprised by Joy,* Lewis recalls the beginnings of a conscious turn toward faith from a conversation with his friend Owen Barfield and Bede Griffiths (a student of Lewis's), in which Lewis refers to philosophy as a "subject."[17] Barfield retorted, "It wasn't a *subject* to Plato; it was a way." "The quiet but fervent agreement of Griffiths, and the quick glance of understanding between these two, revealed to me my own frivolity. Enough had been thought, and said, and felt, and imagined. It was about time that something should be done." And when the moment came for this "something," Lewis says: "Now what had been an ideal became a command. . . . Total surrender, the absolute leap in the dark, were demanded. The reality with which no treaty can be made was upon me. The demand was not even 'All or nothing.' . . . Now, the demand was simply 'All.'"[18] "The commands were inexorable, but they were backed by no sanctions [rewards or punishments, in this life or in the life to come]. God was to be obeyed simply because he was God. . . . If you ask why we should obey God, in the last resort the answer is, 'I am.' To know God is to know that our obedience is due to Him."[19] Indeed, to know God *is* to love and obey Him. This is the kind of "knowing" that we call *faith.*

In his literary works, Lewis also portrays faith in this way: as an act of total surrender, of submission to the compelling commands of God. And, like Kierkegaard, Lewis recognizes that an essential element of this total surrender is a complete assurance that what God wills, will be done. It is this assurance that is the basis for the supernatural "joy" that comes to those with faith. If faith is a gift of the Spirit, then joy is one of the fruits of that gift. As Lewis clearly sees, faith in God, and all one's actions based on that faith, consists not merely, nor primarily, in an intellectual grasp and understanding of certain doctrines, but rather in a "way": a life of active obedience, devotion and charity.

Finally, returning to where we began the chapter, the majority of Lewis's essay "On Obstinacy in Belief" is concerned with what he calls the Christian's

---

[17]C. S. Lewis, *Surprised by Joy* (New York: Harcourt Brace, 1956), p. 225.
[18]Ibid., p. 228.
[19]Ibid., p. 231.

"adherence to [one's] belief," what is properly called *faith*.[20] This "adherence to belief," he says, is where "the charge of irrationality and resistance to evidence really becomes important. For it must be admitted at once that Christians do praise such an adherence as if it were meritorious; and even, in a sense, more meritorious the stronger the apparent evidence against their faith becomes." "Christians seem to praise an adherence to the original belief which holds out against any evidence whatever." But, Lewis argues, "such praise is in fact a logical conclusion from the original belief itself." To show this, Lewis does indeed emphasize the peculiarity of the One in whom we believe. If we believe that God is a Person, definitive of goodness, love, justice, power and order, and that "his intention is to create a certain personal relation between Himself and us," then there must be complete trust.[21] For "to love involves trusting the beloved beyond the evidence, even against much evidence." As Lewis concludes, because of this uniqueness,

> there is no parallel between Christian obstinacy in faith and the obstinacy of a bad scientist trying to preserve a hypothesis although the evidence has turned against it. Unbelievers very pardonably get the impression that an adherence to our faith is like that, because they meet Christianity, if at all, mainly in apologetic works. And there, of course, the existence and beneficence of God must appear as a speculative question like any other. Indeed, it is a speculative question as long as it is a question at all. . . . To believe that God—at least *this* God—exists is to believe that you as a person now stand in the presence of God as a Person. What would, a moment before, have been variations in opinion, now become variations in your personal attitude to a Person. You are no longer faced with an argument which demands your assent, but with a Person who demands your confidence.[22]

---

[20]Lewis, *World's Last Night and Other Essays*, pp. 21, 23.
[21]Ibid., p. 25.
[22]Ibid., p. 26.

10

To Reign in Hell or to Serve in Heaven

C. S. Lewis on the Problem of Hell and Enjoyment of the Good

MATTHEW LEE

I do not myself feel that any person who is really profoundly humane can believe in everlasting punishment.
BERTRAND RUSSELL, IN *WHY I AM NOT A CHRISTIAN*

In Christian morals . . . it is wicked to call a man "damned": but it is strictly religious and philosophic to call him damnable.
G. K. CHESTERTON, IN *ORTHODOXY*

THE PROBLEM

When C. S. Lewis set out to answer the Problem of Evil, he saw that the Christian philosopher's work is not done until she has come to terms with the Christian doctrine of hell. It has traditionally been thought that the sufferings of hell far surpass those of earthly life in duration, if not also in intensity. So even if a solution can be offered for the standard problem of evil, that solution may be quite inadequate as a solution to what we will call the Problem of Hell.

C. S. Lewis wrestled with the Problem of Hell in various writings, and he ultimately came to propound a Christian position that, to the satisfaction of many, answers the Problem of Hell without departing from traditional Christianity. This position is founded upon the Augustinian/Thomistic understanding of human fulfillment in terms of enjoyment of the Good—that is, enjoyment of God the Supreme Good. Many of Lewis's works contain thought-provoking meditations on the nature of the human good and its relation to the divine transcendent Good, and these meditations give rise to a theory of salvation that offers a promising answer to the Problem of Hell.

But before turning to Lewis's answer to the Problem of Hell, it will be helpful to give a rigorous formulation of the problem, presented as an inconsistent set of premises, all of which the Christian is expected to affirm. If the argument is successful, it will prove the Christian position (conceived of as involving *at least* commitment to this set of premises) to be incoherent. Here are the four premises:

(1) If anyone is perfectly good, then that person does not torment anyone (or intentionally and determinately cause anyone to be tormented) eternally.[1]

(2) If anyone is in hell, then God torments that person (or intentionally and determinately causes that person to be tormented) eternally.[2]

(3) God is perfectly good.

(4) There are some people who are in hell.

From (1) and (3) it follows that

(5) God does not torment anyone (or intentionally and determinately cause anyone to be tormented) eternally.

And from (2) and (4) it follows that

(6) God does torment some people (or intentionally and determinately causes them to be tormented) eternally.

But (5) contradicts (6). So (1), (2), (3) and (4) form an inconsistent set.

Christianity itself presumably commits one to (3) and (4). (3) has always been a commonplace among Christian thinkers and seems to have been presupposed by the writers of Scripture. (4) is often taken to be essential to Christianity because it is repeatedly said or implied by Jesus in the most widely accepted translations of the New Testament; it is an explicit commitment of the

---

[1]The parenthetical clause is included to cover the case in which God causes someone to be tormented through intermediaries (such as devils or angels or lesser created beings). In other words, this first premise states that someone who is perfectly good would not torment anyone eternally, either mediately or immediately.

[2]For any Christian who believes in the harrowing of hell (the idea that Christ went to hell after the crucifixion to bring some people out), this second premise will need to be reworked somewhat. Exception would need to be made for Christ himself and for those whom he led out of hell at the harrowing.

Roman Catholic Church and of most major Protestant sects. (1) is a common assumption (even if rarely made explicit) about the nature of perfect goodness. And (2) is a common assumption about hell that has inspired major works of Christian art and literature, as well as the hellfire-and-damnation preaching with which most readers will be familiar. And (1) seems, on the face of it at least, an obvious implication of the concept of perfect goodness.

LEWIS'S ANSWER

Lewis resolves the contradiction by challenging (2), the assumption that if anyone is in hell, then God torments that person (or intentionally and determinately causes that person to be tormented) eternally. It is not that Lewis rejects the traditional notion that hell is a place of eternal torment. What Lewis denies is that *God* is the tormentor, either remotely or immediately.

To understand this answer to the Problem of Hell, it will be necessary to understand what Lewis thinks hell *is*. But Lewis's conception of hell is of a piece with his conceptions of heaven and of the human and divine natures as they pertain to human salvation. We will start with heaven and the divine nature and approach hell by way of descent.

Lewis's view of heaven derives from the beatific-vision tradition, whose membership includes such notables as Thomas Aquinas, Dante Alighieri and perhaps even Plato.[3] The beatific vision is *beatific* in the sense of bestowing a great blessing. And it is a *vision* that is given not by the eyes, but by the intellect. In the beatific vision the human soul grasps God in a way that is more complete and direct than any perception of God that is possible in earthly life. Those thinkers who are in the beatific-vision tradition believe that in heaven a human soul "sees" God and that this seeing bestows on the soul the greatest blessing that a human being can possibly enjoy. "Final and perfect happiness can consist in nothing else than the vision of the Divine Essence."[4]

But some might wonder: What is so good about *seeing* God, whether with the eyes or in some other way? It is a valid question and perhaps impossible to answer in a precise manner. We are in need of an extended conception of see-

---

[3]The argument for including Plato in the beatific-vision tradition derives primarily from the Speech of Diotima in the *Symposium*, esp. 211A-212B.
[4]Thomas Aquinas *Summa Theologica*, trans. Fathers of the English Dominican Province, 2nd and rev. ed., 5 vols. (1920; reprint, Cambridge: Cambridge University Press, 2003), Ia-IIae, q. 3, a. 8; <http://newadvent.org/summa/2003.htm#8>.

ing to give us an idea of what good might be conferred by seeing God. Perhaps we can begin to get at it by thinking about more mundane instances in which we speak of "seeing" (in one sense or another) and in some way enjoying what we see. You see a breathtaking mountain prospect. You see a child playing happily in the snow. You see an old friend at your door. You see the answer to a perplexing physics or mathematics question. These are only hints, but they give us some slight idea of how we can be blessed by in some way grasping something that is interesting or excellent or beautiful in itself. The idea is supposed to be that in the beatific vision we are supremely blessed by grasping the One who is supremely interesting, supremely excellent or supremely beautiful in himself, the very Paradigm of Truth, Goodness and Beauty.

C. S. Lewis places himself squarely in this tradition. In *The Four Loves*, for instance, he writes that the ultimate state of blessedness, which the human soul attains in heaven, consists in "final union with God, vision of God and enjoyment of God."[5]

But Lewis is better known for his characterization of celestial beatitude in terms of *glory*, and we will have to ask whether this is compatible with conceiving heaven in terms of the beatific vision. In what is perhaps his most popular address—"The Weight of Glory"—Lewis presents a number of striking reflections on the scriptural promise that in heaven souls will have *glory*. Lewis characterizes the beatified human soul's glory as "good report with God, acceptance by God, response, acknowledgement, and welcome into the heart of things."[6] It is "to please God, . . . to be a real ingredient in the divine happiness, . . . to be loved by God, not merely pitied, but delighted in as an artist delights in his work or a father in a son."[7]

Is there any connection between the attainment of glory and the beatific vision? Or does heavenly beatitude consist in two great, but separable and unrelated, blessings—like a two-course meal? I think Lewis would answer that they are connected in this way: the attainment of glory is a necessary condition for the beatific vision. For Lewis does *not* think the direct vision of God would in all cases be pleasant. In *Mere Christianity*, Lewis says: "Some people talk as if meeting the gaze of absolute goodness would be fun. They need to think

---

[5]C. S. Lewis, *The Four Loves* (London: HarperCollins, 2002), p. 5.
[6]C. S. Lewis, "The Weight of Glory," in *The Weight of Glory and Other Addresses*, ed. Walter Hooper (New York: Macmillan, 1980), p. 15.
[7]Ibid., p. 13.

again. They are still only playing with religion. Goodness is either the great safety or the great danger—according to the way you react to it. And we have reacted the wrong way."[8] That is, we have reacted the wrong way by disobeying the commands of God, and thus making ourselves his enemies. The great blessedness that attends the perception of the divine essence in the beatific vision cannot be received by creatures in our present state, whose sin is a perpetual affront to that essence. How can we possibly enjoy standing face to face with the Supreme Goodness, who by his very nature "must hate most of what we do"?[9]

If we are ever to *enjoy* seeing God, we are in need of transformation. Lewis writes, "The promise of glory is the promise, almost incredible and only possible by the work of Christ, that some of us, that any of us who really chooses, shall actually survive that examination, shall find approval, shall please God."[10] One might suppose that this means our transformation is up to us, that it is a matter of our own choice. But that would be a gross misreading of Lewis. He thinks the role of the saved to be almost negligible; virtually all the initiative is Christ's: "We, at most, allow it to be done to us."[11] There is a striking illustration in *The Great Divorce:* a ghost whose soul is inhabited by the vice of lust, which in the dream is a lizard on his shoulder, is approached by an angel who wishes to kill this vice for him. The angel asks the ghost's permission to kill the lizard, explaining: "I cannot kill it against your will. It is impossible."[12] The ghost fears that he himself will be killed in the process, but at length he consents: "'It would be better to be dead than to live with this creature. . . . Damn and blast you! Go on, can't you? Get it over. Do what you like,' bellowed the Ghost: but ended, whimpering, 'God help me. God help me.'"[13] That minimal act of consent is enough; the angel kills the lizard, and immediately the ghost gains solidity and becomes a powerful man, who rides off into the mountains of heaven.

This transformation scene conveys a spiritual principle that is key to much of Lewis's philosophy. It is the principle expressed by Jesus in Matthew 16:25: "For those who want to save their life will lose it, and those who lose their life

---

[8]C. S. Lewis, *Mere Christianity* (New York: Simon & Schuster, 1996), p. 38 (hereafter *MC*).
[9]Ibid.
[10]Lewis, "Weight of Glory," p. 13.
[11]*MC*, p. 166.
[12]C. S. Lewis, *The Great Divorce: A Dream* (New York: HarperCollins, 2001), p. 109.
[13]Ibid., p. 110.

for my sake will find it" (cf. Mark 8:35; John 12:25). This principle, the "ultimate law,"[14] runs throughout Lewis's writings, and every, or virtually every, one
of his works contains meditations on it (though it is approached from different
angles in different works). *The Four Loves* states it this way: "The consequences
of parting with our last claim to intrinsic freedom, power, or worth, are real
freedom, power, and worth, really ours just because God gives them and because we know them to be (in another sense) not 'ours.'"[15] It also features in *The
Screwtape Letters* as a principle of which the demons are aware and which they
try to use to destroy human souls; the senior demon advises his junior, "Get
them to turn their gaze away from God to themselves."[16] And perhaps the most
complete statement is Lewis's prophecy at the end of *Mere Christianity:*

> Give up your self, and you will find your real self. Lose your life and you will save
> it. Submit to death, death of your ambitions and favourite wishes every day and
> death of your whole body in the end: submit with every fibre of your being, and
> you will find eternal life. Keep back nothing. Nothing that you have not given
> away will ever be really yours. Nothing in you that has not died will ever be
> raised from the dead. Look for yourself, and you will find in the long run only
> hatred, loneliness, despair, rage, ruin, and decay. But look for Christ and you will
> find Him, and with Him everything else thrown in.[17]

So when Lewis discusses a soul's existence in heaven in *The Problem of Pain*,
he says, "[The soul's] union with God is, almost by definition, a continual self-
abandonment—an opening, an unveiling, a surrender, of itself."[18] But there is
no end to this self-abandonment: "A blessed spirit is a mould ever more and
more patient of the bright metal poured into it, a body ever more completely
uncovered to the meridian blaze of the spiritual sun."[19] Lewis goes so far as to
say that heaven is, in a sense, eternal *dying*, as well as eternal life.[20]

At this point we may be tempted to ask, with the narrator in *The Great Divorce*, "Then those people are right who say that Heaven and Hell are only states
of mind?"[21] (Heaven a state of self-abandonment, hell a state of self-absorption.)

---

[14]C. S. Lewis, *The Problem of Pain* (New York: Macmillan, 1976), p. 149.
[15]Lewis, *Four Loves*, p. 159.
[16]C. S. Lewis, *The Screwtape Letters* (Glasgow: Fount Paperbacks, 1978), p. 25.
[17]*MC*, p. 191.
[18]Lewis, *Problem of Pain*, p. 151.
[19]Ibid.
[20]Ibid., p. 152.
[21]Lewis, *Great Divorce*, p. 70.

The Spirit of MacDonald replies that it is blasphemy to say that heaven is only a state of mind. "Heaven is reality itself. All that is fully real is Heavenly."[22] The state of the soul does, however, make a difference *to that soul.* The self-abandoning soul can accept and enjoy the reality that confronts him. Such a person is at ease in looking into the Face of the Divine Being, for he finds no condemnation there, but only approval. It is for that person a beatific vision.

But the self-absorbed soul is incapable of receiving anything of the heavenly reality. "The choice of every lost soul can be expressed in the words 'Better to reign in Hell than serve in heaven.' There is always something they insist on keeping even at the price of misery. There is always something they prefer to joy—that is, to reality."[23]

The difference is not in God; God is willing that all should be saved and find approval in his eyes. And God will accept the most minimal initial act of submission. He is a heavenly Father who is "delighted with the first feeble, stumbling effort."[24] But that feeble movement of the will, insubstantial though it may be amid the current of divine grace in which it is caught up, is yet *essential* in the scheme of salvation, on Lewis's view. "The happiness which God designs for His higher creatures is the happiness of being freely, voluntarily united to Him and to each other in an ecstasy of love and delight compared with which the most rapturous love between a man and a woman on this earth is mere milk and water."[25]

But this ingredient that is essential for heavenly beatitude is also the very thing that makes hell possible. "Some people think they can imagine a creature which was free but had no possibility of going wrong: I cannot. If a thing is free to be good, it is also free to be bad."[26] And so if we cannot be saved without our voluntary consent, then it must be in our power to "escape" salvation.

We can now return to our question: What is hell in Lewis's view? "Hell is a state of mind. . . . And every state of mind, left to itself, every shutting up of the creature within the dungeon of its own mind—is, in the end, Hell."[27] Whereas heaven is infinitely beautiful, inspiring and interesting, hell is infi-

---

[22]Ibid.
[23]Ibid., p. 71.
[24]*MC*, p. 174.
[25]Ibid., p. 53.
[26]Ibid.
[27]Lewis, *Great Divorce*, p. 70.

nitely dull: there is *nothing* to it.[28] Whereas souls in heaven flower into their full personhood through relationship with God, hell is "the outer rim where being fades away into nonentity."[29] And whereas heavenly beatitude consists in contemplation and enjoyment of the wholly Other, "The characteristic of lost souls is 'their rejection of everything that is not simply themselves.'"[30]

In *The Great Divorce* Lewis pictures hell as a sprawling city, the inhabitants of which continually move farther and farther away from each other because they cannot tolerate one another. They shut themselves off inside houses of their own imagining and gnaw unceasingly on the jealousies, resentments or lusts that have consumed their whole personalities. Each has obtained their own wish—to be the indomitable god of their own world; but the world is the smallest there could possibly be, consisting only of a single soul, or perhaps only the remains of a soul.[31]

Hell, then, is simply the culmination of a pattern of free choice to turn away from God and to be on one's own. God and his creation certainly do not cease to exist; a damned soul "escapes" only by turning her attention away from God and from everything that bears his imprint. The damned soul "has his wish—to live wholly in the self and to make the best of what he finds there. And what he finds there is Hell."[32]

So in Lewis's view, God is not the damned soul's tormentor (contra [2]). The denizens of hell are their own tormentors. They psychotically cling to their addictions, to the wrongs they have suffered, to petty lusts and to their "rights." They will not forgive, will not admit wrongdoing, and will not be ruled; they make themselves miserable, but will not believe that a better way is open to them.

God is perfectly good. A perfectly good God would not torment someone eternally. Some people are in hell. These premises Lewis accepts. He carves out a consistent theodicy of hell by understanding hell as the state of creaturely

---

[28]C. S. Lewis characterizes the Satanic predicament—and by extension the predicament of every damned soul—as a state of "blank uninterestingness" and "infinite boredom," in *A Preface to Paradise Lost* (London: Oxford University Press, 1942), p. 100.

[29]Lewis, *Problem of Pain*, p. 127.

[30]Ibid., p. 123. Lewis here quotes from Friedrich von Hügel, "What Do We Mean by Heaven and Hell?" in *Essays and Addresses on the Philosophy of Religion*, 1st ser. (London: J. M. Dent, 1921).

[31]Like the Jewish mystic Martin Büber, who suggests that a personal *I* cannot exist without a personal *Thou* as its counterpart, Lewis wonders if it is even possible for an utterly isolated soul to have experiences or consciousness at all (*Problem of Pain*, p. 126).

[32]Lewis, *Problem of Pain*, p. 123.

rebellion against God, a state to which misery is intrinsic. In brief: God does not make the damned miserable; but misery is intrinsic to the state that culminates persistent rebellion.

OBJECTIONS AND ALTERNATIVES

There have been other attempts to answer the Problem of Hell from within the tradition of orthodox Christianity. We can identify three well-established alternatives to Lewis's view: the retributionist, the universalist and the annihilationist positions. We will now sketch these three positions and consider how each would object to Lewis's theodicy.

Retributionism. The retributionist denies (1) above and claims that a perfectly good God will in some cases torment a person eternally in hell. These will all be cases in which the person's sins *merit* eternal torment. Retributionists differ over precisely when a person's sins merit eternal torment. Some say original sin is enough to make one worthy of eternal torment; others say that eternal punishment can only be merited by actual sins.

The typical retributionist's objection to Lewis's position is basically that it is too *nice:* it is soft on offenders. A perfectly good God must take himself and his own holiness seriously enough to deal out proportionate retribution to those who do evil. And since every evil act is an offense against an infinitely great God, proportionate retribution for sin must also be infinite.[33] The repentant sinner may receive atonement through Christ, but for those who are incorrigibly unrepentant, it would be unfitting for God *not* to torment them (or see to it that they are tormented) eternally. It is inappropriate for them simply to be left to their own devices, as is the case in Lewis's hell.

Universalism. Like Lewis, the universalist denies (2) above; unlike Lewis, the universalist objects not (necessarily) to the idea that God torments the damned, but rather to the idea that God does so *forever.* Universalism is the view that ultimately all will be saved, that all human beings will eventually end up in heaven.

Whereas the retributionist objects to Lewis's view because it is too nice, the

---

[33]Some retributionists have given a different rationale: an unrepentant sinner develops a hard heart, which has the disposition to sin again and again throughout eternity. It may be that in an ordinary case of sin, a single sin merits only finite punishment. But the person who develops the fixed disposition to continue sinning eternally is worthy of infinite punishment by virtue being disposed to commit an infinite number of sins.

universalist's central objection to Lewis's position is that it is not nice enough. If God is all-powerful and perfectly good, then we can trust that in the end all will be well. But how can all be well if some are cast aside and left out of the blessings of heaven? If pressed on the question of how God can confer heavenly bliss on those who are unwilling to receive it, the universalist simply insists that (as the Godfather might put it), "He has his ways."

Annihilationism. The annihilationist rejects (4), that there *are* some people who are in hell. On the annihilationist view, one can say that some people are in hell only if one is speaking very loosely. Strictly speaking, no one is in hell; going to hell is a matter of being annihilated, being taken out of existence. Slogan: If your destination is hell, you're not going to arrive there.

Interestingly, different annihilationists may object to Lewis's theodicy for different reasons. One annihilationist, being "hard-hearted," will join the retributionist in saying that hell is too soft on the wicked. Another annihilationist, being "soft-hearted," will join the universalist in saying that hell is too harsh. The first kind of annihilationist objects to leaving the wicked to their own devices. Even if their earthly sin was not infinitely bad (by being an offense against an infinitely great God), in their postmortem life they would keep sinning again and again throughout eternity. In either case the appropriate response is infinite punishment.[34] And annihilation constitutes infinite punishment, since it deprives a person of eternal life. Moreover, punishment by annihilation is the only way to ensure that in the end there is peace throughout the created order.

How, then, could a different annihilationist charge that Lewis's hell is too harsh? On Lewis's picture, there is misery where there need be none. Surely God can see whether a person will ultimately repent or not. If God sees that a person will not repent, what is the point of keeping that person in existence

---

[34]"The question has sometimes been raised: "How can annihilation be bad for me? After all, if I'm annihilated, there is no *me* for it to be bad for!" But this does not seem to me so difficult to answer if we consider what I am *deprived* of by being annihilated. If you have been looking forward to your birthday celebration, which is tomorrow evening, and if Death comes to you tonight and asks whether you would like to be annihilated tonight or tomorrow night, you would (all else being equal) choose tomorrow night. And if you have much to look forward to and expect rather little bad to befall you in the coming years, you would want to postpone annihilation much longer. These things are good for you, and being deprived of them is bad for you. Here is another way of arguing the point: Suppose there is a country where everyone is convinced that death is annihilation of the person. Can you imagine finding in that country a jury that is persuaded by a murderer who defends himself on the grounds "I've done no harm to the person I've killed—she has ceased to exist, and so there is no *she* to suffer harm!"?

only to torment him? If God is perfectly good, he will prevent suffering that is unnecessary for any present or future good.[35] So, according to this view, it is more reasonable to think that a perfectly good God would just annihilate souls that are never going to repent.

WHAT LEWIS WOULD (OR COULD) HAVE SAID IN REPLY

These objections are varied and conflicting, and we do not have space to consider each one thoroughly. Yet it will be worthwhile to give some idea of how Lewis would or could respond to these objections.

Lewis would respond to most of the objections mentioned above by insisting on certain *psychological* theses. Again, the controlling idea is that of a beatific vision that is psychologically possible only through voluntary submission to God. To the universalist, Lewis would respond (and *did* respond) that no one will be in heaven against their own will; voluntary self-surrender, though by no means a sufficient condition for bliss, is absolutely necessary.[36] The universalist might suggest that submitting freely is compatible with being determinately caused by God to submit. But Lewis would have said that the idea of being determined but free is just incoherent nonsense.

It is not obvious exactly what Lewis would have said to the retributionist or the hard-hearted annihilationist. Certainly he would have insisted on the psychological thesis that when habitual sin comes to dominate a person, one's experience is characterized by suffering. And Lewis definitely upheld the appropriateness (in principle) of retributive punishment.[37] So Lewis could have agreed with these detractors that retribution is appropriate for persistent rebels and yet maintained that the sort of hell he posits *does* serve a retributive function, since it is a psychological fact that persistent rebellion against God makes one miserable.

On the question of whether the sufferings of hell are everlasting, Lewis

---

[35]There is a complication with this principle so stated. Suppose there is a case in which there is some good that requires one of two possible instances of suffering (but neither one in particular). Then neither of the two is necessary for that good, but it is necessary that one or the other of the two occur in order to bring about the desired good. The principle in question turns out to be quite difficult to state in an unproblematic way. But fortunately, what I have to say about annihilationism does not depend on a bullet-proof formulation of this principle.

[36]See Lewis, *Problem of Pain*, pp. 118-19; idem, *Great Divorce*, p. 75.

[37]See C. S. Lewis's "The Humanitarian Theory of Punishment," in *C. S. Lewis: Essay Collection and Other Short Pieces*, ed. Lesley Walmsley (London: HarperCollins, 2000), pp. 698-709.

pleads ignorance. He flirts with the idea that human souls exist timelessly "after" death.[38] Would a timeless hell satisfy the retributionist's demand for infinite punishment? It is hard to say. But perhaps it is a moot point, for Lewis could simply challenge the notion that rebellious human beings deserve infinite punishment. Even if the amount of punishment deserved is a function of the greatness of the being against which one offends (an assumption that is dubious at best),[39] it does not follow that an offense against an infinitely great being merits infinite punishment. It depends on the function from greatness to punishment merited. Let g be the greatness of a being, p be the punishment due for an offense against that being, and k be a constant. If the correct function is $p = k \times g$, then, yes, when g goes to infinity, p also goes to infinity (assuming k is a positive constant). But suppose the correct function is $p = (k \times g) / (g + 1)$. Then as long as k is a finite constant, p comes out finite *no matter how great* the offended being is. (Then k is the highest magnitude of punishment any sin can deserve.) So if punishment deserved is not a function of the greatness of the offended being, or if the function is not of the right sort, then there is no need to try to satisfy the retributionist's demand for infinite punishment in hell.

We have now seen how Lewis might have responded to the universalist, the retributionist and the hard-hearted annihilationist. What about the soft-hearted annihilationist? The objection, recall, is that in Lewis's hell an incorrigibly unrepentant sinner ends up suffering longer than is necessary, since God can foresee the sinner's "final answer." But notice that it would not make sense to propose that God should (permanently) annihilate a person *now*, upon foreknowing that that person will make bad choices at some time *in the future*. Consider the following three sentences:

1. God (permanently) annihilates Monsieur Z today.

2. Monsieur Z will commit a sin tomorrow.

---

[38] It is quite problematic what "after" could mean here. If my existence in heaven or hell is temporally posterior to my existence on earth, then my existence in heaven or hell is not timeless. Perhaps the best hope for this line of thought is to say that there is some relation of priority *other than* temporal priority in which states of being can stand to each other, and that my earthly life is prior in *that* sense to my existence in heaven or hell. But it is not clear to me whether this is really even intelligible.

[39] Notice that most modern legal systems do not take the moral excellence of the victim into account when assessing penalties for the perpetrator who has harmed the victim. This presumably reflects a widespread intuition that what is relevant to assessing the punishment due for a crime is not the excellence or greatness of the person wronged, but the acts, intentions, beliefs and desires of the perpetrator.

3. God knows that Monsieur Z will commit a sin tomorrow.

Sentence (3) cannot be true unless (2) is true. (You only know something if it is the case.) But (1) cannot be true unless (2) is false. (Monsieur Z won't be doing anything tomorrow if he is permanently annihilated today!) So (3) and (1) cannot both be true. (If they were both true, then [2] would be both true and false, which is impossible.) That is, it cannot be the case both that God knows that Monsieur Z will commit a sin tomorrow and that God (permanently) annihilates Monsieur Z today. Thus, it does not make sense to say that God could foreknow that a person will sin in the future, and then, on the basis of that knowledge, permanently annihilate that person before he commits any more sins.

So what the soft-hearted annihilationist really needs to say is that God should annihilate a person if he knows that that person *would* continue to choose badly in all the choice-situations in which she *could* be involved in the future. The claim must go in the subjunctive mood, not the indicative mood. But then the question is this: Are such facts at all times available for God to know?

Suppose Madame X has persistently rebelled all her life, and upon her death God is deliberating whether or not to annihilate her. If annihilation is a possibility, then God has not yet foreknown any future situation that includes Mme X. So God has available for his deliberation only the present and past states of the world, of himself, and of Mme X and possibly some future states of himself and of the world that do not involve Mme X (states to which she is not essential, though she may be affected by them if she does still exist). God wants to know whether Mme X would come to repent if she were given various future opportunities. If there is a fact of the matter, and if that fact is available to God, it seems it must be because what Mme X would do in those situations is determined or fixed by present and past states of God or of the world or of Mme X herself or by future states of God or of the world that do not involve Mme X. It is hard to see how Mme X could have the sort of voluntary control that Lewis thinks is necessary for such life-and-death choices if her choice is fixed by anything other than herself or aspects of her character for which she is responsible.

So it seems that God's choice about whether to annihilate her will need to be based on the state of her character, or of those aspects of her character for which she is responsible. If Mme X's character has not by the time of her death become so rigidly formed that future repentance is impossible for her, and if there are possible future situations in which Mme X could be offered chances to repent, then it seems that God does not have available to him (at the time of Mme X's death) the resources for determining what Mme X would do in those possible future situations. In light of this, Lewis could argue that God would not annihilate a person until her character was so rigidly set that there is absolutely no hope of her future repentance. There may be many people who are not yet at that point when they die, and so the soft-hearted annihilationist would have God eliminate these people too quickly. In theology, as in medical ethics, mercy killing has a very disturbing downside.

Lewis does not give a clear answer to the question of what God does after the unrepentant sinner has gone beyond the "point of no return." One comment from *The Great Divorce* actually sounds annihilationist: "If there's one wee spark under all those ashes, we'll blow it till the whole pile is red and clear. But if there's nothing but ashes, we'll not go on blowing them in our own eyes forever. They must be swept up."[40] But again, Lewis thinks that there may be a complicated relationship between the time that we inhabit in our earthly lives, and the time (or lack of time) that those in heaven and hell inhabit. This is very obscure, and so I do not think we can say definitively whether Lewis thinks the torments of hell have durations that could be shortened. In any case, the core of his position would be left intact if he were to suppose that there is duration to infernal existence and that God annihilates unrepentant souls after the point of no return.

FURTHER QUESTIONS

We have seen how Lewis could respond to the main objections raised by the retributionist, universalist and annihilationist positions, and many would find these responses promising. Before closing, though, I wish to enumerate a few more questions that a proponent of Lewis's theodicy would need to address. For lack of space, I cannot provide discussion of these questions, but it will be worthwhile to raise them so that it is clear what shape further discussion should take.

Question 1. Is it true that a persistent rebel against God will necessarily be miserable? What is the basis for the psychological claims involved? And could

---

[40]Lewis, *Great Divorce*, p. 77.

not a maximally intelligent God make some little world (or simulated world) for the rebel to enjoy? Would not a perfectly good God rather do this than leave the rebel shut up endlessly (or timelessly) in solitary confinement?

Question 2. Why think that the damned will all shut themselves up in their own minds? Might there not be some who thumb their noses at God but are quite friendly and even generous with other human beings? Might there not be some who hate God and other people, but who are good with animals or plants?

Question 3. Is it really plausible to suppose that a sinner who is miserable in hell might continue forever to endure his torments rather than repent and submit to God? (But note that there still remains the interpretive question of whether Lewis actually supposes this.)

Question 4. Is it right to equate rebellion against God with sin? What exactly is wrong with disobeying a divine command where what is commanded is something that would not otherwise have been morally obligatory (such as keeping the Sabbath)?

Question 5. Is there really something incoherent about the supposition that God could determinately cause a person to perform the voluntary acts of repentance and submission that are necessary for enjoying the beatific vision?

These are contentious issues, and the debates over some of them are as old as philosophical theology itself. In saying that the proponent of Lewis's theodicy of hell must face these questions, I certainly do not mean to suggest that Lewis's theodicy lacks resources for generating answers to these questions or that the burden these questions place on the defender of Lewis's theodicy is especially great (relative to the burdens of most other substantial philosophical positions). Indeed, on most every claim that Lewis advances in his theodicy, he finds himself in very good philosophical and theological company.

THE REAL PROBLEM OF HELL

"And here is the real problem," writes Lewis, "so much mercy, yet still there is Hell."[41] Drawing on biblical, philosophical, theological and psychological resources, Lewis formulated a response to the Problem of Hell that is in many ways promising and that has resonated with numerous readers. But Lewis was by no means concerned only with the philosophical problem. He was even

---

[41]Lewis, *Problem of Pain*, p. 120.

more concerned with the *practical* problem of hell, the problem of living in enemy-occupied territory, where self-choice is a constant temptation. In Lewis's view the problem of hell ought, for each of us, to hit *very* close to home. Like it or not, we are each playing a high-stakes game which is possible to lose.

What must we do to win? Here Lewis's theodicy of hell frames the answer. The chief mark of the lost soul is that the "taste for the *other,* that is, the very capacity for enjoying good, is quenched."[42] If we are not to be lost, we must never lose the taste for the other. Salvation is a work of divine grace, but we must allow it to be done to us; and we can begin with *desire.* "No soul that seriously and constantly desires joy will ever miss it. Those who seek find. To those who knock it is opened."[43]

---

[42]Ibid., p. 123.

[43]Lewis, *Great Divorce*, p. 75. Suggested further reading: Jerry Walls, *Hell: The Logic of Damnation* (Notre Dame, Ind.: University of Notre Dame Press, 1992); Charles Seymour, *A Theodicy of Hell* (Dordrecht: Kluwer Academic, 2000); Jonathan Kvanvig, "Heaven and Hell," in *The Stanford Encyclopedia of Philosophy,* ed. Edward N. Zalta (1955-; Stanford, Calif.: Metaphysics Research Lab, Center for the Study of Language and Information, Stanford University, Winter 2003), electronic resource <http://plato.stanford.edu/archives/win2003/entries/heaven-hell/>.

11

C. S. Lewis on the Necessity of Gratuitous Evil

MICHAEL L. PETERSON

The difficulty of reconciling belief in a God who is omnipotent, omniscient and wholly good with pain and suffering in the world is both a stronghold for atheists and skeptics and a serious challenge for persons of faith. This chapter explores how C. S. Lewis would respond to an important statement of the problem of evil by philosopher William Rowe and, in the process, compares Lewis's thinking to other theistic replies and locates it within his larger vision of God's purposes.

THE EVIDENTIAL ARGUMENT FROM GRATUITOUS EVIL

The problem of evil is typically formulated in one of two basic ways: either as a *logical argument* (which alleges that there is an inconsistency in theistic beliefs that both God and evil exist) or as an *evidential argument* (which alleges that the facts of evil provide a strong reason not to believe in God). Philosophers now widely agree that no version of the logical argument is effective and that the evidential argument deserves critical attention.[1]

William Rowe frames his version of the evidential argument with an initial question: Putting aside whatever reasons there may be for believing that God

---

[1]This is largely due to the work of Alvin Plantinga on the Free Will Defense. See his *God, Freedom, and Evil* (Grand Rapids: Eerdmans, 1977).

exists, do the evils in our world make belief in atheism more reasonable than belief in theism? Rowe answers that, on these terms, evil strongly supports atheism. In other contexts, of course, theists and their critics discuss belief in God as a conclusion to be reached after a comprehensive process of weighing all positive and negative arguments, including the argument from evil. Clearly, the writings of C. S. Lewis provide a "cumulative case" argument that it is more rational to believe theism—and indeed Christian theism—than any other worldview. But we restrict ourselves here to formulating Lewis's response to Rowe's specific challenge.

Rowe's argument is straightforward:

1. There exist instances of intense suffering that an omnipotent, omniscient being could have prevented without thereby losing some greater good or permitting some evil equally bad or worse. (Factual premise)

2. An omniscient, wholly good being would prevent the occurrence of any intense suffering that being could, unless that being could not do so without thereby losing some greater good or permitting some evil equally bad or worse. (Theological premise)

Therefore,

3. There does not exist an omnipotent, omniscient, wholly good being.[2]

Granting that the logic of the argument is valid, the epistemic status of the premises becomes the focus of the dispute. Since we cannot prove the premises or know them with certainty, we have to decide whether each one is more reasonable than not to believe.

Before proceeding, we need a few key definitions. *Restricted theism* is the belief that there exists an all-powerful, all-knowing, perfectly good being (God). *Expanded theism* is restricted theism conjoined with additional propositions, which are generally drawn from one of the three living theistic religions—Judaism, Christianity or Islam—or one of their various traditions. *Moral evil* denotes both moral wrongdoing such as cheating, lying, stealing and murdering and character defects such as cruelty, cowardice, greed and selfishness. *Natural evil* originates independently of human actions and includes disease, hurricanes, famine, blindness and deformity by which many sentient beings are robbed of the full benefits of life. Then, a final definition: *An evil is*

---

[2]William Rowe, "The Problem of Evil and Some Varieties of Atheism," *American Philosophical Quarterly* 16 (1979): 335.

gratuitous if its prevention would not thereby prevent the occurrence of some greater good or permit some evil equally bad or worse. We will shorten this definition throughout and simply say that a gratuitous evil is not necessary to a greater good. Obviously, a gratuitous evil is one without which the world would genuinely have been better.

Rowe thinks that theists, by virtue of being theists, must accept the theological premise and thus that the only way to rebut his argument is to reject the factual premise. This would mean that theists must maintain that God has a justifying reason for permitting every horrendous evil that occurs. God's reason would have to be that there is either some outweighing good that, all things considered, he wishes to realize and cannot realize without permitting that evil—or that there is some equal or worse evil that, all things considered, he wishes to prevent and cannot prevent without permitting that evil. In other words, the debate typically centers on whether there are evils that are necessary for the occurrence of a greater good or prevention of a greater evil.

To support the factual claim that there are indeed gratuitous evils, Rowe often cites an example of moral evil (a five-year-old girl is brutally beaten, raped and strangled in Flint, Michigan) and an example of natural evil (a fawn is horribly burned and dies in a forest fire caused by lightning). His point is not that these two instances are definitive but rather that theists have to believe that *all* such instances of intense human and animal suffering occurring daily in our world are such that an all-powerful, all-knowing being could not have achieved greater goods without permitting them. All evils, then, are necessary according to the definition. This strikes many people, including Rowe, as preposterous, quite beyond our belief, which is why the factual premise has strong epistemic support—that is, the premise seems more rational to believe than not. Assuming the theological premise to be true, the conclusion follows that it is rational to reject theism. This reasoning represents the evidential argument from gratuitous evil.

TWO FAMILIAR THEISTIC RESPONSES

Since most theists accept the theological premise of the argument, they typically attack the factual premise:

> There exist instances of intense suffering that an omnipotent, omniscient being could have prevented without thereby losing some greater good or permitting some evil equally bad or worse.

However, theistic strategies differ in interesting ways. One major theistic strategy argues that we cannot know the premise to be true; another important strategy argues that it can be known to be false. At the popular level many ordinary religious believers embrace one or the other of the technical responses offered by theistic philosophers.

Cognitive Limitation Defense. Playing pure *defense,* Stephen Wykstra argues that Rowe does not and indeed cannot provide any reason to think that the factual premise is true.[3] Wykstra contends that this premise rests on an argument from ignorance that fallaciously concludes that there are no goods justifying God's permission of horrendous evils from the fact that we do not know what these goods might be. Since God's mind infinitely transcends human minds, it is not likely that we could comprehend the goods for the sake of which God permits evils. If such goods do exist, then, we have no reason to think that, given our finite cognitive faculties, we should be able to discern them or that things would strike us differently.

Rowe replies that he is not offering an argument from ignorance but is rather basing the factual premise on our knowledge of many goods combined with our reasonable judgment that none of them justifies God in permitting horrendous evils. The argument for this premise rests on knowledge of what a being of infinite power, intelligence and goodness would be disposed to do and would be capable of doing. Yet it is still *logically possible* that there are goods we cannot comprehend that justify God's permission of horrendous evils. That is why we cannot *prove* the factual premise. Nevertheless, the Cognitive Limitation Defense is not sufficient to defeat reasons for thinking that the premise is *probably* true or reasonable to believe or more reasonable than its denial.

Rowe also challenges Wykstra's claim that restricted theism entails that the human mind cannot comprehend the ways of God concerning evils and their justifying goods. After all, a defense that construes the finite-infinite gap in this way unwittingly smuggles in an interpretation of omniscience and the human epistemic condition that is drawn from a Calvinist version of expanded theism. Restricted theism simply does not provide this kind of information about finite human reason being totally incompetent to make such judgments about God's ways with good and evil.

---

[3]Stephen Wykstra, "The Humean Obstacle to Evidential Arguments from Suffering: On Avoiding the Evils of 'Appearance,'" *International Journal for Philosophy of Religion* 16 (1984): 73-93.

Lewis agrees with Rowe that the Cognitive Limitation Defense fails to attenuate the force of the factual premise. His own view is that it is a mistake to remove God's goodness from human comprehension, a mistake that has one or both of two roots: an extreme interpretation of the effects of sin or an incorrect construal of the gap between finite creature and infinite God. Lewis would say that Wykstra's position has the second root. By contrast, Lewis points out serious difficulties in all positions that either implicitly or explicitly disconnect the human and the divine on matters of moral judgment, insisting that a radical disconnect renders meaningless our claims that God is good and undercuts all moral grounds for loving and obeying him.[4] To reinforce this point, Lewis rejects Divine Command Theory, which bases moral obligation exclusively on divine command or volition, because it reduces the human relation to God to submission to absolute power and will. By contrast, Lewis embraces Natural Law Theory, which affirms a general resonance in created humanity to the goodness and rightness of moral law, as we shall see.

Cognitive Limitation Defense may be given a weaker interpretation: not that our moral judgments and God's are utterly different, but that God simply knows a lot of things we do not, including how justifying goods are connected to evils. However, to be an effective counter to the evidential argument, the Cognitive Limitation Defense must maintain that for any instance of evil for which we cannot think of a justifying good, we are in no position to assume that we should be able to know its justifying good anyway. Thus, we are never in an epistemically appropriate position to call any evil gratuitous. But Lewis rejects this thinking, and he also corrects it.

Lewis affirms that our cognitive and moral powers are endowments of the creation and that neither the taint of sin nor their essential finitude renders them systematically unreliable in making judgments about God's ways with evil. Nevertheless, Lewis would be comfortable in claiming that sometimes our judgments that evils are gratuitous are mistaken, and sometimes they are not. However, as Lewis compares human and divine throughout his writings, he emphasizes the continuities in the dimension of the personal more than the discontinuities that make for the finite-infinite "size-gap" on the metaphysical plane. Echoing the classic Christian doctrine of humanity that we are made

---

[4]C. S. Lewis, *The Problem of Pain* (New York: Macmillan, 1962), p. 37; also see p. 100 for his rejection of Divine Command Theory.

"in the image of God [*in imago Dei*]," he states that humankind is "the completest resemblance to God" who "is the source from which all [our] reasoning power comes."[5] So, if human judgments about gratuitous evil were systematically mistaken and never reliable, this fact would have no good theological explanation and would itself constitute a kind of gratuitous evil!

Furthermore, Lewis would point out the incongruities created by the skeptical-theist approach. Why claim, on the one hand, that finite humanity is not epistemically entitled to claim that evils appearing to be gratuitous are really gratuitous and then claim, on the other, that we can know, for example, the lofty truth of the Trinity? Trinitarian doctrine was developed by accredited church bodies and councils that rationally reflected on key concepts in God's revelation in Scripture as well as on the experience of the believing community. Lewis would presume that the human capacity to make reasonably reliable judgments about good and evil, including whether some evils are gratuitous, is likewise based on the same legitimate powers of judgment and reflection. For other theists to assign a lower rating to human reflection and judgment about matters relating to an infinite deity simply accents the differences between versions of expanded theism, not all of which are equally defensible.

Greater-good theodicy. The second type of theistic rebuttal of the factual premise goes on the *offensive*, seeking to offer a *theodicy:* a positive reason or reasons to justify God's permission of horrendous evils. The enterprise of constructive theodicy assumes that we can have a measure of insight into God's ways, including into the sorts of goods for the sake of which evils are permitted. Drawing from a different version of expanded theism, this enterprise is not as skeptical as Cognitive Limitation Defense about our knowledge of the relation of goods and evils, but it still shares with it the aim of discrediting the factual premise.

The common strategy behind most theodicies is to specify some greater good or goods that outweigh the evil in question and that could not have been otherwise achieved, and thereby justify God in allowing the evil. In light of such goods, then, there really are no gratuitous evils. Theodicists have selected various goods that ground their theodicies or provide key themes within their theodicies. So, we have free-will theodicy, character-building theodicy, best-possible-world theodicy, punishment-for-sin theodicy and a great many more.

---

[5]Lewis, *Mere Christianity* (New York: Touchstone Books, 1996), pp. 139 and 53.

We might say greater-good strategy is the general form of most theodicies, much as a parent is related to its offspring.

Understandably, Lewis articulates insights that have had currency in Christian theodicies over the centuries. For example, he clearly extols the great good of human free will, which is at the root of untold amounts of evil. But for God to eliminate these evils, he would have to abrogate free will, as Lewis explains:

> God created things which had free will. That means creatures which can go either wrong or right. Some people think they can imagine a creature which was free but had no possibility of going wrong; I cannot. If a thing is free to be good, it is also free to be bad. And free will is what has made evil possible. Why, then, did God give them free will? Because free will, though it makes evil possible, is also the only thing that makes possible any love or goodness or joy worth having.[6]

But does Lewis think that all evils are necessary to the good of free will and therefore that we have sufficient grounds to reject the factual premise?

Rowe forcefully argues that free-will theodicy fails to rebut the factual premise. First, while genuine free will may entail the freedom to do evil, no morally responsible person thinks that the good of human freedom is so great as to require that no steps be taken to prevent the flagrant abuses of free choice. Uncurbed abuses of free will often result in suffering and devastation out of proportion to any goods to which they may be connected. Second, free-will theodicy fails to account for natural evils that are not brought about by human free choice (cancer, flood and even the fawn dying in the forest fire). Rowe contends that such evils could have been prevented without losing the great good of free moral choice. Since Rowe believes that all other greater-good type theodicies can be dismantled in a similar fashion—by showing that the relevant evils are in excess of what is needed for the envisioned goods or by citing counterexamples to claims that a particular good justifies all evils— he concludes that it is more reasonable to believe the factual premise than to deny it.

Although formidable for straightforward free-will theodicies, are Rowe's points effective against Lewis's position? If Lewis were claiming that all evils flowing from the misuse of free will are necessary to the great good of free will and in direct proportion to that good, or if he were claiming that the value of free will justifies all evils, perhaps even natural evils, then Rowe's criticisms

---

[6]Ibid., pp. 52-53.

would counter such claims. However, Lewis's position here is complex. He is not arguing that all evils are necessary for free will but that a world of significant free choice is the only environment where great goods—such as joy, love and connection with God—can meaningfully occur. Yet none of his remarks amount to an official greater-good position that denies the existence of gratuitous evils.

It is worth considering and countering two readings of Lewis that take him to be advancing a greater-good theodicy. The first reading focuses on his megaphone and surgeon metaphors, which converge to suggest that pain and suffering can have certain valuable results that God wants for human beings. In *The Problem of Pain* (and even in the film *Shadowlands*), Lewis indicates that pain is God's "megaphone to rouse a deaf world" to realize its need of him.[7] *A Grief Observed* says that the Divine Surgeon "hurts only to heal" the patient's self-centeredness.[8] Remarks like these, if used as the sole exegetical lens through which to view Lewis, make him seem to support the unqualified theory that God directly causes the evils of pain and suffering in order to bring us to himself, discipline us, purify us and the like, again suggesting that evil is necessary for the achievement of these greater goods. But this conflates insightful ideas about God's redemptive use of suffering with an effective philosophical answer to the problem of gratuitous evil.

Lewis's comments about God's causing pain and suffering must be placed in larger perspective in order to frame up his more complete approach to the problem of evil. Lewis argues elsewhere, for instance, that suffering is not good in itself and that we have the strongest duty to minimize it in our fallen world.[9] Moreover, he does not claim that extremely high—perhaps unbearably high—levels of pain are required for whatever goods are connected to the megaphone or surgeon effects and thus leaves open the logical possibility that some levels are unnecessary to achieve those goods. And he clearly admits that pain and suffering are not fairly distributed among individuals or exactly proportioned to any particular outcome. It is at this point, then, that his additional thoughts about the redemptive uses of suffering make best sense. Any given evil, even a gratuitous evil, Lewis argues, can be exploited by God, who can create a "complex good" that includes the evil. God's ability to create this

---

[7]Lewis, *Problem of Pain*, p. 93.
[8]Lewis, *A Grief Observed* (New York: Bantam Books, 1976), p. 49.
[9]Ibid., p. 111.

complex redemptive good relies heavily on our free response. Obviously, free human responses to pain differ, as Lewis knows, driving some to bitterness while spurring others to greater spiritual maturity. So, philosophically, he is just not claiming that all suffering serves the greater good of drawing us to God, much less that all evils are connected to greater goods. Thus, he does not reject the factual premise on these grounds.

Now, the second reading of Lewis argues that he endorses greater-good theodicy, not regarding temporal and finite goods, no matter how great, but regarding the eternal and infinite good of God himself and all he has done for our redemption. In *Perelandra*, the sinister Un-man, speaking through Weston's corpse, cunningly reasons with Ransom and the Green Lady that sin brought the incarnation of Maleldil to earth, making fallen earth and the forbidden knowledge it acquired preferable to unfallen Perelandra and its naive and narrow life. In pondering his response, Ransom thinks of the *felix peccatum Adae* (happy fault of Adam) of the Antiochian Western Easter Vigil. After all, has not the church told us that good came from our disobedience? The Exultet contains the line: "*O certe necessarium Adae peccatum, quod Christi morte deletum est! O felix culpa, quae talem ac tantum meruit habere Redemptorem!* [O truly necessary fault of Adam, which the death of Christ has blotted out! O happy fault, that merited such and so great a Redeemer!]" So, on this view, not only is Adam's sin happy; it also is necessary!

By having Ransom consider the meaning of "Adam's happy fault," is Lewis embracing a whole logic that affirms both the good fortune and the necessity of the fall? Does Lewis's Ransom take the *felix culpa* to entail that the greatest good could come only through sin? Would Ransom in effect affirm that, among all possible worlds, any fallen world that includes incarnation and atonement is better than any unfallen world without them? Does fallenness give rise to more good than is possible with unfallenness? Ransom's thoughtful reply is instructive:

> Whatever you do, He will make good of it. But not the good He had prepared for you if you had obeyed Him. That is lost forever. The first King and the first Mother of our world did the forbidden thing; and He brought good of it in the end. But what they did was not good; and what they lost we have not seen. And there were some to whom no good came nor ever will come.[10]

---

[10]Lewis, *Mere Christianity*, p. 159.

For Lewis, evil is still evil and shows a willingness to disobey God regardless of the specific command in question. The loss caused by this disobedience is great indeed. Yet we cannot deny the beauty and love of God manifest in the Christ-event and dramatically displayed in the crucifixion. How does Lewis negotiate these tradeoffs?

Initially, it is plausible to allow the Easter Vigil some poetic license to express profound gratitude and praise for what Christ has done. Yet Lewis organizes his considered position around God's eternal and unchanging goal for humankind: to make us sons and daughters, to bring us into his own Blessed Life. Nothing can change our ultimate destiny, but the contingent fact of the human fall changed the means by which God pursues it: "The process of being turned from a creature into a [daughter or] son would not have been difficult or painful if the human race had not turned away from God centuries ago." God set for himself "the problem of expressing His goodness through the total drama of a world containing free agents, in spite of, and by means of, their rebellion against him."[11]

For Lewis, then, incarnation and atonement are necessary only given the fact of the human fall, but they are not absolutely necessary because God would carry out his original plan for humanity even without the fall. Lewis would think it absurd to defend the counterfactual claim that, if humanity had not fallen, then we would not have the greatest good, which is God himself. Indeed, Lewis would disconnect incarnation and atonement, since incarnation may still have occurred in a nonfallen world in order to reveal God's nature to us. And when that nature was revealed, it would be the same self-giving, self-sacrificing love demonstrated in the atonement in fallen earth: "God saw the crucifixion in the act of creating the first nebula."[12] Humanity did not need to fall into sin to get the greatest good of God himself or even the goods of "knowledge" to navigate temporal existence.[13] The King explains to Ransom that we need not have experienced the "darker ignorance" of sin and estrange-

---

[11] Lewis, *Problem of Pain*, p. 84.

[12] Ibid.

[13] In *Perelandra*, we see the Green Lady, for example, learn effectively without the loss of moral innocence. In fact, she acquires knowledge of good and evil better by resisting temptation than by succumbing to it. On several occasions, she describes this growth as "getting older." She learns not only new information but also develops a new self-consciousness related to the passage of time, free will, and even of the purposes of God's commands. Lewis also explores the theme of ill-gotten knowledge in *The Magician's Nephew*, in *The Chronicles of Narnia* (San Francisco: HarperCollins, 2001).

ment from God. It was always possible, and always more desirable, not to sin.[14]

At this stage, we offer our most judicious conclusion: the goods that Lewis envisions as able to emerge from evils are not marshaled into a greater-good theodicy. Since he does not endorse Cognitive Limitation Defense either, he really offers no reasons for rejecting the claim that there is gratuitous evil.

LEWIS'S RESPONSE TO THE EVIDENTIAL ARGUMENT FROM EVIL

It is not simply that Lewis does not reject the factual premise; he gives positive reasons for why it is more reasonable to believe the premise than its denial. Furthermore, he rejects the theological premise, which is the reverse of many theistic approaches to the evidential argument. Let us closely examine Lewis's thinking about God and the human condition, which generates a fascinating and insightful response to the evidential argument.

Acceptance of the factual premise. Lewis's version of expanded theism, which reflects his broad, orthodox understanding of Christian theism, leads him to accept the factual premise. First of all, he is a metaphysical and epistemological realist, who believes in an objective reality and in the ability of the human mind to know it. Against idealism, pantheism and related views, he affirms the reality of the physical world, which operates by its own laws and is "a neutral something, neither you nor I," in whose ambit we meet.[15] In *Miracles,* he argues for the general reliability of human rationality and exposes the fallacies of undercutting it.[16] Second, Lewis's confidence in human rationality extends to our ability to make moral judgments about objective moral values and principles, making him a moral realist as well. This moral realism permeates *The Abolition of Man,* which conscripts the term *Tao* to denote the absolute values that are variously called "Natural Law or Traditional Morality or the First Principles of Practical Reason or the First Platitudes."[17] Early in *Mere Christianity,* our awareness of an objective Moral Law even anchors an argument for the existence of God.

So, for Lewis, when many evils strike us as gratuitous, our judgment has strong epistemic status, whereas Cognitive Limitation Defense and greater-

---

[14]Lewis, *Perelandra*, p.179.
[15]Lewis, *Problem of Pain*, p. 31.
[16]Lewis, *Miracles* (San Francisco: HarperCollins, 2001), chap. 3.
[17]Lewis, *The Abolition of Man* (New York: Macmillan, 1947), p. 56; see also p. 84.

good theodicy, in their own ways, cast doubt on our ordinary judgments about the gratuitous nature of many evils. Now, though it is logically possible that there are goods beyond our grasp that justify horrendous evils, and though it is logically possible that there are specifiable goods not beyond our grasp that justify all existing evils, the judgment that at least some evils are gratuitous comes with a great deal of rational support. To use either of the two familiar theistic strategies to overturn evaluative judgments about the gratuity of much evil is to invite a kind of agnosticism about the general reliability of our powers of moral evaluation—and, for Lewis, that is philosophically unacceptable.

Rejection of the theological premise. Although Lewis agrees with the nontheistic critic that the factual premise is more rational to believe than not, he would nevertheless maintain that the evidential argument from evil fails because its theological premise is faulty. Nevertheless, many theists as well as nontheists consider this premise to be implied by restricted theism:

> An omniscient, wholly good being would prevent the occurrence of any intense suffering it could, unless it could not do so without thereby losing some greater good or permitting some evil equally bad or worse.

However, Lewis would argue that both theists and nontheists unwittingly load key attribute terms—particularly *goodness*—with information drawn from some version of expanded theism. In spite of his insistence that he is focusing on restricted theism, Rowe tacitly builds his own version of expanded theism into the formulation of the theological premise, showing that the debate will always require more information than restricted theism provides. Lewis's own reflection on Christian doctrines and teachings leads him to contend that *the theological premise is not essential to theism*, since the conceptual resources of theism per se do not contain enough information about how infinite power, knowledge and goodness would act with respect to evil.

Rowe might respond by claiming that the theological premise is deduced from restricted theism together with some necessary truth or set of necessary truths that all rational persons must accept. The relevant necessary truth would have to be about the nature of moral goodness generally or of divine goodness specifically. But the definition of divine goodness that figures into the theological premise is just not a necessary truth. Many critics suppose, often without sufficient challenge, that God's goodness consists in the fact that God necessarily produces as many good states of affairs, and prevents as many evil states of affairs, as possible, allowing only those evil states of affairs that are necessary to greater goods. This makes God a Cosmic Utility Maximizer, a concept that reduces goodness to mere "kindness." But "love and kindness are not coterminous," Lewis explains, since "kindness, merely as such, cares not whether its object becomes good or bad, provided only that it escapes suffering."[18]

We see now that not even critics can confine themselves to discussing the problem of evil in terms of restricted theism. So, why should faith have to defend itself without the richer resources of Christian theism? Yet there are different versions of Christian theism, some supporting the Cognitive Limitation Defense and others supporting various forms of greater-good theodicy. And some versions of expanded theism accept the theological premise, but Lewis embraces a version which denies that this premise is essential to theism, in which case the theist qua theist is not obligated to accept it.

As a last resort, it might be argued that though the theological premise is not essential to theism, all *Christian* theists do in fact accept it. But again, *the theological premise does not reflect a version of Christian theism that Lewis accepts.* Versions of Christian theism differ in interesting ways—over the nature of perfect goodness, the scope of free will, divine commands as the basis of morality, and even over value theories—that imply different understandings about God's dealing with evil and, consequently, different ways of treating each premise. Since Lewis's understanding of Christian theism leads him to deny the theological premise, he is thereby able to block the evidential argument from going through.

The necessity of the possibility of gratuitous evil. Rejecting the theological premise is tantamount to accepting that gratuitous evil is possible in a world created by the Christian God. One of Lewis's major reasons for this rejection lies in his explication of what it means for God to create a moral order as a framework within which persons can make moral choices and develop character. Affirming libertarian (or incompatibilist) free will, which is incompatible with any form of determination, either natural or divine, Lewis writes:

> Christianity asserts that God is good; that He made all things good and for the sake of their goodness; that one of the good things He made, namely, the free will of rational creatures, by its very nature included the possibility of evil; and that creatures, availing themselves of this possibility, have become evil.[19]

---

[18]Lewis, *Problem of Pain*, pp. 40-41.
[19]Ibid., p. 69.

In the terminology of modal logic, free will means that moral evil is *possible*, but it is *not necessary*.

For moral freedom to be significant and not trivial, persons must have a wide range of potential choices and actions. Indeed, the significant degree of freedom that makes possible great and noble deeds also makes possible the most atrocious actions, including actions that cannot be compensated for by the occurrence of greater goods.[20] God cannot ensure that persons who are significantly free in the libertarian sense will always choose and do what is right: "A world . . . continually underpropped and corrected by Divine interference, would have been a world in which nothing important ever depended on human choice, and in which choice itself would soon cease from the certainty that one of the apparent alternatives before you would lead to no results and was therefore not really an alternative."[21] Lewis knew that eliminating the possibility of gratuitous moral evil means eliminating significant freedom. Put more precisely, no specific moral evil is necessary, as my cryptic title suggests, but *it is necessary that gratuitous moral evil be possible*, including moral evils that cannot be calibrated to the existence of some greater good or the prevention of some greater evil. Without this fundamental condition, morality would be undermined.

Furthermore, Lewis argues that a vital element of the moral order is the *belief* on the part of finite agents in the possibility of real injury flowing from their moral behavior. Framed for the present discussion, this is the belief that one can indeed perform actions resulting in harm to others, harm that is not temporally or even ultimately necessary for a greater good. If one believes that all evils are somehow necessary to greater goods, that is, that no suffering can be really gratuitous, then it is difficult to imagine arousing moral indignation, inspiring the release of moral energy to correct wrongs or exhibiting genuine sympathy and compassion.[22] So, not only the real possibility of gratuitous moral evil but also the belief in that possibility is required to avoid undermining the moral order.

Lewis's careful analysis, moreover, reveals that *a natural order is a necessary*

---

[20]Ransom comes to realize the "true width of the frightful freedom" he has; Lewis, *Perelandra*, p. 126.

[21]Lewis, *Problem of Pain*, p. 71. Also, consider Ransom's insight: "Either something or nothing must depend on individual choices. And if something, who could set bounds to it?" Lewis, *Perelandra*, p. 121.

[22]Lewis, *Problem of Pain*, pp. 113-14.

condition for there being a moral order. His metaphysical realism commits him to the existence of a wide variety of impersonal physical entities, with their own distinctive properties, powers and dispositions to act, react and interact in regular ways, forming a relatively stable context for human life. And certainly, in the hands of Lewis, rich theological themes amplify this insight into the nature of the physical: *creational themes* (that the physical is good as a creature of God), *incarnational themes* (that God the Son came to us in a physical person, Jesus, so that humanity may forever be taken into the life of God), and *sacramental themes* (that grace often comes through quite ordinary experiences in the material world).

Interestingly, a natural order running by natural laws makes it possible for a human person to be an *agent*: "A creature with no environment would have no choices to make: so that freedom, like self-consciousness (if they are not indeed the same thing) again demands the presence to the self of something other than the self."[23] Yet this impersonal realm operates, as it were, of its own accord:

> The inexorable "laws of Nature" which operate in defiance of human suffering or desert, which are not turned aside by prayer, seem at first sight to furnish a strong argument against the goodness and power of God. I am going to submit that not even Omnipotence could create a society of free souls without at the same time creating a relatively independent and "inexorable" Nature.[24]

So, if a natural order is necessary to a moral order, then the natural order, by extension, supports the possibility of moral evil. But a natural order also entails the possibility of natural evil. God cannot simply arrange all natural evils so that they never harm us out of proportion to some higher good at which he aims, since so doing would involve frequent interruption or alteration of the world and thereby jeopardize the very meaning of a natural system. Lewis's conclusion, then, is not that gratuitous natural evils are necessary, as my attention-getting title suggests, but that *it is necessary that gratuitous natural evil be possible.*

---

[23]Ibid., p. 29. It is logically possible some agents are nonphysical beings, or pure spirits. But they must also be individuated in some way and inhabit some environment that supports action and community. Since a human being is necessarily physical, a physical order is necessary for a human being to be an agent and engage in interpersonal relations.

[24]Ibid.

GOODS AND EVILS IN LEWIS'S VISION OF GOD AND THE WORLD

As we have seen, Lewis's rebuttal of the evidential argument from evil employs a sophisticated understanding of human rationality, moral judgment, libertarian free will and natural law. However, these structural features of reality require further explanation within the larger context of God's purposes. Why would the universe include these elements? What is the point of it all? Lewis says that "the whole purpose for which we exist is to be taken into the life of God."[25] Trinitarian doctrine entails that the life of God is inherently personal, interpersonal and social. As classical orthodoxy teaches, participation in this Life is the only way to distinctively human happiness. So, this profoundly relational universe—populated with significantly free beings within a complex natural order—is designed to make possible the highest relational goods. But a universe that has the upside potential of great goods—such as moral character, proper treatment of fellow creatures and surrender of self to God—also carries commensurate downside risks. The human condition is that sin has damaged creation at all levels so that we do not readily live in harmony with God and others, and therefore unnecessary pain and suffering mark our existence.

Lewis's conceptual understanding of the possibility of gratuitous evil plainly conditions his practical approach to life. Being neither agnostic about our judgments that pointless evils exist nor overly sanguine about the connection of all evils to greater goods, he could respond authentically to genuine tragedy in his own experience. *A Grief Observed* reveals a vulnerable Lewis struggling with the unnecessary suffering and death of his wife, Joy. The film *Shadowlands* tries to capture this sense of Lewis when, for example, he sarcastically snaps at colleagues, "Don't tell me it's all for the best," clearly repudiating simplistic answers that all evils are necessary to greater goods.[26] In *Grief,* Lewis shows us that it is more honest to admit and much healthier to feel the utter needlessness of suffering while still allowing it to humble us and letting God use it for our benefit. Without claiming to be biographically accurate, *Shadowlands* ends with a touching scene that is profoundly Lewisian. Lewis and his stepson Douglas are shown just crying together under the weight of their loss, with no hint that the awful extent of Joy's suffering was exactly nec-

---

[25]Lewis, *Mere Christianity,* p. 142; also see pp. 143, 152-53.

[26]*Shadowlands,* dir. Richard Attenborough (Price Entertainment, 1993).

essary to greater goods and yet with no pretense that finite beings are barred from knowing anything about how God might connect goods with evils. On the other side of his sorrow, Lewis tells us, was the realization that God had used the loss of Joy to knock down his "imaginary faith" and to bring about a deeper spiritual transformation.[27]

Although the kinds, amounts and distributions of pain and suffering in our fallen world often bear no proportion to any goods to which they may be connected, God can still use these evils redemptively. Suffering, Lewis writes, has the "tendency to reduce the rebel will," since it shatters the illusion of self-sufficiency so that we might realize our need for God.[28] The theme is pervasive in Lewis that fallen persons are not their "true selves" and that it is worth everything to be brought to healing and wholeness. God will use anything, including pain, to accomplish his nonnegotiable goal of transforming us. This theme is treated in *The Voyage of the "Dawn Treader"* when Eustace is turned into a dragon by his own corruption and can be saved only by Aslan using his terrible claws to tear off the dragon's scales.[29] While suffering is intrinsically evil, Lewis argues that God can use it for our benefit.

Lewis knows that perfect love wills the perfection of its object—and sometimes this love can seem unkind. Yet God's absolute goodness cannot aim at anything but the proper well-being of the creature. In this light, missing our true happiness, not pain, is the ultimate evil. In this relational universe, then, with its unspeakably lofty destiny, *it is necessary that gratuitous evils be possible.* Standing within the Anglican tradition, which comes out of Catholicism and traces back to the oldest traditions of the Christian faith, Lewis says that these thoughts on God and evil rely essentially on "restating ancient and orthodox doctrines."[30]

The question we initially posed was this: All reasons for believing in God aside, do the evils of our world make it more reasonable to deny God's existence than to affirm it? In a manner that is both philosophically credible and theologically informed, Lewis argues that they do not. And his argument is embedded within an incredible vision of a God who offers to share his own

---

[27]Lewis, *A Grief Observed*, pp. 42-44, 61.
[28]Lewis, *Problem of Pain*, p. 112.
[29]C. S. Lewis, *The Voyage of the "Dawn Treader,"* in *The Chronicles of Narnia* (San Francisco: Harper-Collins, 2001), pp. 474-75.
[30]Lewis, *Problem of Pain*, p. 10.

life with finite creatures, is undeterred by their fall into sin, and resourcefully works in all things for their good. It is no wonder that, despite his intellectual engagement with the problem of evil as well as his deeply personal struggle with suffering and loss, Lewis calls the human venture, with all of its joys and sorrows, and yet all of its amazing potential, God's "grand enterprise."[31]

---

[31]Lewis, *A Grief Observed,* p. 84.

Part Three

BEAUTY

12

Evil and the Cosmic Dance

C. S. Lewis and Beauty's Place in Theodicy

Philip Tallon

*In the plan of the Great Dance plans without number interlock,
and each movement becomes in its season the breaking into flower of
the whole design to which all else has been directed. Thus each is
equally at the centre and none are there by being equals, but some by giving
place and some by receiving it, the small things by their smallness and
the great things by their greatness, and all the patterns linked and looped
together by the unions of a kneeling with a sceptred love. Blessed be He!*
C. S. Lewis, in *Perelandra*

BEAUTY AND THEODICY: AWKWARD DANCE PARTNERS?

The perennial problem of evil and its religious response, theodicy, force us to consider the way that we think about God, human life and the rest of reality. Which values we admit to discussion of this theological dilemma will subsequently shape the response we give to the problem. If, as has often been the case, the problem of evil discussion is restricted to religiously neutral values (no mention of heaven, let alone angels and demons), then theodicy can trade in only generic goods such as free will or character development. Although there is merit in such stripped-down defenses of God—they are highly portable and widely applicable—they also force us to defend a less-than-sufficient picture of God's person and purposes.

Likewise, when the problem of evil discussion is restricted to purely moral considerations, theodicy's palette is denied the full range of values with which to paint a picture of God's goodness. When aesthetic considerations are absent from theodicy, we may be forced to defend God as Moral Lawgiver, while ignoring God's role as Creator. Perhaps even worse, an overly austere theodicy may force us to picture God's goodness as somehow alien or antithetical to human flourishing. Like Charles Dickens's Gradgrind, who preached the value of facts without communicating the desirability of the truth, a moralistic theodicy may proclaim the value of goodness without indicating why the good is alluring.

Yet the inclusion of beauty into theological discourse also has its difficulties. Beauty is an evasive concept, yet it commands our attention as fiercely as it eludes our description. Hans Urs von Balthasar describes beauty as "the last thing which the thinking intellect dares to approach, since only it dances as an uncontained splendor around the double constellation of the true and the good."[1] The image of the dance again points to an alluring yet elusive quality at the center of aesthetics. The widespread indifference to aesthetics in academic theodicy is likely due to this quality. It is difficult to dance with beauty—easy as it is to slow her down, step on her toes, and break her rhythm. Theodicists with their sophisticated thinking intellects, perhaps taking von Balthasar's warning, have often not dared to approach beauty as they carefully and slowly do their work.[2]

JOHN HICK: "MERE" THEODICY

But more than being ignored, beauty has sometimes been deliberately excluded. Perhaps the most extended and formidable opposition to allowing a serious place for aesthetic considerations in theodicy comes in the masterful

---

[1]Hans Urs von Balthasar, *The Glory of the Lord: A Theological Aesthetics*, vol. 1, *Seeing the Form*, trans. Erasmo Leiva-Merikakis (San Francisco: Ignatius, 1982), p. 18.

[2]The major recent exception to this is Marilyn McCord Adams, whose recent book, *Horrendous Evils and the Goodness of God* (Ithaca, N.Y.: Cornell University Press, 1999), contains a chapter discussing the way that aesthetic value is useful in showing how God is good to humans. Specifically, Adams highlights the benefits of the beatific vision and the power of the aesthetic imagination to reverse the meanings of evils (pp. 129-51, passim). Her exclusion from this essay is entirely due to space, as I think she forms a helpful triad in this discussion between Hick and Lewis, as she tends, in perfect opposition to Hick, to deemphasize the moral dimension of theodicy. Lewis's work, I believe, equally answers both thinkers, as I argued in a paper presented in 2005 at the Oxbridge C. S. Lewis conference, where I had the terrifying pleasure of receiving feedback from Marilyn Adams herself, who was sitting in the audience.

work of John Hick, *Evil and the God of Love*. Hick, writing against Augustine's vision of cosmic harmony, is unrelentingly stern in emphasizing the priority of moral values.

In his work, Augustine of Hippo repeatedly seeks to justify the beauty of creation despite the presence of metaphysical evil (finitude) and moral evil (sin) in the universe. Reflecting on the inequality of creation, Augustine compares the universe to the "celestial luminaries," of which it would be foolish to ask "that the dimmer ones be done away with or made equal to the brighter ones."[3] Against such "foolishness," Augustine argues that the comparative levels of being in the universe (plenitude) heighten, rather than diminish, its total value. That there are beetles as well as angels, and millipedes as well as men, is no fault to the universe, but its benefit.

Moral evil is likewise incorporated into the beauty of the universe, since happiness perfectly accompanies righteousness, and misery is perfectly visited on those who sin. Thus, as Augustine writes, even sin is forced "to conform to the beauty of the universe as a whole" because the "ugliness of sin is remedied by the punishment of sin."[4] In *The City of God*, Augustine's image is of a painting, which, though it has some black patches, is still beautiful because of the purpose these dark spots serve, to heighten the brightness of the light patches by contrast. In the Augustinian picture, then, punishment and plenitude keep the universe beautifully balanced and wonderfully diverse.

This Augustinian theodicy is antithetical to what Hick desires in a response to the problem of evil. For Hick, it is not primarily that Augustine's use of aesthetic considerations is faulty (though he thinks that as well), but more so that any such considerations distract us from God's *agapē* for human persons. By trying to see the cosmic harmony in creation's variety, or sin's punishment, Hick is arguing, we are losing focus on theodicy's purpose. "A Christian theodicy must be centered upon moral personality," Hick writes, "rather than upon nature as a whole, and its governing principle must be ethical rather than aesthetic."[5]

Because of Irenaeus's heavy influence on Hick, it is ironic that Hick takes his stand not just against Augustine's "aesthetic theme" of perfectly balanced harmony but also against Irenaeus's "aesthetic theme," which includes an es-

---

[3] Augustine of Hippo *On Free Will*, in *Augustine: Earlier Writings*, ed. J. H. S. Burleigh (Philadelphia: Westminster Press, 1953), p. 186.
[4] Ibid., p. 187.
[5] John Hick, *Evil and the God of Love* (San Francisco: Harper, 1978), p. 204.

chatological dimension. The Irenaean alternative to the static Augustinian picture resembles more of a beautiful symphony than a beautiful painting, but even so, Hick warns, this improved version of the aesthetic theme is still open to the same basic objection. "If God is personal," Hick writes, "we must see man as standing in a quite different relationship to Him from that in which the material universe stands to its Creator." The following propositions are that we should see "human life [not] as a link in the great chain of being," but rather as central to God's intention for fellowship; and that we should not be "upholding the perfection of the universe as an aesthetic whole," but rather as "suited to the fulfillment of God's purposes for it."[6] For Hick, God's purposes center around creating persons with whom he can have fellowship.

Theodicy's concern, then, according to Hick, is relational instead of creational, and ethical rather than aesthetic, and hence any cosmic aesthetic, no matter how skillful or sensitive, cannot effectively communicate God's *agapē* for humans. Yet, Hick concedes, even if something could be made of the aesthetic themes of Augustine or Irenaeus, it would be trivial. Such considerations would be peripheral to the rational discussion. "Whatever realms of life and dimensions of meaning there may be beyond our present awareness and concern," Hick writes of the aesthetic theme, since they have little to do with "the high good of man's fellowship with God," they are therefore beyond the scope of theodicy's concern.[7] Aesthetic considerations, if at all possible, are relegated to the scholastic dustbin, with other questions like "How many angels can dance on the head of a pin?"

To begin with, it is hard to quibble with Hick's focus on moral questions. It is primarily a question of God's character rather than God's creativity that drives theodicy. Granting this, however, does not in any way make beauty distracting or irrelevant to the discussion. To the contrary, I will argue that it is possible to keep the priority of theodicy on moral concerns while also recognizing the indispensable role of beauty. The work of C. S. Lewis, I believe, allows us to begin to engage with this problem by connecting creation's beauty with theodicy in significant ways. Lewis's work, though not the last word on this issue, mounts the first line of a defense for a deep commitment to creation's beauty as a pointer to God's goodness, even in the midst of evil.

---

[6]Ibid., p. 202.
[7]Ibid., p. 204.

C. S. LEWIS: IN DEFENSE OF AN AESTHETIC THEODICY

C. S. Lewis's legacy in the recent theodicy discussion is, sadly, somewhat marginal. Though his writings on the problem of evil are certainly substantial (having written theological, autobiographical and fictional treatments of the subject), it is possible to read widely in the contemporary literature on evil without coming across even a mention of his work. One rarely finds his monograph on the subject, *The Problem of Pain,* quoted in the ongoing discussion; though one suspects that this work is read much more than its scanty citations suggest.

That Lewis's theodicy is often ignored is no doubt partly due to the fact that he defends orthodox views, most of which are represented elsewhere in the literature. But what is not easy to find elsewhere is the panoramic and yet unified vision of reality that Lewis possesses. And it is this vision that is such a help in all walks of philosophy, including theodicy. Owen Barfield once wrote about C. S. Lewis that "what he thought about everything was secretly present in what he said about anything."[8] Indeed, the range of Lewis's understanding is often not so secretly present in any of his writings, since Lewis explicitly brings together his cognitive, ethical, and aesthetic faculties to bear on many key issues. For Lewis, beauty was as objective as logic or morality, and their unity was held together at the heart of reality. Human interaction with this reality is, for Lewis, a necessary first principle for philosophy:

> We must, then, grant logic to the reality; we must, if we are to have any moral standards, grant it to moral standards too. And there is really no reason why we should not do the same about standards of beauty. There is no reason why our reaction to a beautiful landscape should not be the response, however humanly blurred and partial, to something that is really there.[9]

If, as Lewis suggests, our experience of beauty is a perception of genuine reality, then it is a source of knowledge, even if we cannot always discern beauty's lesson. "If our religion is something objective," Lewis argues, "then we must never avert our eyes from those elements in it which seem puzzling or repellent; for it will be precisely the puzzling or repellant which conceals all that we do not yet know and need to know."[10]

---

[8]Quoted in Alan Jacobs, *The Narnian* (San Francisco: HarperSanFrancisco, 2006), p. xxi.
[9]C. S. Lewis, "De Futilitate," in *The Seeing Eye* (New York: Ballantine, 1967), p. 96.
[10]C. S. Lewis, "Learning in War-Time," in *The Weight of Glory* (New York: Macmillan, 1980), p. 27.

At the outset, we can see that Lewis's work is marked by a trust in the value of pursuing beauty in the philosophical enterprise. In "The Weight of Glory," Lewis argues that the desire for beauty is "no mere neurotic fantasy," but like the urgings of morality (here he parallels his argument in book 1 of *Mere Christianity*), it has its origin in God. Lewis writes that we can pursue beauty "in the sure confidence that by so doing we are either advancing to the vision of God ourselves or indirectly helping others to do so."[11] As a methodological principle, Lewis's affirmation of beauty's objectivity forms a preliminary response to Hickian skepticism about aesthetic imaginings. Following Lewis here, even if we cannot precisely see where beauty fits into theodicy, we can pursue its study in the sure confidence that we are advancing our knowledge of God's goodness. For any philosopher to restrict theodicy's scope to the purely moral may be marked by a sort of distrust in the deep connections between beauty and goodness.

I also think that Lewis's vision of theodicy successfully answers the explicit doubts of philosophers such as Hick by showing various ways that the moral and aesthetic dimensions of reality are knit together, as well as how the cosmic and personal dimensions intersect. My thesis, simply stated, is that Lewis uses creation's beauty to point to God's goodness. Though space forbids a full examination of the depths of Lewis's views, I want to sketch two key areas in theodicy (eschatology and soul making), which are greatly helped by Lewis's appeals to created beauty, and conclude by showing how Lewis successfully employs the "aesthetic theme," which Hick critiques so strongly.

ADDING WEIGHT TO HEAVENLY GLORY: IN DEFENSE OF "FALLEN IMAGERY"

Lewis fittingly concludes *The Problem of Pain* with a chapter on heaven, citing Paul's invocation of future glory *(doxa)* as a good with which present sufferings cannot be compared (Romans 8:18).[12] He is further emphatic that heaven's delight weighs so strongly in Scripture and tradition that any theodicy ignoring heaven cannot even be called Christian.[13] In this, Hick and Lewis are of one mind, since Hick also defends heaven as "crucial" to Christian theodicy.[14]

---

[11]Ibid.
[12]C. S. Lewis, *The Problem of Pain* (New York: Macmillan, 1956), p. 132.
[13]Ibid., p. 132.
[14]Hick, *Evil and the God of Love*, p. 338.

Alongside the apostle, Hick and Lewis both see the redeemed afterlife as an infinite good capable of outweighing human suffering, but Hick is sadly rather vague on the details of this life, citing the "fallenness" of all our present imagery as a barrier to imagining life eternal. "We cannot visualize the life of the redeemed and perfected creation," Hick writes;[15] instead, "we can think in only very general terms . . . of expanded capacities for fulfillment."[16]

Hick here recognizes a problem for theodicy, produced by our inability to imagine and thus value this future glory. Yet Hick does little to surmount this obstacle, only observing that our attempts to imagine how our expanded capacities for creativity, relationships and knowledge are "probably all but childish guesses." Thus, the fallenness of our images of eternal beatitude leads us to be able to affirm the character of Christian eschatology, as Hick phrases it, "only by faith." Yet, that our apprehension of this future glory remains vague is surely a problem for theodicy, even if it is not a strictly logical problem.

That heaven is also for Lewis an enjoyable experience par excellence is beyond question. Lewis also recognizes that this doctrine suffers from a rather serious public relations problem, which, no matter how strongly we affirm heaven's desirability in principle, prevents us from evoking its desirability in the practice of theodicy. Compared with its infernal counterpart, in the modern imagination, heaven comes off as rather bland.

Lewis acknowledges the difficulties of the doctrine of heaven in "Transposition," observing that our notion of eternal beatitude tends to include undesirable negations.[17] Most Christian accounts of heaven are of a life which, if bodily, is no longer defined by fleshly desire. And difficult and painful as this present life may be, it is hard for us to imagine a future life of satisfaction without the familiar ebbs and tides of yearning and fulfillment. Ostensibly, though we will not starve in heaven, neither can we satisfy our hunger. Though we will all share in perfect love, sensuality cannot play a part of this *agapē*. Even though none of us enjoy a painful rash, it is difficult to imagine normal, bodily life without itches to scratch.

As Lewis sees it, by eliminating certain needs derived from scarcity, insecurity or mortal biology, a redeemed afterlife would also, seemingly, negate the attendant pleasures we currently enjoy (e.g., food, sex or sleep). Against such

---

[15]Ibid., p. 350.
[16]Ibid., p. 352.
[17]C. S. Lewis, "Transposition," in *The Weight of Glory*, p. 66.

worries, Lewis is confident that "the reality of the Beatific Vision would or will outweigh, would infinitely outweigh, the reality of the negations."[18] The problem, then, is not whether heaven can be ultimately satisfying despite these negations, but rather, as Lewis asks, "[Can] our present notion of it [heaven] outweigh our present notion of [the negations]?"[19]

Here is where Lewis the poet comes to the aid of Lewis the philosopher. This repeating theme in his work—of trying to show heaven to be as lovely and desirable as possible—is seen everywhere: from the dynamic excitement of going "further up and further in," into more and more "real" Narnias in *The Last Battle*, to the rugged beauty of heaven in *The Great Divorce*, to his poetic attempts in "The Weight of Glory" to "rip open the inconsolable secret" of our unattained longing.[20] Through fresh appeal to delightful tropes—graceful athleticism, a journey into distant mountains, the sense of youthful nostalgia—Lewis tries to sidestep ethereal clichés and silence the objections of "facetious people" who complain of a tedious afterlife where we "spend eternity playing harps."[21] In essence, Lewis tries to give imaginative weight to the future glory the apostle Paul indicates. In doing so, Lewis helps to tip the scales of theodicy, not by introducing new ideas, but by helping us to value old ideas properly.

Without some allure, the doctrine of heaven adds little to any theodicy. The success with which Lewis combines, as Chesterton phrases it, "an idea of wonder with an idea of welcome," is undoubtedly the result of his ability to allow us to taste some of the delight of heaven through aesthetic descriptors drawn from this-worldly imaginings.[22] That these imaginings are, perhaps, nothing more than "childish guesses," however, is no mark against them, for if they have given us a deeper sense of the possible weight of glory, then they have done their work.

Poetic description of paradise, however, is not the only necessary ingredient for a proper doctrine of heavenly glory. While Lewis winsomely adds welcome to the afterlife, he equally tries to evoke fearful respect for the divine *mysterium tremendum*. In *The Great Divorce*, heaven's outdoorsy beauty is not only bright and fresh but also hard as diamonds to those who have not yet

---

[18]Ibid.
[19]Ibid.
[20]C. S. Lewis, "The Weight of Glory," in *The Weight of Glory*, p. 6.
[21]C. S. Lewis, *Mere Christianity* (San Francisco: HarperSanFrancisco, 2001), p. 137.
[22]G. K. Chesterton, *Orthodoxy* (San Francisco: Ignatius, 1995), p. 15.

become solid. In the Chronicles of Narnia, the lion Aslan may well be good, but he is not "safe." To those who love evil, Aslan is a terrifying figure. As a word of warning against becoming too comfortable with the idea of the beatific vision, Lewis observes in *Mere Christianity,* "Some people talk as if meeting the gaze of absolute goodness would be fun. They need to think again."[23] So Lewis prevents his aesthetic vision of the redeemed afterlife from lapsing into "mere aestheticism" by balancing it with a moral dimension, which I will discuss in the next section.

DEVELOPING A TASTE FOR THE OTHER: IN DEFENSE OF CREATION'S SOUL-MAKING CAPACITIES

The role of soul making plays a part in many contemporary theodicies. Of its recent proponents, John Hick is certainly the best known, though it is notable that the concept of soul making, and even the phrase, is well covered in *The Problem of Pain.* "I have seen great beauty of spirit in some who were great sufferers," Lewis writes. "If the world is indeed a 'vale of soul making,' it seems on the whole to be doing its work."[24] Lewis cites Keats as the originator of the phrase, and in his book *Evil and the God of Love,* Hick cites Keats as well, with no reference to Lewis on this matter.[25] Whatever route Hick came by the concept, it is indubitable that Hick was aware of Lewis's similar use of soul making as a justifier for some amounts of evil, and it is therefore sad that Hick misses out on a vitally important point in Lewis's theodicy: that beauty, as well as suffering, can bring us closer to God by helping us grow morally.[26]

The general thrust of Hick's soul-making theodicy is that God desires us to grow to maturity, into the "likeness of Christ," and that this process of perfection often requires pain and struggle. In his work he skillfully responds to David Hume, who attacks creation, comparing the world to a house where the "windows, doors, fires, passages, stairs, and the whole economy of the house were the source of noise, confusion, fatigue, darkness, and the extremes of heat and cold."[27] If there were an all-knowing, all-powerful Creator, Hume is sug-

---

[23]Lewis, *Mere Christianity,* p. 31.

[24]Lewis, *Problem of Pain,* p. 96.

[25]Hick, *Evil and the God of Love,* p. 259.

[26]Hick twice references *The Problem of Pain* in ibid., pp. 248, 315, both times in notes, though neither time in reference to Lewis's use of the term "soul making."

[27]David Hume, *Dialogues Concerning Natural Religion,* ed. Richard H. Popkin, 2nd ed. (Indianapolis: Hackett, 1998), p. 68.

gesting, then this being would be able to rig all the "secret springs of the universe" in order to avoid pain and keep all humans happy. Responding to Hume, Hick writes: "Such critics as Hume are confusing what heaven ought to be, as an environment for perfected finite beings, with what this world ought to be, as an environment for beings who are in the process of becoming perfected."[28]

Here Hick rightly points out that there may well be good reasons for creating a world with suffering. If God wants to do more than pacify us, indeed to perfect us, then this world may well be the creation of a good God. But the repeated tendency of Hick to avoid discussing the goodness of creation is troubling. When discussing the beauty and variety of all lower forms of life, Hick can take confidence in only two roles for nature to play: to provide the evolutionary material that produced humanity, and to provide a dangerous world in which humans may grow to maturity through difficulty.[29] Hick repeatedly emphasizes that we can really know very little about God's purposes for the rest of creation, seeing only the part of the story that concerns ourselves. That God has a special purpose for us is beyond question, but it seems troubling that God only has a loving purpose for us, and that this loving purpose expresses itself almost exclusively in suffering.

Lewis also sees pain as a tool often used by God for bringing us into right relationship. His famous line, repeatedly quoted in the movie *Shadowlands,* admits that while pleasures can be ignored, pain cannot. "God whispers to us in our pleasures," Lewis writes, "speaks in our conscience, but shouts in our pains: it is His megaphone to rouse a deaf world."[30] But what of a God who only shouts to us and never whispers? That the character-building quality of beauty is lacking from Hick's soul-making theodicy may well lead us to think that God is narrowly concerned only with our moral development, like a domineering parent. That Hick emphasizes the formative aspect of suffering is both appropriate and biblical (Romans 5:3-5), but that he emphasizes this so exclusively leaves his theodicy impoverished. Defending God's goodness solely in moral terms can lead to a picture of God that is cold, harsh and generally not worth defending. What Lewis does so successfully, in including beauty and pain as formative parts of God's creation (God's whisper and God's

---

[28]Hick, *Evil and the God of Love,* pp. 293-94.
[29]Ibid., p. 317.
[30]Lewis, *Problem of Pain,* p. 81.

megaphone), is not only to balance the joys and pains of God's world but also to suggest that pain itself, in its ability to break through our self-centeredness, is thereby helping us to enjoy divine and created beauty.

Our ability to participate in the joys of heaven is, for Lewis, conditional on a deeper transformation of our person. The beatific vision is not a good that exists apart from moral considerations; those who do not love God also will not love the beatific vision. In *The Problem of Pain* he writes, "The joys of heaven are, for most of us in our present condition, 'an acquired taste'—and certain ways of life may render the taste impossible of acquisition."[31] Yet it is not as if moral goodness is a prerequisite for enjoying God's beauty; rather, enjoying God's beauty is an aspect of moral goodness itself. This applies to earthly beauties as well. In *The Abolition of Man*, Lewis argues that the appreciation of objective value is central in personal formation:

> Until quite modern times all teachers and even all men believed the universe to be such that certain emotional reactions on our part could be either congruous or incongruous to it—believed, in fact, that objects did not merely receive, but could merit, our approval or disapproval, our reverence, or our contempt.[32]

The old view of the universe, as Lewis describes it, affirmed not only an objectivity to reality, but also a moral call that this reality placed upon us. Citing Aristotle, Lewis describes the goal of education as making the pupil "like and dislike what he ought." We *ought* to train our emotions in such a way that they conform to reality: to train ourselves such that beauty gives us pleasure, ugliness engenders disgust and so on. Such training is more than a necessary ingredient for being a member of the cultured elite; it is also training in the basics of virtue. Other thinkers have tied together moral and aesthetic taste in similar ways. Atheist literary critic I. A. Richards likewise holds that errors in taste are more than a simple cultural faux pas; they undermine our entire interaction with reality. One hears echoes in *The Abolition of Man* of such statements as "No life can be excellent in which the elementary responses are disorganized and confused."[33] These elementary responses of pleasure, disgust, fear and delight are the raw material that must be worked up by the rational mind to form a virtuous person. Lewis notes that Augustine defines virtue as

---

[31]Ibid., p. 61. Of course, this is also a central theme in Lewis, *Mere Christianity*, as on pp. 81, 92, 118-20, 147-48, 176, 192.

[32]C. S. Lewis, *The Abolition of Man* (New York: Touchstone, 1996), pp. 27-28.

[33]I. A. Richards, *Principles of Literary Criticism* (Orlando, Fla.: Harcourt Brace, 1985), p. 62.

ordo amoris, the ordinate condition of the affections in which every object is accorded the kind and degree of love that is appropriate to it. Virtue, then, is expressed by relating properly to God and the rest of creation.

Loving rightly, or as Lewis phrases it, developing "the taste for the *other,*" requires first that we be broken out of our self-centeredness.[34] Focusing inward, we can neither enjoy true beauty nor true goodness. In *The Magician's Nephew,* it is notable that Uncle Andrew hates the song that Aslan sings as much as he hates Aslan, wishing for a gun to "get that brute shot."[35] Attending to either the song or the singer would require him to attend to something other than himself. Sin, for Lewis and Augustine, is a "movement whereby a creature . . . tried to set up on its own, to exist for itself."[36] Great beauty or great goodness requires a radical decentering that is anathema to the sinful spirit. In *The Great Divorce,* hell is filled with chip shops and second-rate cinemas. It is easy to see why ultimate beauty would be far less desirable to sinners than minor prettiness, because the latter requires of us so much *less.* It is not as if God is withholding from sinners the privilege of ultimate happiness as punishment for disobedience, but rather that the best God has to offer us, by its very nature, cannot be appreciated by those of us who love improperly.

The process of developing a taste for the other, however, requires that we love other things appropriately. And here Lewis finds a personal role for the maligned Augustinian notion of plenitude. The universe contains a great multitude of items, as Lewis describes it: "an immoderate deluge of atoms, orchids, oranges, cancers, canaries, fleas, gases, tornadoes and toads."[37] That this variety of objects deserve varying degrees of approval, reverence or contempt cannot be denied. That we must live in a world with such variety, which we must learn to value properly and ordinately, is, following Lewis, part of our soul making. Thus there may be a personal and ethical principle even within the Augustinian cosmic notion of plenitude, assuming this account of virtue.

If appreciation of creation is part of our development in virtue itself, then, contra Hick, upholding the aesthetic qualities of creation is fully compatible with a person-focused theodicy. That nature is so varied—ranging from rocks

---

[34]Lewis, *Problem of Pain,* p. 111.
[35]C. S. Lewis, *The Magician's Nephew,* in *The Chronicles of Narnia* (New York: HarperCollins, 2001), p. 68.
[36]Lewis, *Problem of Pain,* p. 63.
[37]C. S. Lewis, *Miracles* (New York: Macmillan, 1960), p. 66.

and plants all the way up to animals, humans and angels—does not only signify that we are merely one link in this chain, but rather, that nature also may
have a positive, personal dimension. Yet Lewis goes beyond seeing creation as
something suited for our appreciation: he moves to see us as part of the picture
itself. In the next section I will discuss how Lewis, in the tradition of Augustine, uses artistic analogies to help us see creation as beautiful, but does so in
such a way that avoids marginalizing the personal aspect of theodicy.

"LET ME COUNT THE WAYS": IN DEFENSE OF "THE AESTHETIC THEME"

In "The Weight of Glory," Lewis economically summarizes much of what I
have been trying to say at much greater length. He writes that created beauty
is not only desirable and beneficial, but also formative, and invites us to participate in its activity:

> We do not merely want to *see* beauty, though, God knows, even that is bounty
> enough. We want something else which can hardly be put into words—to be
> united with the beauty we see, to pass into it, to receive it into ourselves, to
> bathe in it, to become part of it. . . . When human souls have become as perfect
> in voluntary obedience as the inanimate creation is in its lifeless obedience,
> then they will put on its glory, or rather that greater glory of which Nature is
> only the first sketch.[38]

The analogy of nature, quoted here as a model for a kind of lovely, though
lifeless, obedience, shows up again in *The Problem of Pain*. God's unfathomable
love is, like heaven's glory, difficult to conceive, and Lewis writes, it "can be
apprehended only by analogies: from the various types of love known among
creatures, we reach an inadequate, but useful, conception of God's love for
man."[39] The first rung on this ladder of analogies is of the love of an artist for
his creation. Peter's analogy of the church as a spiritual house, of which we are
"living stones" (1 Peter 2:5) is, Lewis admits, limited by the static quality of
the analogy. Humans here are only sentient bricks, useful for supporting
something else, but not very valuable for their unique characteristics; what ar-
chitect is concerned about individual stones? This seems exactly the sort of
"aesthetic theme" to which Hick originally objected! For Hick, the problem

---

[38]Lewis, "Weight of Glory," p. 17.
[39]Lewis, *Problem of Pain*, p. 30.

with Augustine's principles of plenitude and punishment, which sought to incorporate humans into an aesthetic scheme, was that they downplayed the dynamic purpose for which God made us.

Yet Lewis does not, unlike Hick, abandon the analogy as useless because it is impersonal. He writes that "it is an important analogy so far as it goes. We are, not metaphorically but in very truth, a Divine work of art, something that God is making, and therefore something with which He will not be satisfied until it has a certain character."[40]

Lewis here affirms the impersonal artistic analogies drawn by Augustine, but overcomes some of Augustine's problems by delving more deeply into the nature of the art that we are. What Lewis sees correctly is that the question is not whether we should see ourselves as God's artwork, but rather, What kind of artwork are we? A decorative ashtray? A limerick? Or an epic poem? In Lewis's view, we are not merely a sketch that God has idly drawn to amuse himself, but a masterpiece, over which "he will take endless trouble" and to which he will "thereby give endless trouble."[41] Lewis thus overcomes some of the problems of Augustine's aesthetic theme, not by making his analogies less aesthetic, but by delving more deeply into the quality of our beauty. Highlighting the deep love God as Creator has for us, Lewis bypasses the facile notion that to be a work of art is always to be dispensable. Who could calculate what *Paradise Lost* was worth to Milton, or the *Mona Lisa* to da Vinci?

Yet Lewis does not stop with artistic analogies; he counts many more ways in which God loves us, as a master loves a dog, as a father loves a son, and as a man loves a woman.[42] Each analogy captures some aspect of the intolerable compliment that God has paid us by loving us so much. Lewis affirms that the romantic analogy is the most useful for theodicy, since it stresses both the commitment of the relationship and the desire within that commitment for perfection; yet Lewis also acknowledges that the romantic metaphor is the most dangerous, since it invites us to imagine that humanity, like the beloved, is the focus of all God's attention. To see humanity only as a work of art would be troublingly incomplete. But to see God only as a lover would be to imagine ourselves equal with God, or perhaps to fancy God as somehow emotionally codependent with his frustrating human creations. Whatever their limita-

[40]Ibid., pp. 29-30.
[41]Ibid., pp. 30-31.
[42]Ibid., pp. 33-34.

tions, then, creational analogues may help to offset the personal analogies, which would collapse the distance between God and humanity.

Finally, it is worth mentioning that Lewis concludes *The Problem of Pain* with a lengthy meditation on a set of aesthetic analogies that should put the criticisms of John Hick to rest. With Augustine, Lewis emphasizes that the world is like a work of art. It is a way for God to "express his goodness through the total drama of a world containing free creatures."[43] But unlike Augustine, Lewis is keen to invest his aesthetic analogies with a deeply personal aspect. For Lewis, dynamic and evolving artworks help us to see that God has the ability to incorporate change, even rebellion and sin, into a beautiful whole. Where some artistic metaphors are relatively rigid, others highlight the flexibility of God's providence: "The symbol of a drama, a symphony, or a dance, is here useful to correct a certain absurdity which may arise if we talk too much of God planning and creating the world process for good and of that good being frustrated by the free will of the creatures."[44]

These artistic analogies are intentionally chosen to make room for humans. Not only are they dynamic and can conceptually make room for human free choices, they also are explicitly anthropocentric. Both dances and dramas *need* people. If Augustine's reflections on the diverse colors of a painting are in fact subpersonal, and therefore limited, the image of the dance or the drama is not likewise restricted.

Throughout his work, Lewis returns often enough to the image of the dance such that it rises above the level of metaphor, to take on the status of a model, or even paradigm. Lewis concludes *The Problem of Pain* with a vision of heaven as a divine dance, in which

> the great master Himself leads the revelry, giving Himself eternally to His creatures in the generation, and back to Himself in the sacrifice, of the Word, then indeed the eternal dance "makes heaven drowsy with the harmony." All pains and pleasures we have known on earth are early initiations in the movements of that dance: but the dance itself is strictly incomparable with the sufferings of this present time.[45]

Here Lewis's aesthetic theme ties together his vision of heaven's delights, with his account of virtue as a "taste for the other" in a way that is not only

---

[43]Ibid., p. 72.
[44]Ibid.
[45]Ibid., p. 142.

personal in focus but also universal in scope, and finally theological in significance. In *Mere Christianity*, Lewis observes that "perhaps the most important difference between Christianity and all other religions" is that "God is not a static thing . . . but a dynamic, pulsating activity, a life, almost a kind of drama. Almost, if you will not think me irreverent, a kind of dance."[46] Is this enough to silence Hick's objections? I believe so. In the face of Lewis's aesthetic vision of God, the cosmos, and the human place within the life of both, any theodicy that seeks to exclude creation's beauty from its considerations should look like gross reductionism.

Hick earlier complained that the inclusion of aesthetic concerns decreased humanity's importance. The above arguments show this to be unfounded. In fact, the kind of *sola moralis* reductionism Hick advocates ends in the attenuation of God's person and purposes, until the anemic result is a cold codependency between God and humans. By cutting out beauty, we cut out theodicy's heart. Lewis's reflections on the Great Dance of the cosmos at the end of *Perelandra* (which provided this chapter's epigraph), remind us that God's condescending love is not just for our lowly estate, but for all facets of his creation, and that we ought not sneer at realms of meaning, however small, with which the greatest of all and the One who is Beauty himself takes delight.

---

[46]Lewis, *Mere Christianity*, p. 175.

13

Lewis's *Miracles* and Mathematical Elegance

RUSSELL W. HOWELL

When C. S. Lewis first published *Miracles* (1947), his aim was to map out a philosophical framework that would be compatible with the notion of miraculous events.[1] Such events, of course, are not viable in a naturalistic worldview, and early on Lewis produced an argument designed to show that naturalism was, as a philosophical system, incoherent. What could his thinking on this issue possibly have to do with mathematical elegance? This chapter explores that question and suggests a very close connection: mathematical elegance poses problems for naturalism—problems that connect with Lewis's own ideas of beauty.[2]

Lewis's third chapter, "The Self-Contradiction of the Naturalist," created quite a storm, and led to a debate with the philosopher Elizabeth Anscombe at the Oxford Socratic Club on February 2, 1948. Anscombe, being Catholic,

---

[1]An earlier version of this chapter first appeared under a different title in the 2006 summer issue of *Christian Scholar's Review*, whose editors have given InterVarsity Press permission to publish this revision.

[2]A chapter on Lewis and the topic of mathematics might remind readers of the difficulties Lewis had in passing his entrance examination on mathematics for Oxford. Despite his mother's impeccable mathematical talents, Lewis himself struggled, especially with basic calculations, and he regretted this deficiency. It is a mistake, however, to think that Lewis did not appreciate the beauty and power of mathematics, especially the higher-order analysis it requires, analysis that Lewis certainly exhibited in his discursive argumentation. For excellent insights into these matters, see David L. Neuhouser's article "C. S. Lewis and Mathematics" (September 25, 2005), posted by the C. S. Lewis Foundation, Faculty Forum Weblog <www.cslewis.org/ffblog/archives/2005/09/c_s_lewis_and_m.html>.

was certainly not a naturalist; she simply thought that Lewis's argument for the incoherence of naturalism was not compelling. The consensus seems to be that Anscombe bettered Lewis in that discussion. Whatever the true situation was, Lewis took Anscombe's criticisms seriously and rewrote the chapter. He renamed it "The Cardinal Difficulty of Naturalism" for a revision of *Miracles* that was published in 1960.

A NOBEL LAUREATE RAISES AN ISSUE

Ironically, an article by the physicist and (later) Nobel Laureate Eugene P. Wigner appearing in that same year also dealt with a miraculous phenomenon of a sort.[3] Wigner's intention was to raise an interesting aspect about mathematics that, as far as the article went, had nothing to do with naturalism. Yet on closer inspection it does, and we will shortly see that spin-offs from the ideas of Wigner, and those of Lewis, are inextricably linked.

Wigner begins with a story about two friends discussing their jobs. One of them, a statistician, is working on population trends. He mentions a paper he has written, which contains a complicated-looking equation on the first page. The statistician tries to explain the meaning of it, as well as other mathematical symbols in the paper. His friend is not trained in mathematics and is thus a bit overwhelmed. Eventually he suspects that the statistician is teasing him. "How can you know that?" he repeatedly asks. "And what is this symbol here?"

"Oh," says the statistician, "this is pi [π]."

"What is that?"

"The ratio of the circumference of a circle to its diameter."

"Well, now you are pushing your joke too far; . . . surely the population has nothing to do with the circumference of the circle."[4]

Wigner uses this story to introduce two issues: (1) the surprising phenomenon that scientists have used mathematics so often to build successful theories relating to the physical world; and (2) the nagging Kuhnian-like question: How can we be sure that completely different theories would not be as suc-

---

[3]Just three weeks after Lewis's death in 1963, Eugene P. Wigner was awarded the Nobel Prize in physics. According to the Royal Swedish Academy of Sciences, the basis for Wigner's selection was his contributions to the theory of the atomic nucleus and the elementary particles, particularly through the discovery and application of fundamental symmetry principles.

[4]Eugene P. Wigner, "The Unreasonable Effectiveness of Mathematics in the Natural Sciences," *Communications in Pure and Applied Mathematics* 13 (1960): 1. Also available at various websites, such as <www.dartmouth.edu/~matc/MathDrama/reading/Wigner.html>.

cessful as the ones now in use, though perhaps concentrating on different phenomena?[5]

Regarding Wigner's first point, he concedes that much of mathematics, such as Euclidean geometry, was developed because its axioms were created on the basis of what appeared to be true of reality. (For example, Euclid's first axiom stipulates that it is possible to draw a straight line between any two points. Indeed, that just seems to be the way things work.) From this viewpoint the applicability of mathematics to the physical world is hardly surprising. But how much of mathematics actually progresses in this manner? A good argument can be made that other factors guide the formation of a large body of higher mathematical theories.

Take the field of complex analysis as just one example. In the 1500s the notion of complex numbers, which involve the square root of minus one, seemed odd to mathematicians. At that time negative numbers by themselves were still being treated with suspicion, so taking square roots of them was all the more problematic. But mathematicians kept using their imagination and "pretended" that complex numbers made sense. They developed logical theories to accommodate these numbers, but this process took time. In fact, it was not until the end of the nineteenth century that complex numbers became firmly entrenched in the corpus of mathematical literature. For our purposes, it is important to observe that no physical phenomenon guided the investigation of complex numbers. Progress came from abstraction, and the manipulation of mathematical symbols in accordance with specified rules of algebra.

Now, however, complex numbers play a pivotal role in helping physicists understand the quantum world.[6] And for Wigner, the early use of quantum mechanics led to a "miracle." It arose when Max Born, Werner Heisenberg and Pascual Jordan decided to use mathematical constructs known as matrices to represent the position and momentum variables in equations involving classical mechanics. Later, Wolfgang Pauli successfully applied this technique to the mechanics of the hydrogen atom. Wigner states that this success was not surprising because the matrix procedure was abstracted from problems dealing with the hydrogen atom in the first place. But then matrix techniques were ap-

---

[5]See Thomas S. Kuhn, *The Structure of Scientific Revolutions*, 2nd ed. (Chicago: University of Chicago Press, 1970).

[6]David Bohm's pilot-wave theory (1952) is an alternative to quantum theory. Its formulation, however, is also based on originally abstract mathematics, so it does not undercut the point being made here.

plied to the helium atom. There was no justification for this move because the calculation rules were meaningless in that context. Yet, the application worked remarkably well. According to Wigner, "The miracle occurred . . . [when] the calculation of the lowest energy level of helium . . . [agreed] with the experimental data within the accuracy of the observations, which is one part in ten million. . . . Surely, in this case we 'got something out' of the equations that we did not put in."[7]

Wigner cites other examples: Newton's law of motion, formulated in terms that appear simple to mathematicians, but which proved to be accurate beyond all reasonable expectations; quantum electrodynamics; and the pure mathematical theory of the Lamb shift. The thrust of Wigner's main point in citing all of these examples can be illustrated by comments he makes near the beginning and end of his paper. Early on he states, "The enormous usefulness of mathematics in the natural sciences is something bordering on the mysterious, and . . . there is no rational explanation for it."[8] In concluding his paper he says,

> The miracle of the appropriateness of the language of mathematics for the formulation of the laws of physics is a wonderful gift which we neither understand nor deserve. We should be grateful for it and hope that it will remain valid in future research and that it will extend, for better or for worse, to our pleasure, even though perhaps also to our bafflement, to wide branches of learning.[9]

Wigner uses the word *miracle* twelve times throughout his paper. In some instances he probably intends it to mean nothing more than "phenomenally surprising." In other places he seems to be pushing for something more than that.

What exactly is a miracle? Lewis defined it as some kind of interference with "Nature" by a "supernatural" agent, and he described a *naturalist* as someone who thinks that nothing exists except Nature. So for a naturalist there are no supernatural powers, and no miracles. Admittedly, the meaning of *Nature* needs clarification (which Lewis spent some time doing), and the term *interference* is a bit awkward for a theist who believes that the "Laws of Nature" themselves are general descriptions of God's continued sustenance of his creation. Lewis was no doubt aware of these difficulties, but going into extensive

---

[7]Wigner, "Unreasonable Effectiveness of Mathematics," p. 9.
[8]Ibid., p. 2.
[9]Ibid., p. 14.

elaboration would have been beyond the scope of his book. Likewise, these definitions will suffice for our purposes. We shall later see that it may be appropriate to use Lewis's definition of *miracle* when reading Wigner's remarks.

A COMPUTER SCIENTIST RESPONDS

Curiously, there was no formal response to Wigner from the mathematical community for twenty years. Finally, in 1980 the well-known computer scientist Richard Wesley Hamming took up the task.[10] Like Wigner, Hamming was impressed with the success of abstract mathematical theories; he had used them in his formulation of an algorithm now known as the Hamming code, which is used to detect (and possibly correct) errors when data are transmitted from one computer to another. Hamming's goal was to tackle the "unreasonable effectiveness" question implied by the title of Wigner's paper, and he offered four "partial explanations" that could account for the applicability of mathematics.

First, scientists see what they look for and craft postulates so that they will produce theories that conform to their prior observations. Because scientists look at the world through a mathematical lens, it is not entirely surprising that they wind up describing it in mathematical terms. Second, scientists select the kind of mathematics to use. The same type of mathematical theory does not work everywhere; different theories are selected in accordance with the phenomenon they seem to describe.

These first two explanations are similar, and each is reminiscent of Wigner's Kuhnian-like question, which we will examine near the end of this chapter. Regarding the selection of mathematics to fit our perception of reality, it has already been acknowledged that some of mathematics develops this way. But not all applicable mathematical theories are generated out of a concern for applicability, so further work must be done, and Hamming indeed gives some additional food for thought.

Hamming's third response is that science actually answers comparatively few problems. To the extent that this assertion is true, the less of a miracle the success of mathematics would appear to be. Wigner, as a physicist, certainly lived with mathematics as an indispensable tool, but other sciences do not

---

[10]Richard Wesley Hamming, "The Unreasonable Effectiveness of Mathematics," *American Mathematical Monthly* 87 (February 1960): 2.

share this same reliance on mathematics. Biology, it is often said, has not yet been successfully dissected by the mathematical scalpel. But whether this observation is true or not—and the statement about biology can be legitimately challenged—it does not help in answering Wigner's main concern. The success of mathematics in physics itself is something that needs accounting, and Hamming's final response suggests an obvious mechanism for doing just that.

It is that evolution provides an explanation for why humans are able to mathematize the physical universe. At face value this claim may seem plausible, but it needs elaboration, and it is not fleshed out beyond Hamming's comment, "Darwinian evolution would naturally select for survival those competing forms of life which had the best models of reality in their minds—'best' meaning best for surviving and propagating."[11] Hamming concludes with the following remark:

> If you recall that modern science is only about 400 years old, and that there have been from 3 to 5 generations per century, then there have been at most 20 generations since Newton and Galileo. If you pick 4,000 years for the age of science, generally, then you get an upper bound of 200 generations. Considering the effects of evolution we are looking for via selection of small chance variations, it does not seem to me that evolution can explain more than a small part of the unreasonable effectiveness of mathematics.[12]

This observation hardly seems compelling. Just as an inclined block needs a critical slope to overcome its friction and start sliding, and once the sliding begins it proceeds rather rapidly, so too one might argue that once science "started" it progressed quickly, but any evolutionary development that occurred before this time was critical and cannot be discounted.

But evolutionary accounts have problems as well, and in any case Wigner acknowledged the possibility of such explanations in his paper. He was after something deeper, hinted at by his remark that he and other scientists create definitions and theories that "appeal to our aesthetic sense."[13] Before turning to spin-offs of Wigner's thinking along these lines—spin-offs that pose problems for naturalism—we will probe some evolutionary models a bit because they tie in with Lewis's analysis in *Miracles*. Specifically, we will consider three theories that have been put forth as viable accounts of human cognition. Their

---

[11]Ibid., p. 89.
[12]Ibid.
[13]Wigner, "Unreasonable Effectiveness of Mathematics," p. 3.

proponents do not necessarily intend that their arguments should apply to *mathematical* cognition, so criticisms leveled against them must be taken with the requisite grain of salt.

SOME EVOLUTIONARY THEORIES

The first explanation can be called the *sexual-selection hypothesis*, as argued by Geoffrey Miller.[14] He claims that excessive capacities or acquisition of resources of any kind may be a sexual display. If one has the energy or time or intrinsic capacity to do things that do not have direct adaptive value—carrying around a set of antlers so big that they are more of a detriment than a defense, or walking around with a big colored tail as a peacock does, or possessing artistic or mathematical brains that are more than needed to solve the problems of survival— then that energy or time or intrinsic capacity by itself may attract mates.

Physical attributes certainly seem to play some role in mate attraction, and artistic brains may as well insofar as they enable people to make attractive artifacts for display. The argument for mathematical brains, however, does not hold up as well. Although Miller does not specifically address the issue of mathematical reasoning, there has been speculation that his thinking might be relevant. Miller states, "The healthy brain theory suggests that our brains are different from those of other apes not because extravagantly large brains helped us to survive or to raise offspring, but because such brains are simply better advertisements of how good our genes are."[15]

But how would a larger brain be evident, and why would such an advertisement be appealing? In this regard a cartoon by Gary Larson comes to mind. It portrays two men competing for the attention of women on a desert island. The one winning the day was able to produce a more impressive array of mathematical equations on a chalkboard! These speculations, while certainly not disprovable, seem to lack good evidence in their support, at least as they might relate to mathematical thinking.

The next explanation is known as the *byproduct hypothesis*, as exemplified by Pascal Boyer.[16] Boyer is an atheist, but many theists are sympathetic with his

---

[14]Geoffrey Miller, *The Mating Mind: How Sexual Choice Shaped the Evolution of Human Nature* (New York: Anchor Books, 2001).

[15]Ibid., p. 104.

[16]Pascal Boyer, *Religion Explained: The Evolutionary Origins of Religious Thought* (New York: Basic Books, 2001).

main approach. He argues against there being a specific module in our brains that accounts for religious conviction, and hypothesizes that many higher cognitive religious functions may not be evolutionary adaptations at all. Instead, they may be byproducts of things that are adaptive and just piggyback on the adaptiveness of these other capacities. For Boyer, such cognition comes from many sources, which explains why religious claims, taken as a whole, produce so many false conclusions.

On the one hand, if the piggyback model holds up, it might be possible to extend it in some way to account for cognition in general and mathematical thinking in particular. On the other hand, some work would have to be done in this regard. How many false conclusions, for example, has mathematical reasoning produced? Additionally, this hypothesis, while plausible, seems to lack any concrete scientific support at this time.

Finally, there is the *module hypothesis*, as argued by Steven J. Mithen. Mithen writes from the perspective of an anthropologist, and he has an enormous amount of archaeological data from which to draw. In many ways his thinking is similar to that of Boyer. He states that integrative and higher level (meta)cognitive processes grew out of the unification of specific evolutionary modules, such as a module for tool use, or a module for interpersonal relations. These modules seem to coincide with spurts of brain enlargement, which are caused by a variety of factors. For example, "In general larger animals have larger brains, simply because they have more muscles to move and coordinate."[17] Mithen further argues that in humans (and only in humans) we also find a structure on top of modules—a general-purpose rationality. Says Mithen, "In summary, science, like art and religion, is a product of cognitive fluidity. It relies on psychological processes which had originally evolved in specialized cognitive domains and only emerged when these processes worked together."[18]

OBJECTIONS TO BLIND CHANCE

Mithen and others who argue along these lines paint a detailed and plausible scenario. But if the scenario were to be cast in a naturalistic framework, then it is precisely here where Lewis, in writing the third chapter of *Miracles*, wanted to put on the brakes. His concern was actually directed against any

---

[17]Steven J. Mithen, *The Prehistory of the Mind: The Cognitive Origins of Art, Religion, and Science* (London: Thames & Hudson, 1996), p. 200.
[18]Ibid., p. 215.

evolutionary theory set in a naturalistic framework, where all the relevant forces involved are nothing more than natural selection, with no oversight by *any* kind of supernatural being—no miracle, if you please.

Briefly, Lewis distinguishes between two ways we use the word *because:* as *cause and effect* (e.g., "Kay is sick because she didn't dress warmly") and as *ground-consequent* (e.g., "Kay must be sick, because she is still in bed"). The latter use expresses an inference. For Lewis, inferences are logically connected thoughts, and are vital components of reasoning. But how does one thought *cause* another thought? With a view that parallels that of the logician Gottlob Frege, Lewis states, "One thought can cause another . . . [only] by being *seen to be* a ground for it."[19] Lewis then thinks it inconceivable that a raw natural selection, which operates solely by rewarding biological responses that enhance survival or reproductive proliferation (i.e., cause-and-effect responses as opposed to ground-consequent responses), could ever transform these responses into acts of insight.

Lewis's views on this matter remain controversial, but many philosophers think that his analysis is, in general, on the mark. In fact, on February 2, 1967 (exactly nineteen years after the Lewis-Anscombe debate), John Lucas engaged Anscombe on Lewis's argument, again at the Oxford Socratic Club. This time, the consensus seems to be that Lucas successfully defended the thrust of Lewis's thinking. More recently Victor Reppert expanded Lewis's views in his book *C. S. Lewis's Dangerous Idea.* Finally, Alvin Plantinga has generated much discussion with his argument, similar to Lewis's argument from reason, that naturalism is self-defeating.[20]

Plantinga, though, gives a probabilistic analysis. He observes, as Lewis did, that evolution selects for survivability or reproductive proliferation. But, to use Hamming's language, even if evolution favors life forms that have "the best models of reality in their minds," *best* is still defined by success in surviving or propagating, *not necessarily* by cognitive reliability. But would not the former imply the latter? No, not according to Plantinga, who spends some time arguing that it is reasonable to suppose, in a hypothetical world, that a high degree of survivability or reproductive proliferation could be found among creatures like us, yet whose beliefs were mostly false. (And many naturalists, ironically,

---

[19]C. S. Lewis, *Miracles* (London: Fontana Books, 1960), p. 21, with emphasis in the original, and bracketed word added.

[20]See Alvin Plantinga, *Warrant and Proper Function* (Oxford: Oxford University Press, 1993), chap. 12.

argue that belief in God, though false, is a quality promoting a high degree of survivability.) Therefore, for Plantinga, the odds are either low or inscrutable that our cognitive faculties are reliable, *given* the tenets of evolution combined with naturalism. So any naturalist, reflecting upon this state of affairs, would not have confidence that one's own cognitive faculties were reliable. But then one could not trust the validity of naturalism itself, a theory that was created by similar cognitive processes. As Darwin himself said,

> With me the horrid doubt always arises whether the convictions of a man's mind, which has been developed from the mind of the lower animals, are of any value or at all trustworthy. Would any one trust in the convictions of a monkey's mind, if there are any convictions in such a mind?[21]

Plantinga's argument has not convinced many naturalists.[22] But however his or Lewis's line of thinking finally plays out, we can at least say that their arguments against naturalism show how beautifully a theistic view—and in particular a Christian theistic view—fits into a framework that justifies trust in the reliability of our cognitive faculties: by whatever process God created us, he did so with the desire that we would come to know and believe in him, rendering it quite likely that "the belief-producing processes from which Christian belief emanates are indeed reliable."[23]

MATHEMATICAL ELEGANCE

The stage is now set to map out, as promised, how mathematical elegance poses problems for naturalism in ways that parallel Lewis's thinking about beauty. Let us suppose that an atheistic evolutionary theory will be able, eventually, to come up with a plausible explanation of our rationality, notwithstanding the arguments by Lewis and others challenging that possibility. If so, any such theory, coming as it does with a naturalistic worldview, would still run up against the arguments of Mark Steiner.[24]

---

[21]Charles Darwin, Letter to William Graham, of Down, July 3, 1881, in *The Life and Letters of Charles Darwin Including an Autobiographical Chapter*, ed. Francis Darwin, 3 vols. (London: John Murray, 1887), 1:315–16 <http://darwin-online.org.uk/EditorialIntroductions/Freeman_LifeandLettersand Autobiography.html>.

[22]See James Beilby, ed., *Naturalism Defeated?* (Ithaca, N.Y.: Cornell University Press, 2002), which contains essays critical of Plantinga's analysis, and Plantinga's responses to them.

[23]Ibid., p. 266.

[24]See Mark Steiner, *The Applicability of Mathematics as a Philosophical Problem* (Cambridge, Mass.: Cambridge University Press, 1998).

We will be focusing Steiner's argument more on aesthetics than he does, but strictly speaking Steiner tries to refute nonanthropocentrism rather than naturalism. If Steiner is correct, however, the naturalist should not take comfort. For any form of naturalism, Steiner muses, is ipso facto nonanthropocentric, in that it would disallow a privileged status for humans in the scope of the universe. If, as Steiner argues, the success of mathematics can be shown to put humans in some sort of a privileged position, then naturalism has some problems to sort out. How does the success of mathematics put humans in such a position?

For Steiner, it is not so much the success of any one particular mathematical theory in an area of science. After all, there have been many failures of mathematics as well. In this respect Steiner agrees with Hamming's third point, and is thus critical of Wigner's approach in citing specific success examples from physics while ignoring error stories. The use of pi (π) by the statistician in Wigner's opening lines ignores all the failures in attempting to predict population trends. What Steiner is talking about is the success of mathematics as a grand strategy. It is a strategy that takes, for example, the raw formalisms of complex Hilbert space theory, and then boldly uses them as tools to make predictions about the quantum world, predictions that subsequently seem to be borne out via experiment.

How is this phenomenon anthropocentric? An analogy may be helpful here. Most cultures use a base-ten numbering system. There is no universal agreement as to why this is the case, but the general consensus is that it has to do with our having ten fingers. (The Mayas, incidentally, used base twenty, and to many this confirms the "appendage hypothesis" for numerical base usage.) Now, what if successful theories of how the universe operates were based on multiples of ten in a fundamental way? That would be anthropocentric to an extreme: the only reason the number ten is special to us is due to how we appear to ourselves.

Suppose, further, that not only did the number ten have special significance, but time and time again other human aesthetic criteria played a significant role in understanding the universe. Such occurrences, when looked at from a metalevel, would surely make one wonder why this privilege seems to fall on the human species. Yet this situation is precisely analogous to what mathematicians and scientists actually do when they rely on human notions of beauty and symmetry in the development of their theories.

In fact, such activity has been a long-standing and consistent strategy. Galileo, for example, pursued this tactic even though the best empirical evidence at the time did not necessarily support—indeed, in some respects it tended to *disconfirm*—his heliocentric theory.[25] He adopted it because it seemed much more elegant than the Ptolemaic model.[26] Most physicists generally admit that elegance, beauty and symmetry hold primary sway in theory development. As Brian Green observes, "Physicists . . . tend to elevate symmetry principles to a place of prominence by putting them squarely on the pedestal of explanation."[27] G. H. Hardy argues that mathematics itself, at least what constitutes good mathematics, is driven primarily by aesthetic criteria such as economy of expression, depth, unexpectedness, inevitability and seriousness, qualities that also seem to form standards for good poetry.[28]

Two of these criteria (unexpectedness and inevitability) appear paradoxical when taken together. In a beautiful mathematical theory, there is certainly the inevitable. A theorem marches toward a conclusion that seems undeniable. But how can something inevitable also be unexpected? The answer lies in the proof of a theorem itself. A beautiful proof has ideas that take the reader by surprise, somewhat like a series of brilliant moves in a chess match. And the surprises, when put in context, become stunningly beautiful. A good poem often has that same effect. The pattern of words forms a symphony that contains many surprises to be sure, but at the end seems paradoxically inevitable in that it had to be stated the way it was.

Lewis believed that poetry could reflect God's character and creation.[29] And in some sense Lewis might say that our earlier use of the phrase "*human* aesthetic criteria" was a bit of a misnomer. For Lewis, our ability to judge something as beautiful is a sign of our bearing God's image, because these judgments point to an absolute Beauty:

The books or music in which we thought the beauty was located will betray us

---

[25]For example, no stellar parallax shift could be detected from observed data, something that certainly would occur if the Earth revolved about the Sun. The problem is that stars are much more distant from the Earth than believed to be in Galileo's time, so the expected shift was not observed. In any case, detecting a shift would not have been possible with the technology then available.

[26]For a good treatment of Galileo, see David C. Lindberg, "Galileo, the Church, and the Cosmos," in *When Science and Christianity Meet*, ed. David C. Lindberg and Ronald L. Numbers (Chicago: University of Chicago Press, 2003), pp. 33-60 and 291-94.

[27]Brian Green, *The Elegant Universe* (New York: Norton, 1999), p. 374.

[28]G. H. Hardy, *A Mathematician's Apology* (Cambridge: Cambridge University Press, 1967).

[29]See, e.g., C. S. Lewis, *Christian Reflections*, ed. Walter Hooper (London: Fount Paperbacks, 1998), pp. 1-13.

if we trust in them; it was not *in* them, it only came *through* them, and what came through them was longing. These things—the beauty, the memory of our own past—are good images of what we really desire; but if they are mistaken for the thing itself, they turn into dumb idols, breaking the hearts of their worshipers. For they are not the thing itself; they are only the scent of a flower we have not found, the echo of a tune we have not heard, news from a country we have never visited.[30]

There is a close connection between beauty and goodness in Lewis's thinking. In *Miracles* he sees the moral judgments we all naturally make as posing further difficulties for naturalists, thereby extending his argument from reason into the realm of value theory.[31] It is not that the moral pronouncements of naturalists are incoherent, but that, on their own view, they can only legitimately be regarded as sentiments, and not genuine expressions of *ought*.

Lewis's fiction also casts God as the source and true locus of beauty and goodness. For example, his book *Perelandra* (originally published with the title *Voyage to Venus*), portrays a beautiful, sinless and freshly created world.

Steiner, too, sees something special in our aesthetic preferences.[32] His book contains several examples of beautiful mathematical systems that subsequently (and, we might say, *miraculously!*) wind up being used in applications to the physical world. His survey includes the use of complex analysis in fluid dynamics, relativistic field theory, thermodynamics and quantum mechanics. One of his examples is worth exploring in some detail. It is well-known among mathematicians and physicists: Maxwell's anticipation of a physical reality.

In 1871 James Clerk Maxwell made a remarkable prediction resulting from his work in electromagnetic theory. He noted that the (experimentally confirmed) laws of Ampere, Coulomb and Faraday, when put in a certain form (known as a *differential form*), contradicted the law of conservation of electrical charge. How could this contradiction be resolved? Maxwell decided to tinker

---

[30]C. S. Lewis, *The Weight of Glory* (New York: HarperCollins, 2001), pp. 30-31. Similar thoughts are also expressed in Lewis's book *Surprised by Joy: The Shape of My Early Life* (New York: Harcourt, Brace & World, 1955).

[31]Lewis, *Miracles*, chap. 5.

[32]As do other thinkers, though perhaps with different conclusions. For example, the American philosopher William James, in "The Sentiment of Rationality," wrote that of two conceptions equally fit to satisfy a logical demand, the one that awakens our active impulses or satisfies other aesthetic demands better than the other will be accounted the more rational conception and will deservedly prevail (William James, *The Will to Believe, and Other Essays in Popular Philosophy, and Human Immortality* [New York: Dover Publications, 1960], pp. 63-110).

with the mathematical equation that represented Ampere's law. He eventually realized that if he added a term to it, the resulting equation would not only be consistent with the conservation of charge law; it also would actually logically imply it. With no other experimental evidence or warrant of any kind, Maxwell then made a bold prediction: his new term would be found to correspond with some physical phenomenon. Maxwell died in 1879. Nine years later Heinrich Hertz demonstrated the reality corresponding to Maxwell's term: electromagnetic radiation.

Richard Carrier is a freelance writer and historian of science who is unimpressed by this episode, claiming that what Maxwell did is entirely consistent with naturalism. First, Carrier states that Maxwell's putting laws in differential form conforms to the naturalistic observation that nature works in continuous—not broken—processes. Second, Carrier argues that Maxwell took a logically sound hypothetical step: if charge is not being conserved, then it must be going somewhere. (Presumably, this logic led Maxwell to add a term to the faulty equation.) Carrier then states:

> Maxwell rightly picked the simplest imaginable solution first . . . which due to human limitation is always the best place to start an investigation, and which statistically is the most likely [since] simple patterns and behaviors happen far more often than complex ones. . . . Maxwell's moves [that] anticipated EM radiation [were] therefore a natural conclusion from entirely naturalistic assumptions.[33]

But with such language Carrier plays into Steiner's hands. Picking a *simple* solution in accordance with *human* limitations is precisely analogous to using the number ten as a means of unlocking secrets to the universe. It is quintessential anthropocentrism.

One wonders if it is difficult for people who are not practicing scientists to appreciate how absolutely uncanny is the continued use of mathematical formalisms by physicists. Green, by contrast, seems to agree with Steiner's main point: at least unconsciously physicists have abandoned a raw naturalism in favor of a theory formation method that has principles of beauty embedded in its core. If they are correct, this approach appears to be an anthropocentric—and by way of implication a nonnaturalistic—strategy.

---

[33]Richard C. Carrier, "Fundamental Flaws in Mark Steiner's Challenge to Naturalism, in *The Applicability of Mathematics as a Philosophical Problem*" <www.infidels.org/library/modern/richard_carrier/steiner.html>.

Or could it be naturalistic after all? Might it not be argued that plausible evolutionary models can be devised that would explain, for example, the human preference for symmetry? Such constructs seem possible, especially considering symmetries that might be adduced in examining our DNA code. But even if some model could be developed that would explain our preference for symmetry, how would the naturalist's form of such thinking explain why such preferences are successful? After all, magical incantations may be symmetrical, but they certainly do not work.

At least three strategies seem possible at this point. The first is to argue for some kind of probabilistic weighting mechanism that would drive physical processes toward the production of sentient life forms, and do so in such a way that their preferences for beauty would coincide with the actual mechanisms of the universe. A second approach would involve an appeal to a primal basic position: it just so happens that the universe evolved in such a way that our notions for beauty work successfully in theory formation. Finally, one might argue (along the lines of Wigner's Kuhnian-like question) that what we call success came only because humans have invested a great deal of energy into science over the last five hundred years. Who is to say that, if similar energies had been funneled in a different direction, there would be operating today a totally different paradigm, yet with the same degree of "success"? The success could be due to effort, not necessarily to some amazing connection humans have with reality.

These are huge issues, and it would be presumptuous to think that they could be settled in the space of this chapter. Nevertheless, we can quickly explore some tentative responses. First, with respect to the probabilistic weighting hypothesis, one might legitimately ask where the evidence is for this claimed weighting. As Keith Ward comments: "A physical weighting ought to be physically detectable, . . . and it has certainly not been detected. . . . In this sense, a continuing causal activity of God seems the best explanation of the progress towards greater consciousness and intentionality that one sees in the actual course of the evolution of life on earth."[34]

Furthermore, if some kind of weighting could eventually be hypothesized and then tested, it may still be asked why such a weighting is biased in favor of humans. To a theist, there is no prima facie reason why God could not work

---

[34]Keith Ward, *God, Chance, and Necessity* (Oxford: Oneworld, 1996), p. 78.

with what appears to be "chance" (although the problem of determining what exactly one means by chance is by no means trivial). For a theist, the human capacity to understand the workings of the universe is due to the creative and purposive activity of God, even if our coming to be this way arose out of some kind of probabilistic weighting scheme.

Next, although primal basic explanations are needed at some level, invoking them in an effort to account for the apparent privileged status of humans in the universe—this is just the way it is and no more needs to be said—appears akin to pulling a rabbit out of a hat. A naturalist may in good conscience choose this option. But for a theist, again, the conviction that human notions of beauty relate successfully to our knowledge of how the universe operates reinforces all the more the belief that human creation is the result of the purposive activity of an intelligent being. Theism makes excellent sense of the epistemic power of aesthetic criteria.

Finally, the idea that our constructs of success are ad hoc appears to be an objection without any realistic alternative. It essentially says, "Well, your theory makes sense, but only if one buys into some of your commonly accepted cultural notions. Other (unspecified) theories would be able to show that the success you claim is really arbitrary—perhaps merely a form of social agreement—and thus not privileged." Such a position, unfortunately, almost shuts down discussion. It may be possible that other theories could be successful, but where are they? More to the point, the effort expended by mathematicians and scientists in developing their (elegant) theories can more plausibly be seen as evidence of bumping into a real world rather than constructing one: many times scientists have tried to explain observed data with a particular theory in mind, only to have reality thwart their attempts. As John Polkinghorne observes (referencing the unexpected but extremely useful byproducts of the Dirac equation), "It is this remarkable fertility that persuades physicists that they are really 'on to something' and that . . . they are not just tacitly agreeing to look at things in a particular way."[35] Furthermore, why is it the case that the development of mathematics seems to be universal across cultures? As the mathematical historian Glen Van Brummelen has observed, premodern China, whose mathematics was independent and virtually isolated from the

---

[35]John Polkinghorne, *Quantum Theory: A Very Short Introduction* (Oxford: Oxford University Press, 2002), pp. 72-73.

rest of the world, exhibits an impressive list of theorems also found in ancient Greece and other cultures, including the Pythagorean theorem, the binomial theorem, the solution of polynomial equations via Horner's method, and Gaussian elimination for the solution of systems of linear equations.[36]

It seems, then, that a theistic explanation might well be the best one to account for the continuing success of mathematical theories that ultimately grow out of human aesthetic criteria. As Lewis observed, "The disorderly [or complex] world which we cannot endure to believe in is the disorderly [or complex] world He would not have endured to create."[37] In assessing these arguments the reader is encouraged to adopt an approach similar to the one suggested by Reppert in his defense of Lewis's thinking: there are valid points to be made by people who disagree with these ideas, which should be looked at not as dogmatic pronouncements, but as a catalyst to weigh various options. Human aesthetic values, and their subsequent use in successful physical theories, dovetail nicely with a Judeo-Christian view that humans are created in the image of God. Whatever being in God's image exactly entails, it seems to include a rational and aesthetic capacity reflective of his that enables humans to understand and admire his creation. While not necessarily a final answer, such a perspective can be put confidently in the marketplace of ideas for appraisal, which is what this chapter has attempted to do.

---

[36]For a fuller account, see Russell W. Howell and W. James Bradley, eds., *Mathematics in a Postmodern Age: A Christian Perspective* (Grand Rapids: Eerdmans, 2001), chap. 2. Similarities in mathematical systems across cultures might remind readers of the cross-cultural moral similarities as chronicled by Lewis at the end of *The Abolition of Man* (New York: Simon & Schuster, 1996).

[37]Lewis, *Miracles*, p. 109, brackets in the original.

14

Beastly Metaphysics

The Beasts of Narnia and Lewis's Reclamation of Medieval Sacramental Metaphysics

MICHAEL P. MUTH

B eauty evokes desire," David Bentley Hart so succinctly tells us,[1] and perhaps no twentieth-century writer stated this truth quite so longingly—and beautifully—as C. S. Lewis:

> We do not want merely to *see* beauty, though, God knows, even that is bounty enough. We want something else which can hardly be put into words—to be united with the beauty we see, to pass into it, to receive it into ourselves, to bathe in it, to become part of it. That is why we have peopled air and earth and water with gods and goddesses and nymphs and elves—that, though we cannot, yet these projections can enjoy in themselves that beauty, grace, and power of which Nature is the image. That is why the poets tell us such lovely falsehoods.[2]

This seemingly erotic, and yet beyond erotic, desire for the beautiful, "to be united with the beauty we see, . . . to bathe in it, to become part of it," explains, I believe, the powerful attraction of Lewis's own "lovely falsehood": the world he creates in the Chronicles of Narnia. The attraction of the Chronicles is at least twofold. First, the skillful use of the conventions

---

[1]David Bentley Hart, *The Beauty of the Infinite* (Grand Rapids: Eerdmans, 2003), p. 19.
[2]C. S. Lewis, *The Weight of Glory and Other Addresses* (New York: Macmillan, 1980), p. 16.

of children's literature—the avuncular tone of voice, the conversational asides, the simple and direct plots, the lovely and loving descriptions of creatures and scenes—makes the texts themselves a delight to read, attracting with their simplicity both child and adult. Second, the imaginary world of Narnia is a powerfully attractive place—mystery, beauty, glory, even terror are so close to the surface in Narnia, making up the very fabric of the world. It is hard to resist the desire to be there—who would not want to sail to the Lone Islands and on to the Very End of the World, to stand in defense of Old Narnia with Trufflehunter, even to face the wrath of the White Witch?

In short, Lewis's Narnia is a beautiful world, and since beauty evokes desire, so Narnia evokes our longing. In what lies its attraction, its beauty? To answer this, we need to consider what beauty is and why it attracts, and to address these considerations we must look further at the sort of broader vision of reality—a metaphysics—to which Lewis himself is committed.

It is my contention that Lewis's Narnia exerts its attractive force because it is a literary instantiation of a certain kind of metaphysics: a metaphysics of participation, of superfluity of being, of sacrament, in which beauty plays a central role. Lewis refers to this metaphysics as Platonic, though it is really Neo-Platonism as transformed by the Christian thinkers of the Middle Ages, with all of their sacramental, trinitarian and incarnational commitments. It is a metaphysics that envisions the world as a place where every creature bears within itself the marks of its Creator, so that the beauty and glory of the Creator shines out from the very being of each creature—a world in which "Nature is the image" of God. It is this sense of superfluity that Lewis attempts to instantiate in Narnia, crafting a world where the Creator's "beauty, grace and power" (normally requiring the effort of discernment to recognize) visibly erupts in the text—at any moment the trees could dance, the stars sing, or Aslan roar (and who knows what delight or terror that could bring). Narnia is constantly on the edge of slipping beyond the boundaries we expect of the world and showing forth a beauty childlike in its innocence yet lovely beyond imagination.

Central to the success of Lewis's literary instantiation of sacramental metaphysics are the beasts of Narnia—Reepicheep, the Beavers, Trufflehunter, Jewel: those delightful, even beautiful, characters that populate Lewis's world. These beasts, and their literary connections to medieval bestiaries, will serve as our point of entry into this examination of Lewis's metaphysical commitments, their instantiation in the Chronicles and the beauty of Narnia. Through this beastly door we will see how Lewis, in his literary Narnia, addresses certain philosophical and theological challenges posed for the Christian committed to a Platonic metaphysics and along the way discover that Lewis presages certain contemporary rumblings in philosophy and theology that have revived and reimagined this sacramental metaphysics. Perhaps the metaphysical world of self-proclaimed "dinosaurs," such as Lewis, is not hopelessly dead.[3] For beauty's sake, I hope so.

BESTIARIES AND METAPHYSICS

The beasts of Narnia may seem an odd place to focus metaphysical and theological reflection on beauty. Surely, someone might say, talking animals are too trivial for much philosophical reflection. First, talking animals are common didactic tools of children's stories—consider, for instance, Beatrix Potter's naughty Peter Rabbit and H. A. Rey's Curious George, who function as stand-ins for the young child, or Leo Lionni's poetic field mouse Frederick, who is a source of homely wisdom. Second, Lewis's use of bestiary materials to flesh out many of Narnia's beasts may seem merely to add a quaint medieval and fantastic flavor to his imaginary world. The bestiaries' strange stories together with their moralizing "allegories" seem unlikely grounds for an ontology. Further, though this chapter will focus on the connection between Narnia's beasts and medieval bestiaries, Lewis clearly draws on other sources as well—classical mythology, English folklore and other children's literature (surely Trufflehunter owes something to Mr. Badger of Kenneth Grahame's *The Wind in the Willows*).

Though many Narnian creatures come from nonbestiary sources, Lewis places them into a world quite different from classical mythology or English folklore: the symbolic, sacramental world of the bestiaries, which are Lewis's prime examples in *The Allegory of Love* of literary expressions of sacramentalism.[4] The bestiaries, which became immensely popular beginning in the twelfth century, have their inception in the *Physiologus*, a work of unknown

---

[3]In his inaugural address at Cambridge, C. S. Lewis claims to be a dinosaur: *"De Descriptione Temporum,"* in *They Asked for a Paper* (London: Geoffrey Bles, 1962), pp. 9-25. It is also quoted in Peter Kreeft, *C. S. Lewis: A Critical Essay* (Grand Rapids: Eerdmans, 1969), p. 46.
[4]C. S. Lewis, *The Allegory of Love* (Oxford: Oxford University Press, 1936), p. 46.

origin, probably written in Greek in Alexandria and dating sometime between the second and the fifth centuries A.D.[5] The title of the work refers to a person, the "natural philosopher" or "the one who studies nature." Setting the pattern followed by the bestiaries of the Middle Ages, the *Physiologus* describes the physical characteristics and behaviors of a number of animals, plants and stones, drawn from numerous ancient sources. Many of the animals, such as the beaver and lion, are real, though others, such as the unicorn and phoenix, are not, and many of the behaviors described are imaginary as well (if not simply bizarre). These descriptions and behaviors, however, form the basis for what is distinctive about the work: the *Physiologus*'s Christian symbolic interpretations.

The *Physiologus* and later bestiaries approach the creatures as "texts" to be "read" as signifiers of important religious and moral truths, discovering in and through these textual beasts a level of reality beyond the apparent. An excellent example of the *Physiologus*'s method, and one relevant to Narnia, is the section "On the Beaver":

> There is an animal called the beaver who is extremely inoffensive and quiet. His genitals are helpful as a medicine. . . . When the beaver sees the hunter hastening to overtake him in the mountains, he bites off his own genitals and throws them before the hunter. . . . O, and you who behave in a manly way, O citizen of God, if you have given to the hunter the things which are his, he no longer approaches you. If you have had an evil inclination toward sin, greed, adultery, theft, cut them away from you and give them to the devil.[6]

Here the imaginary behavior of the beaver is to be read as a sign for an important aspect of the righteous Christian life, a reflection of Jesus' statement to his followers: "If your hand causes you to stumble, cut it off; it is better for you to enter life maimed than to have two hands and to go to hell, to the unquenchable fire" (Mark 9:43). The clear connection here may make us suspect that the reported behavior is fictitious, and it is unclear just how medieval readers received these stories, whether they thought them accurate scientific data or rhe-

---

[5]Michael Curley lists five reasons why this seems most likely, including the fact that a number of the legends can be traced to Egyptian folk beliefs and that the allegorical method found in *Physiologus* was centered in the Jewish and Christian communities of Alexandria. See Michael J. Curley, trans., *Physiologus* (Austin: University of Texas Press, 1979), introduction, pp. xvi-xvii.
[6]Ibid., p. 52.

torical tropes.[7] But in either case, the approach is to see God's creatures as texts, so that in these creatures the bestiarists encounter a world overflowing with meaning, a world of superfluity, in which the very being of the animals "stretches" beyond their physical existence toward some further reality—without, however, canceling out the existence or reality of the animals themselves.

The beasts of Narnia are integral parts of the sacramental character of Lewis's imaginary world, important elements in its ontological superfluity, and so quite unlike Peter Rabbit and more like the sacramental animals of the bestiaries. Narnia's beasts are certainly important characters that advance Lewis's narrative, yet they also push against the confines of that narrative, just as the animals of the bestiaries transcend their appearances. For example, Trufflehunter the badger is a delightfully drawn character with an important role to play in leading Caspian toward his destiny as king of Narnia, including the arming of the young king with dwarfish armor and weapons. But through a subtle use of bestiary material, Lewis moves us beyond the confines of this particular narrative moment. When the dwarf smithies offer Trufflehunter arms and armor like those given to Caspian, the badger refuses: "The badger could have had the same if it had liked, but it said it was a beast, it was, and if its claws and teeth could not keep its skin whole, it wasn't worth keeping."[8] Trufflehunter reports here precisely what the bestiaries say is the fundamental nature of being a beast: "The name 'beast' applies, strictly speaking, to lions, panthers and tigers, wolves and foxes, dogs and apes, and to all other animals which vent their rage with tooth and claw."[9]

Lewis uses this bestiary definition as a means of distancing Narnia's beasts from technologies—unlike human beings and dwarfs, they neither need nor desire technology to promote their existence—and harkens back to the original gift Aslan gave the beasts in their creation: "Creatures," says Aslan to the newly created and speaking animals, "I give you yourselves."[10] So Trufflehunter's reference here to his own bestiality, as defined by the bestiaries, bumps the reader out

---

[7]By the seventeenth century these stories are seen as scientifically false, though symbolically useful. Thomas Browne (1605-1682) claims of them: "As for the testimonies of ancient fathers and ecclesiastical writers, we may more safely conceive therein some emblematical than any real story" (*Pseudodoxia epidemica* 5.1.338-40). See *Sir Thomas Browne: Selected Writings*, ed. Claire Preston (New York: Routledge, 2003), pp. 49-50.

[8]C. S. Lewis, *Prince Caspian* (New York: Macmillan, 1970), p. 71.

[9]*The Aberdeen Bestiary*, ed. Michael Arnott and Iain Beaven <http://www.abdn.ac.uk/bestiary/>, esp. *Incipit*, folio 7r <http://www.abdn.ac.uk/bestiary/translat/7r.hti>.

[10]C. S. Lewis, *The Magician's Nephew* (New York: Macmillan, 1970), p. 118.

of the immediate and apparent narrative moment into an awareness of the creatures' being as a gift from their Creator, as a sacrament of their Creator's gifting love. In ways such as this, as well as the use of bestiary materials in the crafting of Aslan and other characters, Lewis draws on the sacramental character of the bestiaries to help develop and heighten the sacramentalism of Narnia.

THE BOOK OF NATURE

So, through the beasts, Lewis draws on the medieval vision that the world is "a book written by the finger of God,"[11] "reflecting, representing, and describing its maker, the Trinity."[12] Creation, like other texts, has layers of meaning: it points or signifies beyond itself. Further, the beauty and light of God shine through every creature: "In every creature is the refulgence of the divine Exemplar, though mixed with shadow."[13] But how can what is true of texts—that they have multiple layers of meaning—be true of animals as well? How could such a metaphor as this—the universe as "the book of nature"[14]—come to be taken seriously, in any sense other than purely poetic? Lewis points us in the right direction in *The Discarded Image,* identifying two primary sources for the sacramental existence of animals:

> If, as Platonism taught—nor would Browne himself have dissented—the visible world is made after an invisible pattern, . . . the expectation that an anagogical or moral sense will have been built into the nature and behaviour of the creatures would not be a priori unreasonable. To us an account of animal behaviour would seem improbable if it suggested too obvious a moral. Not so to them. Their premises were different.[15]

---

[11]Hugh of St. Victor *De tribus diebus* 4; in Migne, Patrologia latina, 176.820.

[12]Bonaventure *Breviloquium* 2.12.1; in *Opera omnia,* 5 vols. (Quarrachi, Italy: Collegium S. Bonaventurae, 1882-1902), 5:230; *The Works of Bonaventure,* trans. José de Vinck, vol. 2 (Paterson, N.J.: St. Anthony Guild Press, 1963), p. 104.

[13]Bonaventure *Collationes in Hexaëmeron* 12.14; in *Opera omnia,* 5:386.

[14]This notion of the universe as a book continued into the early modern period, as in the works of Galileo and Thomas Browne, whom Lewis references in the next extended quotation. But the metaphor is subtly changed. The focus is no longer on the sacramental character of the beaver or pelican, since the stories about them are false anyway, but now rather on the reader's "admiration" of God's intelligence and power in creating a regular and rational universe. See, for instance, Thomas Browne *Religio Medici* 1.16 (a readily available edition of the text can be found in *Sir Thomas Browne: Selected Writings,* ed. Claire Preston [New York: Routledge, 2003], pp. 15-17). This is not intended to diminish in any way the beauty and importance of Browne's work, though this new interpretation of "the book of nature" does eventually lead to the rather banal design arguments (Watchmaker analogy) of William Paley and others.

[15]C. S. Lewis, *The Discarded Image* (Cambridge: Cambridge University Press, 1964), p. 152.

The sacramental vision of the "world as text" arises at the intersection between two modes of thought: on the one hand, the Platonic/Augustinian metaphysics of participation and sacrament ("the visible world is made after an invisible pattern"); and on the other, the characteristic method of medieval biblical exegesis, in which exegetes discover (where appropriate) symbolic levels of meaning, including a moral (anagogical) meaning, hidden under the literal signification of a biblical text.

BEING "SOBERLY DRUNK" IN "GOD'S DINING ROOM": THE "DEPTH" OF SCRIPTURE

For medievals like the bestiarists, the Bible is surely the text of texts, the text whose layers of meaning necessarily overflow the literal meanings of the words. The Bible, as Bonaventure refers to it, quoting James 1:17, is "the perfect gift, . . . coming down from the Father of lights," God's revelation of himself and all that is necessary for the salvation of the wayfaring human being.[16] But if it is to be the self-revelation of an infinite God—a God of infinite truth, beauty and goodness—the Bible must possess a richness or superfluity of meaning unparalleled by any other text. Lewis captures this idea in his essay "Transposition": for the richer system (God and heaven) "to be represented in the poorer system" (the physical world), each element of the poorer system must be given "more than one meaning."[17] So Hugh of St. Victor likens the Sacred Scriptures to "a honeycomb, for while in the simplicity of their language [the Sacred Scriptures] seem dry, within they are filled with sweetness," with meanings and beauty beyond the literal surface of the text.[18] Peter Comestor uses an even more delightful metaphor: "Holy Scripture is God's dining room, where the guests are made soberly drunk," a dining room built out of several different modes of interpretation: "History is the foundation, . . . allegory the wall, . . . tropology the roof."[19]

Though Peter Comestor mentions only three modes, the "depth" of Scripture, the excess of meaning found in Sacred Scripture, expressed itself

---

[16]Bonaventure *Breviloquium*, Prologus; in *Opera omnia*, 5:201; de Vinck, *The Works of Bonaventure*, 2:2.
[17]Lewis, *Weight of Glory*, p. 60.
[18]Hugh of St. Victor *Didascalicon* 4.1; in *The "Didascalicon" of Hugh of St. Victor*, trans. Jerome Taylor (New York: Columbia University Press, 1991), p. 102.
[19]Peter Comestor *Historia scholastica*, Prologue; in Migne, Patrologia latina, 198:1053. See Beryl Smalley, *The Study of the Bible in the Middle Ages* (Notre Dame, Ind.: University of Notre Dame Press, 1978), p. 242.

to the medievals more often in four layers of meaning.[20] The first, foundational level of meaning is the historical, or literal, level of interpretation, in
which we find "not only the recounting of actual deeds but also the first
meaning of any narrative which uses words according to their proper nature."[21] The other senses are symbolic or figurative. These include allegory,
in which "one thing signifies another thing which is in the realm of faith";
tropology, or a moral level, in which "from something done, we learn another
thing that we must do"; and anagogy, in which "we are given to know what
to desire, that is, the eternal happiness of the elect."[22] Care must be taken to
find meanings only where they actually exist: "It is necessary, therefore, so to
handle the Sacred Scripture that we do not try to find history everywhere,
nor allegory everywhere, nor tropology everywhere, but rather that we assign
individual things fittingly in their own places, as reason demands."[23] This
care is necessary because not every text has all levels of meaning, as Hugh
informs us:

> Similarly, in the divine utterances are placed certain things which are intended
> to be understood spiritually only, certain things that emphasize the importance
> of moral conduct, and certain things said according to the simple sense of his-
> tory. And yet, there are some things which can suitably be expounded not only
> historically but allegorically and tropologically as well.

Hugh thus claims that "certain things" are "placed" in the "divine utterances," and we are to "find" history, allegory and tropology in their fitting
places. The guiding idea here is that God put the many layers of meaning
in the Scriptures. Medieval biblical scholars did not believe that they were
adding anything to the Scriptures when they interpreted them in symbolic
or figurative ways. They were convinced that they were only discovering
the meanings that God had hidden within the text, the refulgent beauty of
God shining through the text of Scripture. Hence, Hugh's honeycomb
metaphor is apt: The exegete is only drawing out the honey that is already
there.

---

[20]This is Bonaventure's term for the superfluity of meaning in the Bible. See *Breviloquium*, Prologus;
in *Opera omnia*, 5:201; de Vinck, *The Works of Bonaventure*, 2:4.
[21]Hugh *Didascalicon* 5.3, in Taylor, *The "Didascalicon,"* p. 137.
[22]Bonaventure *Breviloquium*, Prologus; in *Opera omnia*, 5:205; de Vinck, *The Works of Bonaventure*,
2:13-16.
[23]Hugh *Didascalicon* 5.2, in Taylor, *The "Didascalicon,"* p. 121.

SACRAMENTAL METAPHYSICS

What explains the presence of the sweet honey hidden within the comb of Scripture? The overflowing honey of Sacred Scripture is an expression of the infinite being, power, goodness and beauty of its divine Author. This same superfluity is found in God's original text—the universe:

> [God] created this perceptible world as a means of self-revelation so that, like a mirror or a divine footprint [*vestigium*], it might lead man to love and praise his Creator. Accordingly there are two books, one written within, and that is [inscribed by] God's eternal Art and Wisdom; the other written without, and that is the perceptible world.[24]

Here we meet in full form the sacramental metaphysics that informs the bestiaries and that Lewis instantiates in Narnia, a metaphysics that begins with the creatureliness of the creature, focusing on the creature's ontological dependence on its Creator. Being and the other transcendentals—unity, truth, goodness and beauty—are possessed by every being; in fact, they are constitutive aspects of the very existence of creatures, gifts from their Creator God. So all of the transcendentals exist in every creature, and the Source of them can be seen in and through every creature as well. Let us begin our exploration of this metaphysics by looking at Plato, since Lewis himself directs us there.

PLATO

At the conclusion of *The Last Battle*, Lord Digory (also known as Professor Kirk) refers to Plato in order to explain to Peter and the others their experience of a new Narnia. The Narnia they had experienced before, he tells them, "was not the real Narnia. That had a beginning and an end. It was only a shadow or copy of the real Narnia, which has always been here and always will be here."[25] Lord Digory then mutters under his breath, "It's all in Plato, all in Plato," which, as Lewis is well aware, is not completely true, though Plato's philosophy is foundational for later transformations of Platonism.

Plato famously divides reality into two worlds: the realm of Becoming, the ever-changing world of physical objects, which "are rolling around as intermediaries between what is not and what purely is"; and the realm of Being, the never-changing, eternal world of the Forms, which truly exist and on which

---

[24]Bonaventure *Breviloquium* 2.11, in *Opera omnia*, 5:229; de Vinck, *The Works of Bonaventure*, 2:101.
[25]C. S. Lewis, *The Last Battle* (New York: Macmillan, 1970), pp. 169-70.

the things of the physical world depend for whatever being they have.[26] Plato actually gives us two slightly different ways to understand the relationship between physical instantiations and the Forms, though both of them involve the dependence of the former on the latter. According to *Republic*, books 5-7 (a work of Plato's middle period), in the same way that shadows and reflections are dependent on physical things for their being, so physical things are dependent on the Forms for theirs. Thus physical things are imaged as "shadows" of Forms cast into space and time. However, in *Timaeus* (a work of Plato's later period), Plato gives a more complex explanation of the physical realm: space is an eternal existent (like the Forms) that is given structure by an artisan god (the *demiourgos*, demiurge) who looked to the Forms as models for this ordering of space. So a physical entity resembles a Form as the result of the initial structuring of space by the demiurge. In Plato's metaphysics, then, each individual physical entity resembles the Form that it instantiates, either as a shadow or a copy, and so Plato's metaphysics becomes the basis for sacramentalist metaphysics—each shadow or copy is a sign pointing to its ontological source (the Form it copies).

In both *Republic* and *Timaeus*, however, Plato sees the particular physical individual as possessing almost no ontological integrity. This is especially true of the account in *Republic*, where physical entities are only shadows in space and time and thus as ontologically tenuous as all shadows and reflections. The *Timaeus* account seems to give greater reality to physical things: space exists eternally and, though its order is initially imposed from outside, the physical world seems capable of continuing that order by itself indefinitely without the demiurge tinkering with it. Yet even in *Timaeus*, though the dynamic order is an integral part of space, the things produced in space—the individual copies—are merely momentary existents about which we can know nothing:

> The material world is subject to never-ending change. Everything in it is in continual process: bodies are unceasingly formed and dissolved and are incapable of maintaining a stable identity. Material things are too evanescent and ambiguous for anything true to be said or known about them.[27]

The physical instantiations, the appearances, are always "intermediate" en-

---

[26]Plato *Republic* 5.479d, in *Plato: Republic*, trans. G. M. A. Grube, rev. C. D. C. Reeve (Indianapolis: Hackett, 1992), p. 155.

[27]Dominic O'Meara, *Plotinus: An Introduction to the Enneads* (Oxford: Oxford University Press, 1993), p. 12.

tities, "intermediate between what purely is [i.e., the Forms] and what in no way is," whose ontological and epistemological importance is exhausted in being a sign of the Form it instantiates.[28] Among non-Forms only rational souls are not such intermediate entities. All of this means, then, that beauty is not really in things; physical things are not beautiful. Beauty itself is a Form that can be momentarily reflected in physical things, but its presence in the world of becoming is as tenuous as that of the being of the physical entities.

MEDIEVAL CHRISTIANITY: THE AUGUSTINIAN SACRAMENTALISM OF BONAVENTURE

The "Platonism" Lewis instantiates in Narnia is not the Platonism of Plato, in which the individual entities of the physical realm are mere shadows or copies, even if Lewis uses the language of both shadow and copy and attributes his metaphysics to Plato. Though Lewis certainly accepts Plato's basic ontology of dependence, he, like other Christian theologians, does not think that it quite satisfies certain Christian convictions about the Creator God and the world that God created. In the Chronicles we find Lewis wary of two things in Plato's metaphysics: first, the tendency to erase individual creatures as mere appearances or intermediate entities, since they do not have the reality of the Forms, and their consequent inability for beauty to be in them; and second, the impersonal nature of the source of being: Plato's Forms, even the Form of the Good, which he calls the "ground of being," are impersonal abstractions (including, then, beauty). Before we examine Lewis's handling of these issues in Narnia, let us develop in greater detail the metaphysical vision underlying Lewis's work, by looking at an important Augustinian thinker, Bonaventure (ca. 1220-1274).[29]

Lewis's "Platonism" is a version of an Augustinian and medieval sacramental metaphysics (like Bonaventure's) in which a personal, triune God—who is absolute Being, Truth, Unity, Beauty, Goodness and Love—creates the universe out of nothing. These characteristics, though in created things distinguishable and even separable, are not separable qualities of God, but rather different ways of talking about God's essence. God's essence, however, is not

---

[28]Plato *Republic* 5.477a, in Grube and Reeve, *Plato: Republic*, p. 152.

[29]The following account is derived primarily from Bonaventure's *Commentaria in quattuor libri sententiarum*, books 1-2; in *Opera omnia*, vols. 1-2). Bonaventure claims to be simply developing insights already made by Augustine of Hippo, incorporating material from Pseudo-Dionysius and others.

static, but dynamic, since it involves Goodness and Love, which are, as Pseudo-Dionysius claims, self-diffusive.[30] This means that their nature is to pour out of their source (the lover, Goodness itself) toward the other (the beloved). In the divine economy, this is expressed as the Trinity, God the Father (the Lover), God the Son (the Beloved) and God the Holy Spirit (the Bond between them).[31] God is thus highest Beauty, because "beauty is the cause of harmony, of sympathy, of community," all of which the Trinity expresses in its fullest form.[32]

Since God possesses these characteristics—Goodness, Being and Love—in overabundance, he wills them to overflow as creation, following the pattern dictated by the Divine Ideas, Plato's Forms now transferred to God's reason, into the Logos.[33] Every creature, then, possesses being and goodness, as well as a form or nature, as gifts of God's goodness and love. Thus, as in Plato, they do not exist independently of their Source, as completely autonomous entities; rather, their being, goodness and nature are always possessed as pure gift. Nor can creatures be like anything other than their triune Creator, since all that they are comes from and remains dependent upon that Source.

So the being, essence or nature of every creature—every lion, beaver and badger, as well as every human being—comes from the triune Creator as a gift and signifies or points back to that source. As God is a Trinity, God is the triune Cause of what he creates—God is Father, Son and Holy Spirit, and thus also efficient cause, exemplary cause and final cause. The result is that every creature possesses a trinity of characteristics, for which Bonaventure (following Augustine) gives two coordinated lists: limit, form and order; and measure, number and weight.[34] Through this threefold mark the creature "stretches" beyond it-

---

[30]Pseudo-Dionysius the Areopagite *The Divine Names* 4, in *Pseudo-Dionysius: The Complete Works*, trans. Colm Luibheid (New York: Paulist Press, 1987), pp. 71-75.

[31]This discussion of the Trinity appears in several medieval thinkers, including Richard of St. Victor and Bonaventure. It has its origins in Augustine's *On the Trinity*.

[32]Ibid. See Luibheid, *Pseudo-Dionysius*, pp. 76-77.

[33]This solution to the problem of the ontological status of Plato's Forms comes from Augustine, *De diversis quaestionibus octaginta tribus* q. 46.1 (in Patrologia latina, 40:29-30): "In fact, Ideas are the primary forms, or the permanent and immutable reasons of real things, and they are not themselves formed; so they are, as a consequence, eternal and ever the same in themselves, and they are contained in the divine intelligence." Augustine often refers to the Divine Ideas as the *rationes aeternae*, the "eternal reasons." See Vernon J. Bourke, ed., *The Essential Augustine* (Indianapolis: Hackett, 1974), pp. 62-63.

[34]See Bonaventure *Breviloquium* 2.1, in *Opera omnia*, 5:219; de Vinck, *The Works of Bonaventure*, pp. 69-71.

self, back to its Creator. It is through its very being, then, that the creature can be read as a text signifying, at several levels of being, its Author. God's power, being and beauty are inscribed into the creature, so that beauty, in such a metaphysical scheme, "refers most properly to a relationship of donation and transfiguration, a handing over and return of the riches of being."[35]

In the sacramentalist view of reality, the world as it appears is held up— "suspended," to use a term from Radical Orthodoxy—on an ontological web of relationships with a Source that is ultimately responsible for its existence and meaning. This means that all creation overflows—the being, goodness, truth and beauty of the ultimate Cause pours out into the world through the suspended creature. Or to put it another way, we can experience the being, goodness, truth and beauty of the ultimate Cause in and through the suspended creatures. But the creature is not erased as a result.

ERASURE AND THE INTEGRITY OF CREATION

For Plato, an individual entity, such as a beaver, lacks creational integrity: it is *only* a shadow or copy of a Form, and its epistemological and ontological importance is exhausted once we have grasped the Form; yet a sacramental metaphysics is committed to the reality of God's creation and so resists the erasure of the particular. We can see such resistance in the bestiaries, where the animals never disappear behind the symbolism. The behaviors and characteristics of the animals (no matter how strange) are carefully described and always stand with the anagogical readings. Also, almost all of the bestiary animals have characteristics and behaviors that are not read symbolically; and some of the animals, such as the badger in the Bodleian bestiary, are given no symbolic reading at all.[36] The exuberant and colorful illuminations give further evidence of this resistance, as they picture the animals themselves and not what they figure. The surface or appearance of the animals is not negated by the symbolism: the depths of being give the appearance a reality, and the appearance is the means by which the depths shine forth. Under the surface are depths of meaning, beauty, goodness, truth; but the depths do not negate or overwhelm the surface—they support and glorify it, so that surface and depth, depth and surface, support each other, shining through each other. So too in Narnia, the

---

[35] Hart, *Beauty of the Infinite*, p. 18.

[36] Richard Barber, trans., *Bestiary: Being an English Version of the Bodleian Library, Oxford M. S. Bodley 764* (Woodbridge, U.K.: Boydell, 1999).

beasts of Narnia are not mere symbols; they possess a certain fictional integrity as characters, though they remain ontologically dependent on their Creator's gift of being. Thus beauty is *in* both the bestiary beasts and the Narnian beasts, at the same moment that Beauty itself is seen *through* them.

Plato's is not the only metaphysical theory that threatens to erase the particular creature, nor is Lewis the only one concerned. For instance, as Milbank, Ward and Pickstock argue in their introduction to *Radical Orthodoxy*, contemporary approaches to metaphysics—postmodernism and scientific reductionism, each appearing in numerous forms—deny the existence of the very entities they claim to explain, erasing creatures into the void of postmodern nihilism or into a falsely static ontological scheme. Milbank, Ward and Pickstock argue that only something like a sacramentalist metaphysics can save the individual creature, that is, only if the creature is ontologically "suspended" on its gifting Creator can we encounter it as an integral other: "For the phenomena to really be there, they must be more than there. . . . This is to say that all there is *only* is because it is more than it is."[37] David Bentley Hart is similarly concerned with erasure of the particular. Lewis's Narnia has already given this dense sacramental ontology literary form. The reality of the particular individuals of Narnia—of Reepicheep, Jewel, Mr. Tumnus, even Beaversdam and Mount Pire—is suspended on the gift of being from their Creator, but they never disappear behind the gift itself.

Reflecting the ultimate expression of Christian commitment to God's gift of ontological integrity to dependent creatures in Christian eschatology (especially the doctrine of the resurrection of the body), Lewis pushes further against the erasure of the creature by projecting their continued existence in an eschatological Narnia. Into the "heavenly" Narnia, Aslan brings all the good creatures of Narnia: "All of the old Narnia that mattered, all the dear creatures, have been drawn into the real Narnia through the Door."[38] In fact, in the "real England," "the England within England," even Professor Kirk's old country house still exists. This is not Plato, where the instantiation has hardly

---

[37]John Milbank, Catherine Pickstock and Graham Ward, *Radical Orthodoxy: A New Theology* (London: Routledge, 1999), p. 4. The argument of Hart's *Beauty of the Infinite* shows a similar concern for erasure behind postmodern thinking. Hans Ulrich Gumbrecht, in *Production of Presence* (Stanford, Calif.: Stanford University Press, 2004), also complains against the loss of the Other, including texts, though his concern is with the hegemony of interpretation, which attempts to replace the Other with interpretation itself.

[38]Lewis, *The Last Battle*, p. 169.

any existence and certainly none after death or dissolution. This is a sacramental ontology that allows an integrity to the creature, without denying its creaturely status; the gift of being is sustained even after the end of the world.

THE REAL LION AND THE PERSONAL CREATOR

According to Plato's metaphysics, the Source of reality is ultimately impersonal: the Forms, including the Form of the Good, the "ground of being," are not rational or mindful beings. In the *Republic* account, there is no mindful or intelligent creation at all; the physical universe is merely the set of shadows cast by the Forms. The *Timaeus* account, however, introduces an intelligent designer, who imposes order on the chaotic state of preexisting matter in space by looking to the Forms as the paradigm.[39] This account, then, does introduce a personal element into Plato's view of creation; Plato gives this artisan god some personal characteristics, calling the being "god" and describing this god as "without envy," as well as both "judging" and "wishing" for an end.[40] Yet this artisan god, the demiurge, is significantly different from the God of Christian sacramentalism.[41] The demiurge does not create ex nihilo, but only orders that which preexists. Most important, the plan for the ordering is also not an aspect of the artisan god, but the Forms, which exist independently of the demiurge, so that the physical universe resembles, not the demiurge, but the impersonal Forms. Nor does the demiurge relate itself to the physical world after the initial ordering; in fact, the demiurge is not responsible for the creation of human beings, animals and plants, but only for the larger order of the cosmos, the basic elements, and the subordinate deities, who were given the task of fashioning the other living things. So in the end the Source of the physical world, which it resembles, is impersonal Being, that is, the Forms.

Lewis's Narnia instantiates not this impersonal source, but the personal source of Christian sacramentalism, and here we must consider Aslan. Lewis borrows quite heavily from the bestiaries to craft Aslan. According to the

---

[39]In *Phaedo*, Socrates expresses concern that an account of reality following Anaxagoras's focus on Mind would be the best account, though he claims that Anaxagoras failed to carry through such an account. In *Timaeus*, Plato seems to be trying to make up for Anaxagoras's failure by introducing the *demiourgos*.

[40]Plato *Timaeus* 29e-30d, in Plato *Timaeus and Critias*, trans. Desmond Lee (New York: Viking Penguin, 1971), pp. 42-43.

[41]Plato uses the following words for the artisan god: *demiourgos*, "artisan, skilled workman, maker, creator, producer"; *tektainomenos*, "builder, maker"; *poiētēs*, "maker, workman, author"; *patēr*, "father"; *theos*, "god."

Physiologus, lion cubs are born dead and are only animated when the father lion breathes on them on the third day,[42] a story Lewis draws on in "the ransacking of the Witch's fortress," when Aslan's breath reanimates the creatures turned into stone.[43] Also, the bestiaries call the lion the king or prince of beasts and claim that the lion "loves to roam amid mountain peaks"—Aslan's country is a range of mountains beyond the end of the world—and is merciful, sparing those who prostrate themselves before him, as Aslan shows mercy to the repentant traitor Edmund. So Lewis draws quite heavily on this sacramental bestiary literature in order to flesh out Aslan.

But Aslan is not *a* lion; Lewis says that he is *the* Lion: "The Real Lion."[44] Aslan then is not an instantiation of a Form, but, if anything, *a Form itself,* the one of which all other lions are signs or sacraments. In Aslan, the fullness of a Form lives, takes on flesh and all that entails, with his creatures. Now, Platonic Forms are impersonal abstractions—Unity, Equality, Beauty, Justice, Leonicity. But the Source of Lewis's Narnia is not an abstraction—he is the living personal godhead of Narnia. Here we see Lewis breaking with Plato in favor of something Augustinian, medieval, even biblical—not the static, abstract Forms of the *Timaeus* and *Republic,* but the living, incarnational God of the Bible and the church's confessions is the Form of being, truth, goodness and beauty in Narnia. Beauty itself, the source of all beauty in Lewis's imaginary world, is alive in Narnia. He is the living exemplar of beauty: "And then she [Lucy] forgot everything else, because Aslan himself was coming, leaping down from cliff to cliff like a living cataract of power and beauty."[45] As living beauty, Aslan is the object of final and rightly ordered desire: "A brightness flashed behind them. All turned. Tirian turned last because he was afraid. There stood his heart's desire, huge and real, the golden Lion, Aslan himself."[46] In the incarnated God-Beast of Narnia, we see Lewis's highest expression of his imaginary sacramental world, by which the reader is drawn out of

---

[42]*Physiologus,* chap. 1; On the Lion, see Curley, *Physiologus,* p. 4: "The third nature of the lion is that, when the lioness has given birth to her whelp, she brings it forth dead. And she guards it for three days until its sire arrives on the third day and, breathing into its face on the third day, he awakens it. Thus did the almighty Father of all awaken from the dead the firstborn of every creature." The reference to Jesus as "the firstborn of every creature" is found in Colossians 1:15: "He is the image of the invisible God, the firstborn of all creation."

[43]C. S. Lewis, *The Lion, the Witch, and the Wardrobe* (New York: Macmillan, 1970), pp. 164-68.

[44]Lewis, *The Last Battle,* p. 100.

[45]Ibid., p.183.

[46]Ibid., p. 146.

our world into Narnia, and then out of Narnia back into our world, but now mediated through the grace, mercy, beauty and love of Christ, the God-Man, of whom Aslan is a beautiful literary sacrament.

AND NOW, WHAT OF BEAUTY?

A sacramentalist metaphysics is uncongenial to, if not simply impossible within, our present intellectual environment, which, at the extremes, tends to cut one of two ways. On the one hand, we find the rejection of metaphysics and meaning in the nihilism of the postmodern void, a view that denies any claim to inherent meaning or signification in the things of the world.[47] On the other hand, we find a lean, minimalist metaphysics designed to support the reductionist practices of science and the market economy that sells the technologies science spawns, a view that objectifies and commodifies the things of this world. Neither tendency can imagine the physical world as a realm of creatures, of symbols, sacraments or "cop[ies] of an invisible world."

It is not clear how beauty fits into either view, except as the object of capricious and market-driven desire.[48] On the first view, beauty, like everything else, is meaningless, if not perhaps distasteful: the attempt to use a pretty ornament to hide a violent and chaotic world. The second view banishes all value, including aesthetic value, from objective reality, leaving us with a world populated by desiring machines.[49] Neither view can give desire an object worthy of our most profound sense of longing. Instead, we are faced with desires that result from accidents of evolutionary forces, guided, if by anything, by self-interest expressed quite often in violence. Such groundless and purposeless desires are prey to the manipulations of propaganda and advertising, mere tools of the marketplace—our longing aimed now toward the dubious beauty of the surgically altered bodies presented in film and television. Beauty's ability to survive in this toxic mix is uncertain. Lewis the dinosaur, and those who have followed him in his concern for sacrament and beauty and even God, point us to a better hope.

---

[47]Lewis, *Allegory*, p. 45.
[48]See the argument of part 1 of Hart's *Beauty of the Infinite*.
[49]Thomas Hobbes states this baldly, and many thinkers since have developed the view; for example, Charles Darwin.

15

Lewis and Tolkien on
the Power of the Imagination

GREGORY BASSHAM

C. S. Lewis's Chronicles of Narnia and J. R. R. Tolkien's *The Lord of the Rings* are among the most popular works of imaginative fiction written in the twentieth century, beloved by millions of readers and now by legions of film-goers as well. The imaginative power of these works was hardly accidental. As colleagues and friends, Lewis and Tolkien often discussed the role of imagination in literature, myth, philosophy and religion, and each had strongly held (and deeply unfashionable) views about the role imagination does and ought to play in fantasy and other kinds of literature. In this chapter I explore these writers' views on the literary, moral, epistemic and religious power of the imagination and address briefly the common criticism that these views are objectionably "escapist."

WHAT IS IMAGINATION?

Imagination is "the power of the mind to consider things which are not present to the senses, and to consider that which is not taken to be real."[1] Following Kant, it has been customary to distinguish two types of (imagistic) imagination: *reproductive* and *productive*.[2] Reproductive imagination is the

---

[1]Michael Martin, "Imagination," in *The Oxford Companion to Philosophy*, ed. Ted Honderich (New York: Oxford University Press, 1995), p. 395.
[2]Immanuel Kant, *Critique of Pure Reason*, trans. Norman Kemp Smith (New York: St. Martin's Press, 1961), pp. 142-43.

power of reproducing mental "copies" of objects that have previously been perceived (e.g., recalling what one's fourth-grade classroom looked like). Productive imagination, by contrast, is explicitly creative and constructive.[3] This is the faculty of "fancy," the power of recombining perceived originals into new and sometimes fantastical combinations, such as a winged horse or a golden mountain.

Lewis distinguishes three kinds of productive imagination. *Reverie* involves brief, episodic daydreaming or castle-building, usually featuring oneself in some pleasing or wish-fulfilling scenario (like imagining oneself hitting a home run in Yankee Stadium or going on a Caribbean cruise). *Invention* involves creating an imagined world or narrative that is more detailed than is typically the case with mere reverie, which may or may not be pleasing, and which generally does not include oneself as a protagonist. Trollope's Barsetshire, Stevenson's *Treasure Island*, and Plato's ideal republic are examples of invention. Finally, *fantasy* (in the literary sense) is a form of imaginative invention that involves "impossibles and preternaturals," such as elves, trolls, wizards, unicorns, dragons or time travel.[4] Swift's *Gulliver's Travels*, Tolkien's *The Lord of the Rings* and Lewis's Narnia books and Space Trilogy are works of fantasy in this sense. In this chapter, I focus primarily on Lewis's and Tolkien's views on the power of imagination in literary fantasy. As I read them, Lewis and Tolkien suggest six ways in which fantasy can excite and expand the imagination.

FANTASY BROADENS OUR PERSPECTIVE AND ENLARGES OUR SENSE OF WHAT IS POSSIBLE

As Lewis notes, one of the special attractions of works of science fiction and fantasy is their power to give us "sensations we never had before, and [to] enlarge our conception of the range of possible experience."[5] Such works can help us see through other eyes; reveal possibilities outside the range of our limited, workaday lives; and satisfy deep-seated human desires to "hold communion with other living things" and to encounter true "otherness."[6]

[3] C. S. Lewis, *Surprised by Joy: The Shape of My Early Life* (New York: Harcourt Brace, 1955), p. 15.
[4] C. S. Lewis, *An Experiment in Criticism* (Cambridge: Cambridge University Press, 1961), p. 50.
[5] C. S. Lewis, "On Science Fiction," in *Of Other Worlds: Essays and Stories*, ed. Walter Hooper (New York: Harcourt Brace Jovanovich, 1966), p. 70.
[6] J. R. R. Tolkien, "On Fairy-Stories," reprinted in *The Tolkien Reader* (New York: Ballantine Books, 1966), p. 15.

Both realist literature and works of fantasy are able to excite our imaginations. But in giving us "sensations we never had before" and enlarging "our range of possible experience," fantasy is indisputably superior to realist literature. What would it be like to be an ordinary bear like Lewis's Mr. Bultitude, or a fifteen-inch-high creature like Reepicheep? How would a naturally immortal or long-lived being such as Legolas or Treebeard look on the passing flow of time? What kind of flora and fauna might exist on another planet? What would it be like to be an "unfallen" creature, such as Lewis's *hrossa*, or a being, such as Tom Bombadil, who lacks all possessiveness and all desire to dominate other wills? All of these imagination-expanding questions are posed in Lewis's and Tolkien's fiction.

FANTASY CAN REENCHANT THE ORDINARY WORLD

In his dense, diffuse but brilliantly suggestive essay "On Fairy-Stories," Tolkien suggests that fantasy can bring "recovery," a restoration of our Wordsworthian ability to see ordinary things ("stone, and wood, and iron; tree and grass; house and fire; bread and wine"[7]) with fresh, childlike wonder.[8]

In Tolkien's *Lord of the Rings*, it is primarily the elves who symbolize the sanative power of recovery. Like the mysterious nature-divinity, Tom Bombadil, Tolkien's elves possess a remarkable ability to take delight in things simply because they are "other." As virtual immortals, the elves dwelling in Middle-earth are grieved by the flow of time, but do not easily succumb to ennui, or boredom. Unlike humans, who have, as Tolkien says, a "quick satiety with good," the elves have an almost endless appetite for poetry, songs, gazing at the stars and walking in sunlit forests.[9] Whereas humans see a beautiful sunset and say "ho-hum," the elves see it with ever-fresh wonder and delight.

How does fantasy help us rediscover wonder and delight in "the other"? It does so by helping us pierce what Tolkien calls the "drab blur of triteness and familiarity."[10] By juxtaposing the enchanted with the familiar, the magical

---

[7] Ibid., p. 59.

[8] The following three paragraphs are adapted from my essay: Gregory Bassham, "Tolkien's Six Keys to Happiness," in *The Lord of the Rings and Philosophy: One Book to Rule Them All*, ed. Gregory Bassham and Eric Bronson (Chicago: Open Court, 2003), pp. 58-59.

[9] J. R. R. Tolkien, *The Letters of J. R. R. Tolkien*, ed. Humphrey Carpenter (Boston: Houghton Mifflin, 1981), p. 344.

[10] Tolkien, "On Fairy-Stories," p. 57.

with the mundane, fantasy provides vivid contrasts that help us see the world
with fresh eyes. Having encountered ents and towering mallorns, we forever
see ordinary elms and beeches differently. Rock and tree, leaf and branch,
shadow and sunlight become again, as they were in childhood, wondrous and
strange. The blue ocean and green earth once again become "mighty matter[s]
for legend."[11] We pierce what Lewis calls the "veil of familiarity" and begin to
see the world as elves see it: as miraculous and charged with the grandeur of
Ilúvatar the Creator.[12]

FANTASY CAN ACTIVATE OUR MORAL IMAGINATIONS

Tolkien once remarked that one of his objectives in writing *The Lord of the
Rings* was "the elucidation of truth, and the encouragement of good morals
in this real world, by the ancient device of exemplifying them in unfamiliar
embodiments, that may tend to 'bring them home.'"[13] As a work of moral fiction, *The Rings* belongs with Bunyan's *Pilgrim's Progress* and Dickens's *David
Copperfield* in the front rank of English literature. Baylor professor Ralph
Wood, who regularly teaches courses on Tolkien, reports that many of his
students "have confessed that they feel 'clean' after reading *The Lord of the
Rings*." By this, says Wood, they refer "not chiefly to the book's avoidance of
decadent sex but . . . to its bracing moral power: its power to lift them out of
the small-minded obsessions of the moment and into the perennial concerns
of ethical and spiritual life."[14]

The "bracing moral power" of *The Rings* works chiefly on two levels. First,
Tolkien's heroes inspire us as moral exemplars. When we read of the selfless,
dogged persistence of Frodo, the indomitable courage of Sam, the loyalty of
Merry and Pippin, the nobility of Aragorn, the repentance of Boromir, or the
humility of Galadriel, we feel the allurement of goodness that Plato classically
describes in the *Symposium*. We are moved, energized and uplifted. We dream
of better things and desire to grow.

---

[11]J. R. R. Tolkien, *The Twin Towers* (New York: Ballantine Books/Del Ray, 2001), p. 29.

[12]C. S. Lewis, "The Dethronement of Power," repr. in *Tolkien and the Critics: Essays on J. R. R. Tolkien's
"The Lord of the Rings,"* ed. Neil D. Isaacs and Rose A. Lombardo (Notre Dame, Ind.: University of
Notre Dame Press, 1968), p. 15.

[13]Tolkien, *Letters*, p. 194.

[14]Ralph C. Wood, *The Gospel According to Tolkien: Visions of the Kingdom in Middle-Earth* (Louisville:
Westminster John Knox Press, 2003), pp. 75-76.

A second way in which *The Rings* fires our moral imaginations is by showing us visions of utopian and dystopian realities. In Hobbiton we feel the charm of a close-knit, rustic community in a bygone age, when there was "less noise and more green."[15] In the hobbits' love of simple things—well-ordered and well-farmed countryside, good friends, good food, good pipe-weed and good beer—we are ruefully reminded of our own frazzled, macadamized, gadget-filled lives. By contrast, in Mordor's hellish moonscape and Isengard's smoking pits, we see terrifying visions of a future that could be ours if humanity's courage or wisdom fail. By means of such starkly contrasting visions, Tolkien activates our imaginations as no reasoned argument could.

If one of Tolkien's aims in writing *The Rings* was "the encouragement of good morals," this motive is even more apparent in Lewis's Chronicles of Narnia. As Gilbert Meilaender remarks, the Narnia tales "are not just good stories. Neither are they primarily Christian allegories. . . . Rather, they serve to enhance moral education, to build character. They teach, albeit indirectly, and provide us with exemplars from whom we learn proper emotional responses."[16]

Similarly, Meilaender points out that the Narnia stories are the direct embodiment, in fiction, of views on moral education that Lewis defends in *The Abolition of Man* (1944). In that work, Lewis critiques moral subjectivism and argues for a classical view of ethics as grounded in self-evident moral axioms. He also defends a classical view of how moral character is best developed. According to this classical model, moral growth requires three things: *instruction* in basic moral principles; *role models* to provide support, inspiration and concrete guidance; and the development of good moral *habits*, or *virtues*, through repeated performance of morally correct actions.[17] Each of these requirements of moral growth is featured prominently in the Chronicles. The children are frequently instructed on ethical fundamentals by wise preceptors, such as Aslan, Puddleglum, Dr. Cornelius, the Professor, Coriakan and the Hermit of the Southern March. They learn from a variety of role models: Reepicheep, Mr. and Mrs. Beaver, Prince Rilian, King Tirian, among others. And the children grow morally—become braver, kinder, wiser and more confident—by

---

[15]J. R. R. Tolkien, *The Hobbit* (New York: Ballantine/Del Rey, 2001), p. 3.

[16]Gilbert Meilaender, *The Taste for the Other: The Social and Ethical Thought of C. S. Lewis* (Grand Rapids: Eerdmans, 1978), p. 213.

[17]Bill Davis, "Extreme Makeover: Moral Education and the Encounter with Aslan," in *The Chronicles of Narnia and Philosophy*, ed. Gregory Bassham and Jerry L. Walls (Chicago: Open Court, 2005), pp. 109-10.

passing successfully through a variety of trials and adventures that test their moral mettle and enable them to form habits of virtuous response.

According to Plato and other defenders of the classical model of moral education, *stories* play a crucial role in moral development. Stories engage our moral imagination, provide vivid moral exemplars and activate our affections in ways that instruction or reasoned discourse (especially when directed at children) often does not. Stories are a primary means of teaching children the "right responses" to morally charged situations before they have reached the age of "reflective thought." Beyond the rollicking adventures, beyond the religious symbolism, the Chronicles of Narnia is a "book of virtues" that seeks to fulfill this classic educational function in a world that, Lewis believed, was increasingly morally and imaginatively impoverished.

In the Narnia tales, this ethical and imaginative impoverishment is symbolized chiefly by Experiment House, the modern, "up-to-date" school that Eustace Scrubb and Jill Pole attend. At Experiment House children are allowed to do what they like, bullies are regarded as interesting psychological cases, and fuzzy, "nonfactual" subjects like myth, poetry, fiction, ethics and religion are largely excluded.[18] As a result, students at Experiment House tend to be, like Uncle Andrew and the Witch Jadis, "dreadfully practical" (*The Magician's Nephew*, p. 75). (Eustace, we are told, "liked animals, especially beetles, if they were dead and pinned to a card. He liked books if they were books of information and had pictures of grain elevators and of fat foreign children doing exercises in model schools" [*The Voyage of the "Dawn Treader,"* p. 425].) The moral effects of such schools, Lewis believed, are disastrous. Having "read none of the right books" (*Voyage*, p. 463) and totally lacking the "emotions organized by trained habit into stable sentiments"[19] that are essential to good moral character, Eustace becomes a "record stinker" (*Voyage*, p. 426): stuck-up, lazy, insensitive, resentful and totally self-absorbed. It is only when he enters the morally rich atmosphere of Narnia, suffers the isolating and dehumanizing effects of being turned into a dragon, and is subsequently cured through the painful "baptism" of Aslan (*Voyage*, pp. 465-76), that he is set on the right moral path.

---

[18]C. S. Lewis, *The Silver Chair*, in *The Complete Chronicles of Narnia*, illustrated by Pauline Baynes (New York: HarperCollins, 2001), pp. 549-51. All other citations to individual books in Lewis's Chronicles of Narnia in this chapter are taken from this source.

[19]Lewis, *Abolition of Man*, p. 34.

As we have seen, Lewis believed that the classical model of moral education—stressing the threefold process of instruction, role modeling and habitual response—is one tried-and-true approach to moral development. The Narnia stories not only *illustrate* this classical model; they also seek to *apply* it.

Lewis accepted a classical natural-law approach to ethics.[20] He thus believed, like Augustine of Hippo and Aquinas, that certain objective moral values and fundamental moral principles are evident to every rational creature (even "fallen" ones such as ourselves). On this view, *instruction* plays a crucial role in moral education by helping to bring latent moral principles to full consciousness in young minds, by reminding young (and not so young) people of important ethical truths, by correcting false moral opinions that can arise from corrupting social influences or willful moral blindness, and by helping us to correctly apply general moral principles to complex concrete situations (an intellectual virtue that the classical tradition calls "prudence").

The children in the Narnia tales are instructed by many wise elders, such as Dr. Cornelius, King Lune and the Professor. But the principal moral teacher in Narnia, as befits his Christlike role, is Aslan. It is Aslan who instructs Lucy on the wrongfulness of eavesdropping (*Voyage*, p. 498), Jill on the dangers of showing off (*The Silver Chair*, p. 555), Aravis on the evil of harming the innocent (*The Horse and His Boy*, p. 299), Digory on the importance of not taking foolish risks (*The Magician's Nephew*, pp. 79-80) and on taking responsibility for one's mistakes (*Nephew*, 83), and Frank the Cabby on the duties of true kingship (*Nephew*, 81-82). As a moral teacher, Aslan is always awe-inspiring and demanding, but also kindly and sympathetic.

In addition, the Narnia stories feature many ethical *role models* that greatly assist the children in their moral development. Reepicheep is the very soul of chivalrous courage, Mr. and Mrs. Beaver of good-hearted hospitality, Puddleglum of incorruptible faithfulness, Dr. Cornelius of scholarly rectitude, Frank the Cabby of cheerful humility, Rilian of commanding boldness, and Tirian of kingly integrity. Lewis believed, as did Plato, Aristotle and other exponents of the classical model, that role models, for good or ill, play a crucial role in moral education. As Plato notes in the *Symposium*, good ethical role models not only provide patterns of embodied excellence for us to emulate, but also inspire, encourage and sometimes shame us into virtuous behavior. And this effect is

---

[20]Ibid., chap. 1; and C. S. Lewis, *Mere Christianity* (London: Fontana Books, 1955), book 1.

achieved, Lewis believed, not only by real-life role models but by fictional ones as well. From Tolkien's hobbits, for instance, we learn what true courage, persistence, friendship and loyalty are. Many avid *Rings* fans (myself included), when confronted with sticky moral situations, have asked themselves, "What would Frodo do?" Tolkien believed that "there is indeed no better medium for moral teaching than a good fairy-story (by which I mean a real deep-rooted tale told as a tale, and not a thinly disguised moral allegory)."[21] Lewis agreed, noting that fantasy tales featuring talking beasts, dwarfs, centaurs and other humanlike nonhuman creatures provide "admirable hieroglyphic[s]" that convey "psychology, types of character, more briefly than novelistic presentation and to readers whom novelistic presentation could not yet reach."[22] Fantasy, Lewis and Tolkien believed, has a kind of imaginative *potency* that few other literary genres possess. Through such fantastical "hieroglyphics" as Reepicheep, Saruman and Sam Gamgee, children can learn, quickly and memorably, important moral and psychological lessons.

Finally, the classical model of moral education stresses the importance of developing good ethical habits or dispositions—in short, moral *virtues*, such as honesty, courage, diligence, generosity and responsibility. Virtues, in the classical tradition, are admirable states of characters, settled habits of appropriate moral response, that enable persons to lead happy and fulfilled lives of sustained moral excellence. Virtues play a crucial role in the moral life. In early moral education, they enable children to do what is right long before they understand *why* it is right. As we become older, we acquire, through consistent performance or practice, virtues that function much like good habits in tennis: they enable us to do what we ought to do easily, readily and largely unthinkingly. Good habits are actually much more important in morality than they are in tennis, not only because the stakes are much higher but because there is no analogue of original sin in tennis. One doubts whether Roger Federer is ever strongly tempted to hit a lazy backhand.

Lewis fully agrees with the classical emphasis on forming good moral habits, and this is reflected at many points in the Narnia stories. In *The Lion, the Witch, and the Wardrobe*, we are told that Edmund was "becoming a nastier person every minute" (*Lion*, p. 129) as his treacheries deepened. Shasta, about

---

[21]J. R. R. Tolkien, "Sir Gawain and the Green Knight," in *The Monsters and the Critics and Other Essays*, ed. Christopher Tolkien (Boston: Houghton Mifflin, 1983), p. 73.

[22]Lewis, *Of Other Worlds*, p. 27.

to go into battle for the first time, says to himself: "If you funk this, you'll funk every battle all your life" (*Horse*, p. 292). Lewis, speaking as the narrator, comments that Digory, despite the terrible temptation he faced, probably would not have taken the magic apple that would have saved his mother's life, because "things like Do Not Steal were . . . hammered into boys' heads a good deal harder in those days than they are now" (*Nephew*, p. 92). But the most salient example of Lewis's stress on forming good moral habits is the episode of the "four signs" in *The Silver Chair*.

In that book, Aslan brings Jill Pole and Eustace Scrubb to Aslan's Country (the Narnian equivalent of heaven) and gives Jill four signs to guide her and Eustace in their quest to find Prince Rilian. After Aslan has told her the signs, he admonishes Jill to

> remember, remember, remember the signs. Say them to yourself when you wake in the morning and when you lie down at night. . . . And whatever strange things may happen to you, let nothing turn your mind from following the signs. And secondly, I give you a warning. Here on the mountain I have spoken to you clearly: I will not often do so down in Narnia. Here on the mountain, the air is clear and your mind is clear; as you drop down into Narnia, the air will thicken. Take great care that it does not confuse your mind. And the signs which you have learned here will not look at all as you expect them to look, when you meet them there. That is why it is so important to know them by heart and pay no attention to appearances. (*Silver Chair*, pp. 559-60)

Jill embarks on her quest, and as Aslan had warned, amid the temptations and murky confusions of Narnia, she does find it increasingly difficult to remember the signs. She gives up the habit of repeating the signs to herself every morning and night (*Silver Chair*, p. 591), and she soon was "no longer so 'pat' in her lesson as to be sure of reeling them off in the right order at a moment's notice and in the right order" (*Silver Chair*, p. 596). Luckily, her faithful guide, Puddleglum, is better at remembering the signs and is able to lead them to a successful fulfillment of their quest.

In the little morality tale of the four signs, Lewis is reminding us that on earth, as well as in Narnia, the air is thick, confusions and temptations abound, Aslan rarely speaks clearly, and it is not always easy to keep or to follow one's moral compass. Good ethical habits make possible the kinds of "stock responses" we need to stay on the straight moral path.

FANTASY CAN BAPTIZE OUR IMAGINATIONS

When he was seventeen, Lewis read a book that stirred him deeply: George MacDonald's *Phantastes: A Faerie Romance*. After he became a Christian, Lewis became convinced that MacDonald's book had "baptized" his imagination by the allure of spiritual goods.[23] Many years later, Lewis tried to achieve a similar effect in his Narnia stories. His purpose in writing these stories, he told his friend George Sayer, was "to make it easier for children to accept Christianity when they met it later in life." "I am aiming," Lewis said, "at a sort of pre-baptism of the imagination."[24] As we shall see, Tolkien also believed that literary fantasy touches on vital religious concerns.

How can works of fantasy, such as the Narnia tales or *The Lord of the Rings*, baptize our imaginations? Primarily in two ways, Lewis believed. First, they can stir and trouble us with a longing for we know not what, "a dim sense of something" beyond our reach that, "far from dulling or emptying the actual world, gives it a new dimension of depth."[25] In short, they can make us feel the beauty of holiness. Such an attraction, Lewis held, can act as a kind of spiritual "homing signal," calling us to higher things. The joy we feel when we read of Aslan's resurrection or the destruction of the One Ring is a voice, a call. If pain, as Lewis says, is God's megaphone to rouse a deaf world, the spiritualized emotions aroused by good works of literary fantasy are his violin, sweetly calling us home.[26]

Second, Lewis believed that fantasy can baptize our imaginations by making us more likely to accept Christian truth and to respond to it fittingly. Intellectually, fantasy can act as a *preparatio evangelica* by helping us understand the place of Christianity in the human quest for the divine. Many critics have argued against Christianity by observing that other religions and mythologies have also featured stories of dying and rising gods, miraculous births, sacramental meals and so forth. Lewis, like Tolkien, argues that such parallels are precisely what one would expect if Christianity were true.

In addition, Lewis believed, fantasy can help us overcome spiritual sloth and respond to Christian truth with the proper attitudes of awe, joy, repentance, gratefulness, "passionate inwardness" and the like. Lewis wrote the

---

[23]Lewis, *Surprised By Joy*, pp. 181, 179.
[24]George Sayer, *Jack: A Life of C. S. Lewis* (Wheaton, Ill.: Crossway, 1994), p. 318.
[25]Lewis, *Of Other Worlds*, p. 29.
[26]C. S. Lewis, *The Problem of Pain* (San Francisco: HarperSanFrancisco, 2001), p. 91.

Narnia stories, he says, because he thought he saw how stories of this kind could steal past the "watchful dragons" of religious sloth and indifference.[27] Countless readers can attest that the Lewis Chronicles do succeed in communicating, or restoring, the "potency" of central Christian teachings.

Lewis's views on the religious significance of myth and fantasy were strongly influenced by conversations with Tolkien, as well as by reading Tolkien's 1939 lecture, "On Fairy-Stories." It was Tolkien and Hugo Dyson who, in a famous late-night stroll on Oxford's Addison's Walk, convinced Lewis that pagan myths are not "lies" but partial glimpses or foreshadowings of truths that achieved complete expression only in Christian revelation. Humans come from God the Creator, and the myths and fantasies "woven by us, though they contain error, will also reflect a splintered fragment of the true light, the eternal truth that is with God."[28] One of the recurrent truths reflected in many myths and fairy tales is what Tolkien calls the "eucatastrophe"—the sudden joyous turn in which good improbably triumphs over evil, producing a "happy ending" to the story. In Tolkien's and Lewis's fantasies, eucatastrophes play a critical role in the plots. The supreme eucatastrophe in *The Rings* is certainly the scene on Mount Doom when, just as all seems lost, the Ring is destroyed and Sauron is overthrown. But Tolkien also included several mini-eucatastrophes in his tale, including Gandalf's return from death, the sudden appearance of Gandalf, Erkenbrand and the trees of Fangorn at the Battle of Helm's Deep, and the arrival of Aragorn and the ghost army at the Battle of the Pellennor Fields. Lewis, too, included sudden joyous turns in his Narnia stories, from the resurrection of Aslan in *Lion*, to the rescue of Prince Rilian in *Chair*, to the final reunion of all the Narnian heroes in Aslan's Country in *The Last Battle*.

The various eucatastrophes in *The Rings* and the Narnia stories help to pre-baptize the religious imagination because they provide, as Tolkien says, "a far-off gleam or echo of *evangelium* in the real world."[29] Tolkien writes:

> The Gospels contain a fairy-story, or a story of a larger kind which embraces all the essence of fairy-stories. They contain many marvels—peculiarly artistic, beautiful, and moving: "mythical" in their perfect, self-contained significance; and among the marvels is the greatest and most conceivable eucatastrophe....

---

[27]Lewis, *Of Other Worlds*, p. 37.
[28]Humphrey Carpenter, *Tolkien: A Biography* (Boston: Houghton Mifflin, 1977), p. 147.
[29]Tolkien, "On Fairy-Stories," p. 71.

> The Birth of Christ is the eucatastrophe of Man's history. The Resurrection is
> the eucatastrophe of the story of the Incarnation. . . . But this story . . . is true.
> Art has been verified. God is the Lord of angels, and of men—and of elves. Leg-
> end and History have met and fused.[30]

In this way, Tolkien suggests, "*Evangelium* has not abrogated legends; it has
hallowed them."[31]

FANTASY SATISFIES PRIMORDIAL HUMAN DESIRES

As youths, Lewis and Tolkien were captivated by tales of mythology (particularly Norse mythology), and both later tried to understand and explain the
psychic roots of this deep attraction. The deepest sources, they concluded,
were spiritual. For Lewis, tales of "Northernness" frequently produced feelings
of "joy"—brief stabs of inexpressible, poignant longing—that Lewis later
identified as yearnings for the divine. For Tolkien, such tales (and tales of fantasy generally) satisfy "certain primordial human desires."[32] Among these are
desires "to hold communion with other living things," "to survey the depths of
time and space," and most important, to imitate the divine creativity by engaging in a derivative kind of making that Tolkien calls "subcreation."

Only God, "maker of heaven and earth, of all that is seen and unseen," Tolkien believes, can engage in "primary creation"—the making of something from
nothing. Humans, though fallen, are created in the image of God and partake
in God's creative impulse to share his love, goodness and reality with other beings. Humans' creative impulses are reflected in many kinds of makings, including "subcreation": the construction, in imagination, of an entire "Secondary
World" that possesses "the inner consistency of reality."[33] Successful literary
subcreation creates in readers a mindset that Tolkien calls "Secondary Belief"—
a kind of "spell" or "enchantment" in which the reader enters fully into a Secondary World and believes it, as it were, as if one "were inside."[34] Subcreation
that involves what Lewis calls "impossibles and preternaturals" (elves, orcs,
ents, dwarves, Olympian gods, etc.) is fantasy. And fantasy, Tolkien says, "remains a human right: we make in our measure and in our derivative mode, be-

---

[30]Ibid., pp. 71-72.
[31]Ibid., p. 73.
[32]Ibid., p. 13.
[33]Tolkien, "On Fairy-Stories," p. 47.
[34]Ibid., p. 37. Yet Tolkien does not fall into the delusion that the Secondary World is real.

cause we are made: and not only made, but made in the image and likeness of a Maker."[35] This, according to Tolkien, is why humans in all ages are inveterate myth-makers and tale-weavers, why myths and fairy tales usually contain "splinters" of truth, and why great fantasy like Tolkien's *Lord of the Rings* and Lewis's Chronicles has such power to move and delight us.

FANTASY OFFERS HEALTHY FORMS OF ESCAPE

One of the common charges against works of literary fantasy is that they are escapist in some harmful, irresponsible, or otherwise objectionable way. Lewis and Tolkien certainly agree that fantasy is escapist. However, they deny that it ordinarily has any of the bad effects critics claim. On the contrary, they argue, the modes of escape that fantasy offers are generally healthy and beneficial.

"Why should a man be scorned," Tolkien asks, "if, finding himself in prison, he tries to get out and go home? Or if, when he cannot do so, he thinks and talks about other topics than jailers and prison-walls?"[36]

In this passage we touch on the deepest roots of Tolkien's Catholic and profoundly antimodernist worldview. When, at the most literal level, is "escape" most reasonable and even praiseworthy? When one is imprisoned or enslaved. And that, Tolkien says, is precisely the human condition in this fallen world, particularly in this post-Christian age.

Both Lewis and Tolkien believed that humans are held captive, at the deepest level, by sin and the consequences of the Fall.[37] Bradley Birzer, in *J. R. R. Tolkien's Sanctifying Myth,* has recognized how deeply the idea of the Fall entered into Tolkien's thinking and writing. As Tolkien remarks in a letter, there were at least four "falls" in Middle-earth before the events described in *The Lord of the Rings:* the rebellion of the elves of Middle-earth under Fëanor; the attempt by the elves of Middle-earth to freeze or "embalm" time; the first defection of humans, shortly after their creation, from the worship of Ilúvatar; and the corruption and idolatry that resulted in the destruction of the Atlantis-like island of Númenor.[38]

Although Tolkien presents these tales as myths, he believed that something like these fictional Falls actually did occur in human history. As a consequence,

---

[35]Ibid., p. 55.
[36]Ibid.
[37]Bradley Birzer, *J. R. R. Tolkien's Sanctifying Myth* (Wilmington, Del.: ISI Books, 2002), pp. 95-101.
[38]Tolkien, *Letters,* pp. 148-54.

humans have fallen captive to sin and death, and need liberation—that is, Escape. For Tolkien and Lewis, certainly, Christ is the true Liberator. He is the one who has given his life as a "ransom for many" (Matthew 20:28) and freed those who were in thrall to sin (John 8:34). But they also believed that Christians can assist in their liberation, and indeed that works of fantasy can provide less fundamental forms of "escape" to Christians and non-Christians alike. One such lesser escape is the short-lived "satisfaction and consolation" that works of fantasy often provide for the common ills of fallen humanity: "hunger, thirst, poverty, pain, sorrow, injustice, death."[39]

In "On Fairy-Stories," Tolkien also identifies a more important nonreligious form of escape that fantasy can provide: an escape from the "noise, stench, ruthlessness, and extravagance of the internal-combustion engine" and other unhappy features of our modern urbanized, industrial societies.[40] As Patrick Curry argues in *Defending Middle-earth,* Tolkien's writings (especially his letters) are infused with strong environmental messages and a thoroughgoing dislike for virtually all aspects of modernity, including (but not limited to) factories, machines, modern armaments, Big Government, "modern" (that is, postmedieval) literature, refrigerated foods, pasteurized beer and French cooking.[41] In places like Hobbiton and Rivendell, we see a true picture of the kinds of premodern societies he much preferred. In these places, and indeed in the whole of his imagined Middle-earth, Tolkien found a refuge—an escape—from what he called (quoting Catholic historian Christopher Dawson) the "rawness and ugliness of modern European life."[42] And myths and fairy tales, he believed, often afford imaginative solace and refreshment for those who, like him, hanker for simpler, greener and less-mechanized ages.

But the value of fantasy goes well beyond simply providing imaginative refreshment, Tolkien believed. At times fantasy can provide modes of escape that "may be heroic."[43]

Anyone who shares Tolkien's strong distaste for modern civilization might be driven to acts of nonconformity that some might consider as heroic (think of a Taoist hermit, for example, or Thoreau's withdrawal to Walden Pond).

---

[39]Tolkien, "On Fairy-Stories," p. 66.
[40]Ibid., p. 65.
[41]Patrick Curry, *Defending Middle-earth* (London: HarperCollins, 1998), passim.
[42]Tolkien, "On Fairy-Stories," p. 63.
[43]Ibid., p. 60.

But almost surely Tolkien's true subtext here is again religious. As mentioned, Tolkien disliked nearly all aspects of modernity, but as a devout, traditionalist Catholic, he was particularly saddened by the growing secularization of nominally Christian societies. As a result, he believed that it is incumbent on Christians today to be dissidents—"not [to] be conformed to this world" (Romans 12:2)—not only in their repudiation of the "rawness and ugliness" of modern industrialized societies, but far more important, also in their rejection of secularized standards and values. In fantasies and fairy tales, we encounter worlds that "have not been flattened, shrunk, and emptied of mystery."[44] In today's cultural climate, such works are inevitably condemned as "escapist." Yet as Ralph Woods observes, great fantasies like Tolkien's *Lord of the Rings* in fact allow us to "escape *into* reality" by dealing with eternal verities and fundamental issues of human existence.[45]

Lewis also denies the charge that fantasy is objectionably escapist. He makes several points in fantasy's defense.

First, he says, fantasy is an excellent source of "innocent recreation."[46] Books like *The Lord of the Rings* and the Narnia stories make great vacation reading because they are rollicking good stories that are at once relaxing, diverting and absorbing. Good works of fantasy provide all the action and adventure of a Tom Clancy novel with all the stress-reducing escapist qualities of a good historical romance. Moreover, as Lewis maintains, reading such works is an *innocent* form of recreation which, unlike many forms of human entertainment or recreation, involves no vice or folly.

Second, it is false to suggest that adults who enjoy fantasy are "childish" or suffering from "arrested development." As Tolkien shows in "On Fairy-Stories," most classic tales of fantasy were originally intended for, and enjoyed by, audiences of all ages. It is only recently that such works have been pigeonholed as "children's literature." Moreover, not all childhood tastes are bad.[47] "Arrested development" consists in failing to add new likes and interests, not in refusing to abandon all old ones. Why must I lose my taste for ice-cream cones and magic shows because I now also enjoy Guinness Stouts and Shakespeare's plays?

---

[44]Wood, *Gospel According to Tolkien*, p. 6.
[45]Ibid., p. 1.
[46]C. S. Lewis, *Letters of C. S. Lewis*, ed. W. H. Lewis (New York: Harcourt Brace Jovanovich, 1966), p. 182.
[47]Lewis, *Of Other Worlds*, p. 25; cf. Lewis, *An Experiment in Criticism*, p. 69.

Third, it is a mistake to think that works of fantasy are somehow dangerous because they lack "realism" and therefore give a false impression of life. Because the make-believe atmosphere of fantasy stories is so transparent, readers are almost never deceived. The really deceptive stories (Dan Brown's *The Da Vinci Code* comes to mind) always have at least a superficial realism.[48]

Finally, because all reading is literally a withdrawal from immediate, concrete reality, "escape" is "common to many good and bad kinds of reading."[49] The relevant questions, therefore, are always "What are you escaping *from?*" and "What are you escaping *to?*" If by escapism we mean "a confirmed habit of escaping too often, or for too long, or into the wrong things, or using escape as a substitute for action when action is appropriate," then of course escapism is something to be avoided.[50] Many realist critics charge that fans of fantasy literature are (often) escapists in this pejorative sense. Whether this is true, Lewis argues, depends largely on whether fantasy fans are escaping "into the wrong things." And this in turn depends heavily on one's metaphysical and theological worldview.

From a theistic perspective, Lewis argues, fantasy provides a healthy form of escape for the reasons we have discussed. Fantasy can help to reenchant the ordinary world, evoke stabs of "joy" that point us heavenward, restore "potency" to spiritual truths and, as Tolkien suggests, fulfill deep-seated desires to participate in the properly human function of "subcreation."[51] From a secular point of view, such modes of escape certainly may be suspect at best. But for Lewis, there could be no real conflict among imagination, intellect and spirit, any more than among truth, goodness and beauty. On the contrary, a fertile imagination is a great help to any Christian philosopher.

---

[48]Lewis, *Of Other Worlds*, p. 30; Lewis, *Experiment in Criticism*, pp. 67-68.
[49]Lewis, *Experiment in Criticism*, p. 68.
[50]Ibid., p. 69.
[51]Lewis, *Of Other Worlds*, p. 27.

Contributors

David Baggett is associate professor of philosophy at Liberty University. He's coeditor (with Shawn Klein) of *Harry Potter and Philosophy* (2004) and (with William Drumin) *Hitchcock and Philosophy* (2007). He's written articles in ethics, philosophy of religion, philosophy and popular culture, and epistemology, and he's currently collaborating with Jerry Walls on a book on ethics and its foundations.

Gregory Bassham is chair of the Philosophy Department at King's College (Pennsylvania), where he specializes in philosophy of law and critical thinking. He wrote *Original Intent and the Constitution: A Philosophical Study* (1992), coauthored *Critical Thinking: A Student's Introduction* (3rd ed., 2008), and coedited *The Lord of the Rings and Philosophy: One Book to Rule Them All* (2003), *The Chronicles of Narnia and Philosophy: The Lion, the Witch, and the Worldview* (2005), and *Basketball and Philosophy: Thinking Outside the Paint* (2007).

Jean Bethke Elshtain is a political philosopher who, since 1995, has been the Laura Spelman Rockefeller Professor of Social and Political Ethics at the University of Chicago. She has authored or edited twenty books and written some five hundred essays, and she is a contributing editor for *The New Republic*. She has delivered several hundred guest lectures in universities in the United States and abroad. Professor Elshtain has been a Fellow at the Institute for Advanced Study, Princeton; a Scholar in Residence, Bellagio Conference and Study Center, Como Italy; a Guggenhein Fellow; a Fellow of the National Humanities Center; and in 2003–2004, she held the Maguire Chair in Ethics at the Library of Congress. She also was appointed by President George W. Bush to the Council of the National Endowment for the Humanities. In 2006, Professor Elshtain delivered the prestigious Gifford Lecturers at the Universities of Edinburgh. In 2008 she received her second presidential appointment, to the President's Council on Bioethics.

Antony G. N. Flew earned an M.A. from St. John's College, Oxford University. Later he received his D.Litt. from the University of Keele. During his lengthy and distinguished career, he taught at Oxford University (Christ Church), the University of Aberdeen (King's College), Keele University and Reading University in the United Kingdom. His many books, such as *God and Philosophy* and *Hume's Philosophy of Belief,* became influential philosophical texts. In recent years he shocked his readers by turning from atheism to deism.

Gary R. Habermas is Distinguished Research Professor and chair of the Department of Philosophy and Theology at Liberty University. He has authored, coauthored or edited thirty books (including fifteen on the subject of the resurrection of Jesus). He has also contributed more than fifty chapters or articles to other books, plus more than 100 articles in journals and other publications. During the past ten years or so, he has been a visiting or adjunct professor at about fifteen different graduate schools and seminaries in the United States and abroad. He and his wife, Eileen, have seven children and six grandchildren, all living in Lynchburg, Virginia.

David A. Horner is associate professor of philosophy and biblical studies at Biola University. His primary research interests are in ancient and medieval philosophy, particularly the ethics of Aristotle, Augustine and Thomas Aquinas. He is a graduate of Oxford University (M.Phil., D.Phil.), where he lived a stone's throw from C. S. Lewis's favorite Addison's Walk.

Russell W. Howell is on the faculty of Westmont College, Santa Barbara, California. His academic interests include mathematics, philosophy and theology. He did his undergraduate work at Wheaton College (B.S., mathematics) and graduate studies at the University of Edinburgh (M.Sc., computer science) and the Ohio State University (Ph.D., mathematics). He counts it as a privilege to be in a position to help educate students who are eager to bring their Christian perspectives into a needful world.

Kevin Kinghorn follows in the footsteps of C. S. Lewis in a strict, literal sense. As philosophy tutor at Wycliffe Hall, University of Oxford, he travels to work each day along some of the same footpaths that Lewis once walked. Kevin is also assistant professor of philosophy at Asbury Theological Seminary. He has published articles in moral philosophy, metaphysics and philosophy of religion, and is the author of *The Decision of Faith: Can Christian Beliefs be Freely Chosen?* (2005).

Peter Kreeft has taught philosophy at Boston College for over forty years and is the author of over fifty books, including *C. S. Lewis: A Critical Essay*, *The Shadowlands of C. S. Lewis* and *C. S. Lewis for the Third Millenium*. His most recent book is *The Philosophy of Jesus* (2007).

Matthew Lee is a Ph.D. student in philosophy at the University of Notre Dame, focusing on metaphysics, epistemology and philosophy of religion. He is a Texan, born and bred, and believes that most of his biographical details should be deducible from that one fact. Matthew is a newlywed and counts himself lucky that his beautiful South African wife, Adél, is not only tolerant but even supportive of his philosophical activities (as long as he doesn't bring them in the house).

Michael P. Muth is associate professor of philosophy at Wesleyan College (the world's first college for women and the first college to grant a degree to a woman). Besides C. S. Lewis, his research interests include medieval bestiaries, medieval metaphysics, gothic architecture and the thought of St. Bonaventure, who argues (fairly convincingly, actually) that angels cannot laugh.

Michael L. Peterson is professor of philosophy at Asbury College. His books include *Evil and the Christian God*, *God and Evil: An Introduction to the Issues*, *Philosophy of Education: Issues and Options* and *With All Your Mind: A Christian Philosophy of Education*. He is editor of *The Problem of Evil: Selected Readings*. He is senior author of *Reason and Religious Belief: An Introduction to Philosophy of Religion* and senior editor of both *Philosophy of Religion: Selected Readings* and *Contemporary Debates in Philosophy of Religion*. He is general editor of the Blackwell series Exploring Philosophy of Religion. He is managing editor of *Faith and Philosophy: Journal of the Society of Christian Philosophers*. Dr. Peterson is also director of the Lilly Transformations Center at Asbury College, which aims at relating the classical Christian understanding of vocation to undergraduate education.

Victor Reppert is an adjunct professor of philosophy at Glendale Community College in Arizona. He is the author of *C. S. Lewis's Dangerous Idea: In Defense of the Argument from Reason* (2003) and numerous academic papers in journals such as *Christian Scholar's Review, International Journal for the Philosophy of Religion, Philo* and *Philosophia Christi*. He is a philosophy blogger with two blogs, <www.dangerousidea.blogspot.com> and <www.dangerousidea2 .blogspot.com>.

David Rozema is professor of philosophy at the University of Nebraska at Kearney. He has coauthored (with Gene Fendt) a book on the dialogues of Plato, *Platonic Errors: Plato, a Kind of Poet* (1999) and has published essays on the works of Lewis, Solzhenitsyn, Kierkegaard, Wittgenstein, Camus, Conrad and Plato. He is currently working on a book showing the harmony of thought between C. S. Lewis and the philosopher Ludwig Wittgenstein.

Philip Tallon is the director of the Christian Studies Center at the University of Kentucky. Among his publications, Philip has a number of essays in Open Court's Pop Culture and Philosophy series, including *Hitchcock and Philosophy* and *Superheroes and Philosophy*. Philip has also written a re-creation of the Lewis-Anscombe debate (with Jerry Walls), which was performed at Oxbridge, a C. S. Lewis Conference, as well as a stage adaptation of *The Great Divorce*, which was performed at the University of Kentucky in 2005. He is a Ph.D. candidate in divinity at the University of St. Andrews, where he is studying in the Institute for Theology, Imagination, and the Arts.

Jerry L. Walls is professor of philosophy at Asbury Seminary. Among his books are *Hell: The Logic of Damnation* (1992); *Heaven: The Logic of Eternal Joy* (2002); *The Oxford Handbook of Eschatology* (ed. 2007); *C. S. Lewis and Francis Schaeffer* (with Scott R. Burson, 1998); *The Chronicles of Narnia and Philosophy* (ed. with Gregory Bassham, 2005). He was the coordinator for the Philosophy Symposium at Oxbridge 2005.

Index